Life in the G

Alex Squadron

LIFE IN THE G

Minor League Basketball *and the* Relentless Pursuit *of the* NBA

Foreword by Andre Ingram

UNIVERSITY OF NEBRASKA PRESS   LINCOLN

The University of Nebraska Press is part
of a land-grant institution with campuses
and programs on the past, present, and
future homelands of the Pawnee, Ponca,
Otoe-Missouria, Omaha, Dakota, Lakota,
Kaw, Cheyenne, and Arapaho Peoples,
as well as those of the relocated Ho-
Chunk, Sac and Fox, and Iowa Peoples.

Library of Congress Cataloging-
in-Publication Data
Names: Squadron, Alex, author.
Title: Life in the G : minor league basketball and the relentless pursuit
of the NBA / Alex Squadron ; foreword by Andre Ingram.
Description: Lincoln : University of Nebraska Press,
2023. | Includes bibliographical references.
Identifiers: LCCN 2023008524
ISBN 9781496235855 (hardback)
ISBN 9781496237941 (epub)
ISBN 9781496237958 (pdf)
Subjects: LCSH: Birmingham Squadron (Basketball team) | NBA G League. |
Minor league basketball—United States. | Basketball—United States. |
BISAC: SPORTS & RECREATION / Basketball Classification: LCC
GV885.52.B57 S73 2023 | DDC 796.3230973—dc23/eng/20230413
LC record available at https://lccn.loc.gov/2023008524

Set and designed in Garamond Premier Pro
by Mikala R. Kolander.

For Mom, Dad, Jake, and Sam

Contents

Foreword

Andre Ingram

The G League has been my home for fourteen years. It doesn't feel right to say that, but not for the reason you may think. When I finally look back on my professional career, it won't be the G League that I think about; at least initially, it will be the D-League, or the Development League.

I'll remember driving the Utah Flash team van to and from practice, to and from the airport, to and from our apartments, and to the mall or wherever most of our guys were grabbing food. Back then, the team staff consisted of three coaches and one trainer. There were no interns, managers, or ball boys around to help players get shots up after practice or even to take them to practice—the players had to do those things for each other. There was no strength coach, travel coordinator, or massage specialist—your trainer had to be all those things. Our practice facility was a security building with one of the rims bent down so much that the height of the basket was closer to nine-and-a-half feet than ten. The D-League was all about making the most out of whatever you were given, and I absolutely loved it!

I came from a midmajor school that bused to every road game. So when I was asked, *as a player*, to drive our team van to the airport for road trips, I just thought it was cool that we'd be flying. We had guys who loved being in the gym and only cared about getting better, so it was no problem for us to rebound for each other. Whatever the issue was, it didn't matter—all I cared about was being one step away from becoming an NBA player. In one way or another, that's all any of us G League players think about. The reason we play in this league is to be one step, one game, one opportunity away from the NBA. And for some, like the twenty-one-year-old I was, that's enough to look past anything that could use improving within the league and to just enjoy the experience of a season. You'll read about that youthful energy and hopefulness in this book, but you'll also read about players like the twenty-six-year-old I was, struggling with starting one week and then playing significantly less the next because the team's affiliate sent down a couple rookies to get action. Still, I was crazy enough to stick around—and at the age of thirty-two, after ten seasons of competing in the G League, I finally made it to the NBA!

But my story isn't the only story. There are players who paid to go to a G League team's local tryout, battled their way to a roster spot in training camp, and then became a key part of the team's success. Beyond that, I've played with and against guys who went from a G League tryout to becoming an NBA player *in the same season*.

You may know the names Alex Caruso and Gary Payton II; you may not know that they went undrafted, signed in the G League, made the NBA, and then became rotation players on NBA championship teams. There are too many stories to count—too many stories you don't know—many of which are highlighted in these pages.

And then there are the things that only happen in the G League. They happen on and off the court, and they're funny only when looking back on them. Our team once had a nine-hour layover in Phoenix trying to travel back to Los Angeles (I remember doing a math tutoring session over Skype to pass some of the time). We had a Conference Finals game in Austin that was stopped midway through the third quarter because the floor was too slick (we played the rest of the game the next day). Those are just a couple of the endless stories I've either experienced or heard through the years, and no doubt there are more to come.

Like any minor league, the main challenge for players in the G is elevating as an individual, in and through a team setting. It's not uncommon to feel excited (internally) after a loss because you played well individually or to feel like you wasted an opportunity when your team won because you didn't put up the numbers or get the minutes that you wanted. I'm often asked what's the best advice I've ever been given or would give to a player entering the G League. A lot of things come to mind: "Control what you can control" or "When the team does well, everyone looks better." But there's no better advice than what Coach Casey Owens told our team in 2015: "If you don't like your situation, give it a week. And if you like your situation, give it a week."

Everything changes in the G League—your roster, your minutes, your emotions, your play—and not always for the better. Staying even-keeled, continuing to work hard, not riding the emotional roller coaster, even *expecting* constant change, will go a long way toward keeping you spiritually, mentally, and physically right and having the best season you can.

The reality of the NBA is that there are only so many spots on a roster. Countless G League players have been told the numbers just aren't there for them to receive a call-up—and that was the truth. But the magnitude of talent in the G may be the one thing that's stayed consistent throughout the years, and the one thing I wish everyone knew about our league. You can't find an NBA roster without multiple guys with G League experience on it. You can't even find a roster without a former G League player who is a significant part of the team's rotation. A league producing those types of players needs to be covered and needs to be known. And that's not just the case now—it's been that way for fourteen years! Whenever I hear someone mention the G as a punchline intended to mean you're not good enough or nowhere near the highest level, it's just silly to me. The talent in this league is something I've always wished the masses could see, understand, and know about—and now, thankfully, you can.

Author's Note

When I told people that I was writing a book about a basketball team called the Birmingham Squadron, the response was usually something like, "Oh, cool! Is it *your* team?" Of course, I understand the confusion. Why wouldn't that be the response? I love basketball; I write about basketball for a living; my last name is Squadron; the team's name is Squadron. It all made too much sense. At the same time, though, I really hope that people don't think I would buy a basketball team, name it after myself, and then write a book about it.

So no, it is not *my* team. I had an idea to write a book about the NBA G League, and there happened to be a team (a brand new one too!) called the Squadron. I mean, come on! It would have been far more ridiculous for me to ignore something like that, right? I chose to follow the Birmingham Squadron as opposed to the Sioux Falls Skyforce or the Rio Grande Valley Vipers or the Delaware Blue Coats or the Wisconsin Herd because it felt like destiny. There, I said it.

It has always been my dream to write a book. I was drawn to this one for so many reasons, including the fact that I share a name with the team at the center of it. But I must make clear before you go any further that I have absolutely no professional connection to the Birmingham Squadron.

Okay, that covers it. You can start the book now. I may not be crazy enough to buy a basketball team and name it after myself, but I am just crazy enough to believe you might actually enjoy what I've created here.

Life in the G

INTRODUCTION

Malcolm Hill doesn't really believe in luck. For someone in his position, that presented a bit of a conundrum. *Luck* is a word you hear a lot when you're a professional basketball player fighting to get to the NBA. "To make it, you have to get lucky," everyone says. A little bit of luck is an essential piece of a very complex equation:

$$Talent + Athleticism + Hard\ work + Sacrifice +$$
$$Opportunity + Luck = NBA$$

Take luck out of the equation, and everything falls apart. It becomes unsolvable.

But after reading about and ruminating on the subject, Hill stopped believing in luck. He believes in taking all the necessary steps to pursue his goals, regardless of how uncomfortable those steps may be. He believes in willing things into existence through his actions. Believing in luck is much easier; it relinquishes control. Hill's process is strenuous. It puts the onus squarely on his shoulders, and requires patience, persistence, and discipline—an *absurd* amount of discipline. But in his mind, if he fully commits to it, then he leaves nothing to chance.

He wouldn't get lucky.

He would make his own luck.

Given where he was at the beginning of 2021, and where he intended to be by the year's end, most others would have said that Malcolm Hill needed a treasure chest filled with horseshoes and four-leaf clovers. They probably would have said he needed a miracle. Hill, then twenty-five years old, was playing for Hapoel Jerusalem of the Israeli Basketball Premier League—well, not exactly *playing*. Most of the time, he was sitting on the bench in street clothes.

It was peculiar. Hill wasn't a huge name in the basketball world, but he was still the third all-time leading scorer at his illustrious alma mater—the University of Illinois—and had been dominant in other pro leagues throughout Europe and Asia. This was his fifth year overseas. He was established, his game had steadily improved, and the six-foot-six forward was probably in the best shape of his life. And now he wasn't even getting a chance to play? He wasn't even wearing a uniform? How did that make sense?

There were a few possible explanations. Hill had suffered a broken hand early in the season that stifled his initial progress. Hapoel Jerusalem had a stacked roster, so Hill wasn't the primary option as he had been for much of his career, which was an adjustment. And the organization was in disarray, shuffling through multiple head coaches over a six-month span.

Still, it didn't make sense that Hill wasn't in the team's rotation. "I don't know the games that they were playing with him over there, but I knew he wasn't the fit for them," Hill's father, Malcolm Sr., later reflected. "And that was the first time overseas where he wasn't the fit. When they did insert him a couple times, he would have a breakout game where he had 23 points or 19 points and you're wondering, *Was that enough?*"

It wasn't. It never was.

The situation was frustrating, of course. Back in the United States, Hill's stepbrother, Clayton Hughes, was blown away by how calm his sibling remained. "He kept his mind straight—to not flip out. If that was me, I would've said something," Hughes remarked with a laugh. "That's why me and Malcolm are two totally different people. I was mad *for him*, because it's a situation that he can't control. And I know how good he is. It was just the fact, like, why are they treating him like that? That was my thing.

"He's a different type of human being," Hughes added. "I don't know how he kept his cool."

Hill was accustomed to not getting the recognition he deserved, dating back to his days dominating at Belleville East High School, where he scored over 2,000 points. He received little buzz while at the University of Illinois, despite being one of the top players in the Big Ten Conference. No matter what jersey he was wearing, his game always seemed to fly under the radar.

But this was a new type of obstacle, perhaps the greatest test yet of his belief in himself. Hill was up for the challenge. In the middle of possibly the biggest setback of his career, he made a curious decision: he aimed higher. Instead of tempering expectations, he chose to become even more ambitious. Sitting in his apartment in Jerusalem one January day, he picked up a pen and wrote down a goal: "Make the NBA by the end of 2021."

Ha!

At one point, it wasn't such a far-fetched target—it was actually there for the taking. Hill had a chance to be selected in the second round of the 2017 NBA Draft. A few teams were prepared to pick him, but none were a great fit. Rather than get tied down by one organization, Hill did what many in his position do: he bet on himself. He kept his options open, eventually signing lucrative contracts in the Philippines, Germany, Russia, and Kazakhstan with the hope of winding his way back to the NBA. But in Israel, that light at the end of the tunnel—the light he had been chasing all along—had begun to dim.

"Make the NBA by the end of 2021" now seemed like a laughable target—to people not named Malcolm Hill, that is. He saw it as attainable, and he was willing to take all the necessary steps in its pursuit.

"I'm a believer in dynamic thought, just that thoughts can play a huge role in what goes on in one's life," Hill said. "Thoughts of disbelief or doubt—that can kind of mess up the flow of things. If you study or come across some people who have done some amazing things that you would call miracles, it'll be like, how can I explain this? You would think there's no way. You gotta believe in yourself before anybody believes in you. The more you progress along in your journey, the more that the universe will align things or people your way that will help you achieve [your goals], whether they know your goals or not."

During the COVID-19 pandemic, Hill had adopted a more regimented approach. He read numerous self-help books about the importance of establishing a routine. Favorites included *The 10X Rule* by Grant Cardone and *Think and Grow Rich* by Napoleon Hill—a near-century-old bestseller that begs the question "What makes a winner?" He regularly listened to motivational speakers like Les Brown, Earl Nightingale, Steve Harvey, and Jim Rohn. He spent a lot of time studying successful people from various walks of life, not just athletes. He found that he could learn from all of them and apply their philosophies to his own profession.

"They all kind of say essentially the same thing just in a different way, relating to their careers and what they do," Hill explained. "*The routine and daily habits that you do over time are what allow the man to become who they are in the present moment.*"

So Hill focused on his routine. He built it out gradually, adding more and more practices. It incorporated meditation and prayer, an hour of yoga, forty-five minutes of breathing exercises, grounding (a therapeutic technique in which Hill walked around barefoot on the grass to electrically reconnect to the earth), multiple basketball workouts, weightlifting, and writing in a journal. He read and reread his goals every single day:

Make the NBA by the end of 2021.
Make the NBA by the end of 2021.
Make the NBA by the end of 2021.

"Once I wrote down that particular goal, I just started challenging myself personally—what can I do within my daily routine and habits that will help me attain my goal?" Hill said. "My AAU coach always told me, 'Every decision that you make is either helping you or hurting you go towards your goal—every single decision that you make in life throughout the day.' That's tough for a lot of people. A lot of that comes down to being able to change up your routine, which puts you in an uncomfortable situation and position. That's not easy at all. It's tough to have faith in something when you're not sure how it's going to look." Or, put differently, it's tough to have faith in something when you're not sure how it's going to *work*.

"I would just always tell him, 'I wouldn't let the circumstances determine my work ethic, because you want to have the work ethic for where you're trying to go,'" said Machanda Hill, Malcolm's mom. "'So even if you're not playing, you want to continue working on your game, because when that opportunity presents itself, you want to be ready for it. And you don't know when it's going to happen or what it's going to look like, but when it happens, you want to be ready.' And honestly, when he was in Israel, in street clothes, I didn't know how it was going to happen. But you just have to trust the process and do the work and trust that it will happen."

Malcolm trusted. He trusted the process. He trusted the work. He wholeheartedly believed in his new routine—that it could help deliver him from point A (sitting on a bench in Jerusalem) to point B (making an NBA roster) if he just stuck with it. But the path between those two points? That part remained a mystery.

• • •

About 4,400 miles from Jerusalem, in the bustling city of Beijing, China, Joe Young was also fixated on the NBA. Unlike Hill, Young had been there before: three years and 127 games with the Indiana Pacers, after being selected in the second round of the 2015 NBA Draft. He was in Beijing now in part because he hadn't fully cherished those three years and 127 games. He wished he had done things differently, of course, but he was younger then. Less mature. Slightly overeager. A couple of mistakes here and there had contributed to his fall from the NBA.

In 2018 the Pacers had decided not to pick up the fourth-year option on his contract, which came as a surprise to Young. No other NBA teams expressed significant interest in signing him. Young knew he couldn't let a year go by without playing, so he agreed to a deal with the Nanjing Tongxi Monkey Kings of the Chinese Basketball Association (CBA) and boarded a plane bound for the other side of the world.

There, Young quickly became a star—the type of star he dreamed of becoming as a kid. Only this was in China, and he had never pictured himself in China. He had pictured himself in the NBA, where his dad, Michael Young, played three seasons in the 1980s, following a stellar career as a member of the University of Houston's legendary "Phi Slama Jama" team. Because of Michael, Joe was exposed to basketball at a very young age.

"He really loved the game," Michael said. "I told him, 'If you want to play at the NBA level, if that's your dream, it's a lot of work.' And the thing was, at an early age, he understood what I was saying. I'm telling you, early in the morning, the sun hadn't come out, you could hear him out there pounding that ball. This was in elementary school. He went out there on his own."

Michael put him in track early on, knowing how important it was that Joe be in elite shape. By the time he was nine years old, Joe was training like a mini–Rocky Balboa, waking up at 5:00 a.m. to do twenty minutes on the treadmill, twenty minutes on the elliptical machine, and twenty minutes on the StairMaster. He was okay with the work—enthusiastic about it, even. He understood the bigger picture: to be like his father, to do what his father did, the work was necessary.

"He really comprehended it," added Michael, who also served as the strength and conditioning coach at Houston for almost a decade. "I mean, you're talking about a kid who in middle school was making a thousand shots in all different kinds of ways. That's a lot of work, man."

Joe didn't do all that to play in the CBA. Still, it was hard not to grow at least somewhat comfortable with his new situation—he was making millions of dollars, averaging over 36 points per game seemingly in his sleep (he even had a historic 74-point performance), and beginning to gain the attention and fame he had always imagined. The NBA never completely slipped his mind, but it had—both literally and figuratively—grown more distant.

By 2021, however, after another three years had somehow come and gone, he was done with it. All of it. The CBA wasn't the dream. This was only meant to be a detour. Young was partly to blame for prolonging it—he had passed on a few nonguaranteed training-camp offers from NBA teams through the years. COVID was also partly to blame, making movement in and out of the NBA even more difficult. Young realized, though, that the longer he strayed down this path, the further he was getting from the NBA. And he was nearing the point of no return.

His life in China, while comfortable, was often secluded. For American players overseas, it tends to be that way. Time tends to slow down. Thoughts tend to race. That's especially true in a place as foreign as China. Young passed many hours alone in his room, just reflecting on his brief stint in the NBA. The distance and separation allowed him to analyze things through a more honest lens. "Being honest with yourself can bring you a long way," he later said. "I was just sitting there and maturing. Like, *Yo, you shouldn't have done that. You should've done that better.* I would just put stuff on paper and write down what's going on, how can I get through it, and what did I do to put myself in this position here."

He joined a new CBA team for the 2020–21 season: the Beijing Royal Fighters, coached by former NBA All-Star and CBA legend Stephon Marbury. That season, more than the previous two, motivated him to get back to the NBA. It was played in a bubble—all teams lived and competed in the same city (Zhuji, Zhejiang), isolated from the rest of society—due to the pandemic. That bubble was far stricter than the one put together by the NBA in Orlando, Florida. This wasn't Disney World—it was more like the Loneliest Place on Earth.

Nobody could leave the hotel in Zhuji, except when shuttling to and from the gym. Players and coaches had to wear Li-Ning gear (or brands with no visible marks) and ate basically the same foods every day. They were completely separated from friends and family and could do practically nothing of their own accord.

More isolation meant more time to think, and overthink, and dwell on every little thing he might have messed up with the Pacers. On the court, Young was still taking care of business, leading the Royal Fighters in points, assists, and steals on most nights. At the hotel, though, his mind was elsewhere, brooding over his experience in the NBA. His belief that he belonged there—not in the far-less-talented CBA—was strengthened by the entire Royal Fighters' staff. It was a theme often reiterated by Marbury and two of his assistant coaches, Jay Humphries and Korey Harris.

"Being an international coach over the years, you see what type of players come through China—some on their last legs, some that don't have the ability to play in the [NBA]," said Humphries, who was an NBA player from 1984–95 and an assistant coach for the Brooklyn Nets in 2014–15. "When you have a player that has the ability to play in the [NBA], puts in the work ethic, you tell him those things and brighten his future and keep him motivated to try to play at the highest level because as a kid, that's what he wanted to do. You just continue to preach those things to him to get the best out of him—for you, but then the best out of him for himself, so that he doesn't get stagnant and just become an overseas player. He can always be an overseas player."

"My verbiage every time I spoke to him or any time we had some type of film session was constantly reassuring and reaffirming, like, 'You're an NBA player. You're better than your situation,'" added Harris.

Marbury constantly challenged Young as well. The two shared many emotional conversations, discussing their individual careers and how they both encountered unforeseen obstacles—in basketball and in life—that led them to China. Some of those conversations brought Young to tears. Marbury pushed him to fight through the adversity and raise his game to a level needed to get back to the NBA. Hearing that, especially from someone of Marbury's stature, sparked something in Young. He wanted to go for it—to *really* go for it. Whatever it took.

It would take a lot. A lot of sacrifice. A lot of commitment. A lot of resolve. That was the message Michael had for his son when they talked over the decision. Joe was twenty-nine years old. He would be turning down millions of dollars, accepting a lesser role, and giving up stardom.

But his mind was made up long before that talk ever happened. Joe had traveled this road long enough. His dream had slipped away three years prior. Now it was time to chase it again.

• • •

Like Joe Young, Zylan Cheatham was supposed to follow in his father's footsteps. In this case, that meant taking over the family business—a local mechanic shop in Phoenix, Arizona. As Young was learning basketball, Cheatham was supposed to be learning engines and transmissions and oil filters and disk brakes.

None of that really interested him, though. Cheatham wanted something different for his future. What, exactly, was still unclear. He was trying to figure it out while constantly being on the move. His parents were divorced and living in different parts of Phoenix. At the age of twelve, he moved from the West Side to the South Side with his mom. "That's kind of when things got real for me," he said.

South Phoenix was a more perilous part of the city, overrun by gangs and plagued by violence. Cheatham was exposed to it all right away. His mom worked long hours, so he was often on his own after school. That independence was more of a curse than a blessing, especially at such a formative stage of his life.

"I'm out in the city. I'm moving around, gangs, doing all that," he said. "I wasn't a druggie, but I was definitely in the streets. I'm fighting and all kinds of shit. All my friends—the dudes I was hanging out with when I went to school—were all gang-affiliated, all smoking before class. That's all I hung out with every day. To this day, they're still in the hood, trapping, doing what they do—or dead, or in jail."

Cheatham was an exceptional football player, a bruising running back with striking athleticism. He began dreaming of a future in the NFL—of a life as a superstar athlete, not a mechanic. He played some basketball, too, but mainly just for fun and to stay in shape. Football had his full heart and full attention—until a shocking development during his eighth-grade season. Cheatham's coach unexpectedly quit on the team that year, frustrated with his players' lack of discipline. The season was cut short, and Cheatham was devastated. What was he supposed to do now? Where was he supposed to turn?

In South Phoenix, those were not questions one wanted to be asking. Thankfully, Cheatham found a new hobby right away. His best friend, Darvis Fletcher, was obsessed with basketball and encouraged Zylan to make the transition to the court. That transition would save Cheatham from venturing down a dangerous path.

"Zylan was hanging out with some young gangsters. They were all street kids," Fletcher recalled. "We all grew up together; we're all from different parts of South Phoenix. But he was kind of in that pack and going down that path. It wasn't looking too good for him at a young age, I'm not going to lie to you. But I don't know—he likes to give me credit for the basketball thing. I was just playing it. I wasn't like, 'Here, you should play basketball.' It was kind of unspoken."

"Darvis literally changed my life," Cheatham said. "He taught me how to play basketball. He's not gonna say it, but I am. I'm gonna tell it like it is."

At that point, Cheatham wasn't particularly skilled at basketball. He had little knowledge of the game, but all the physical tools were there. He was fast, strong, agile, athletic. He and Fletcher began training together, developing a daily routine. The minute school let out at 3:00 p.m., they would hustle to the

Central Avenue bus and ride it straight up the street to the South Mountain Community Center. They were usually the first two people to arrive at the gym. They would shoot around, play one-on-one, mimic moves they had seen on TV. Zylan would try to dunk, springing toward the rim but coming up *just* short, over and over and over again. Older kids—sometimes grown men—would trickle in. They would split into teams and scrimmage full court. Zylan and Darvis typically stayed at the facility until the doors were closing around 10:00 p.m. Their blossoming love for basketball kept them in the gym, as did their understanding of what existed just outside—the many negative influences that threatened to steer them off course.

"The crazy part about it is, when I first picked up a ball, there were no hopes of making it to the NBA. There were no dreams of getting a DI scholarship offer," Cheatham said. "It was just, either I pick up this ball and stay in the gym all day, or I go run the streets with my friends and get in trouble. It was that decision, man. I feel like I picked the right one. And I fell in love with it."

"We knew kids who were really active in gang activity early on in their lives," Fletcher added. "You see it every day. A lot of fighting. A lot of killings. Kids entered things that you wouldn't think a kid would be involved in. It's easy to fall into that. But we fell in love with the game of basketball, and it made it kind of easy to keep that where it was."

The more they played, the better they got. And the better they got, the more they started dreaming of the NBA. It helped that Zylan hit a massive growth spurt around this time, shooting up from five feet ten to six feet four. Now he was fast, strong, agile, athletic, *tall, and skilled*. He was also determined. Albert Ramirez, who coached Zylan and Darvis in AAU (Amateur Athletic Union) basketball, used to pick up a bunch of kids from the South Side to take them to the YMCA before school. His phone would ring around 4:30 in the morning.

"Coach, I'm ready," Cheatham would say. "Come get me."

"Zylan's one of the only kids that would call me at 4:30," Ramirez remembered. "And that was on a constant basis. I never called him or ushered him to go work out. He always initiated the call. To us, we knew that he was going to play at the next level. Just how far, we didn't know."

By junior year of high school, it was clear that Cheatham would go at least as far as the college level. He had sprouted to six feet eight and become a top-100 recruit in the nation, with scholarship offers from major Division I programs across the country. San Diego State eventually won his favor. Cheatham spent two memorable years with the Aztecs and two more at Arizona State before setting his sights on the highest level—the *farthest* level he could possibly reach.

Cheatham understood, even after he signed with a premier agency in Roc Nation Sports, that he was likely to find himself on the fringes of the NBA. After going undrafted in 2019, he got an opportunity with the New Orleans Pelicans—a modest opportunity, but an opportunity nonetheless. He appeared in four games and logged fifty-one total minutes during his rookie season, which was suspended in March due to COVID. Under normal circumstances, he would have been on track to find a home and carve out a role in the NBA. But these were not normal circumstances.

Entering the summer of 2021, more than two years since he had left college, those four games and fifty-one minutes remained his only taste of NBA action. Zylan had touched an NBA floor, but he hadn't "made it"—not in the way he and Darvis had talked about since childhood.

He was right on the doorstep, though, which, considering when and where this had all started, was extraordinary. Of course, it wasn't enough. Cheatham hadn't made it out of South Phoenix just to lay down on the doorstep. He had much bigger plans.

"One of Zylan's biggest statements—we were out in California. We were at the Anaheim Complex, at a tournament," Ramirez recalled. "He said, 'Coach, when I make it to the NBA, I'm getting you a gym, we're getting it in, and we're gonna help all the South Side kids.' I said, 'Right on, son. That's good.' He always had a vision of being something bigger than what he was and being able to afford to come back and give back to the community."

• • •

Basketball didn't become the center of Zylan Cheatham's life until he was a teenager. For Jared Harper, the situation was different—*very* different. Basketball was to be the center of his life from the day he was born: September 14, 1997.

Patrick Harper, who played college basketball at Elizabeth City State University in North Carolina, had hatched a plan. He was going to be married by thirty and have two sons, both of whom would be basketball players. Jared was the firstborn.

"I think the dream of playing basketball and making it to the NBA was probably settled before Jared was born, before he ever knew who he was," said Patrick. "I was a college basketball player, so I was planning everything before I even knew his name. That planning goes back a long way. But I think at one year old, he would sit in the swing and not cry, not do anything, and we would just sit and watch games for hours. At a young age, he could just sit in front of the TV and stare at basketball, before he knew what it was."

Patrick didn't have to steer Jared toward the game—his son seemed to gravitate to it on his own. When he was two, Jared would play outside their home in the quiet suburb of Mableton, Georgia, dribbling a ball for hours. They had a little Nerf hoop, and he would surprise guests by sinking ten shots in a row. By four, he was dribbling two balls at the same time, up and down the sidewalk. In his first organized game at the age of five, parents and coaches had to introduce a new rule because he was dominating so easily. Jared had to wait at half-court until the defense was fully set before attacking.

"Always having a ball and always advanced," Erica Harper, Jared's mom, recalled, "and always working to perfect whatever he was working on. I remember at a young age, maybe even when he was two, he would keep shooting until he shot a high percentage of baskets."

"As long as I can remember, I've always been around basketball," Jared said. "It just always came naturally. I remember after school in kindergarten, first grade, my dad used to take me to the gym every day, going there, working on ball handling, just working on simple fundamentals and knowing that those little things would help me in the long run."

That type of training started early for a reason. Patrick understood, based on his and Erica's heights, that Jared was likely to be undersized for basketball. So his son would have to be more skilled, more polished, more knowledgeable than everyone else. Patrick purchased instructional videos made by Dave Hopla, who worked as a shooting consultant and coach in the NBA. Jared learned all the proper forms and techniques from studying those tapes. Then, with the guidance of Patrick, he tackled all the game's fundamentals—shooting, dribbling, passing, defense—in painstaking detail.

The plan was working to perfection; Patrick and Erica even had a second son, whom they named Jalen. The two brothers would often play on the Nerf hoop together, wearing uniforms and official NBA socks. Jared even added accessories at times: a headband and an arm sleeve, just like Allen Iverson, one of his favorite players. They would turn on the fan in the nearby bathroom to simulate crowd noise, the loud hum echoing through their play area. In their minds, they were transported to a large, packed, rowdy NBA arena. They would toss each other alley-oops or pretend the clock was winding down . . . *3, 2, 1* . . . and launch long-distance shots at the buzzer. *It's good! Harper hits the game-winner! It's all over!*

Basketball was fun for the boys, but it was also hard work. Patrick didn't take it easy on either of them. From the time he was little, Jared always played at least one level up. He was small for his age, so as a fourth grader running with middle school kids or a seventh grader running with the junior varsity squad, he was *extremely small*. Some of his jerseys looked like night gowns, draping to his knees. Some of his opponents would be six, seven, even eight inches taller.

That was all intentional, all part of the plan. Jared's dream was to make it to the NBA, and to give him a shot, Patrick knew that his son needed to be constantly challenged, both mentally and physically.

"I had to adjust to Patrick being so hard on him and Jared playing with older kids, being knocked down and all of that," said Erica. "It was probably more of an adjustment for me than it was for him. But that's what he wanted to do."

"The opponents used to always try to capitalize on his size," Patrick explained. "Like, 'Hey guys, you gotta play physical with him. You gotta rough him up.' Which, in my mind, I'm like, great, that's exactly what I want, so he can learn and have that toughness. So the plan kind of worked. Was it challenging? Yes. His training regimen was tough. I'm a very tough, hard coach."

It was tough, sure; but over time, it paid off. People constantly overlooked Jared because of his height—on multiple occasions, he was warming up and the referees asked Patrick, "What's this little kid doing on the court?"—and then he would nonchalantly bury five three-pointers and break down defenses with ease.

"His abilities would always be questioned," Erica added. "And I would be in the stands, and that's what I would hear." She got used to the murmurs: *What is he doing here? Who can he guard? Why is he on the floor?* "And then it would immediately stop after he started playing."

Part of Patrick's elaborate plan was also exposing Jared to the highest levels of basketball. The Harpers went to watch high school championships, AAU championships, SEC (Southeastern Conference) championships, the Final Four, the NBA. They observed more like students in a classroom than fans in a gym. Seeing those stages, experiencing those atmospheres, imagining himself in those situations was important for Jared's development too.

Of course, others encouraged Jared to dream smaller. Making the NBA was a near-impossible feat for anyone to achieve. And for someone his size? *That* was impossible. Somehow, none of that noise seemed to get under Jared's skin. He knew what he was capable of. He had competed against some of the best prospects in the country—Jayson Tatum, Jaylen Brown, De'Aaron Fox, Bam Adebayo, to name a few—and more than held his own. He was crowned co-MVP of the high-profile Nike EYBL (Elite Youth Basketball League) Peach Jam Tournament in 2015, recording 34 points and 8 assists against Tatum's St. Louis Eagles in the title game. "Of course, you always hear, 'Oh, you need to have a backup plan.' *Blah, blah, blah,*" Harper said. "But I don't think I ever really listened to that. I feel like my entire life, I always believed I would be in the NBA."

"Never wavered on it. There's no plan B. I'm going to the NBA and that's what it is," said George Washington, Harper's head coach at Pebblebrook High School in Mableton. "He's been that way forever—ever since I met him. 'I'm going to the NBA.' *Dude, you're five feet five, what are you talking about?* 'I'm going to the NBA.' And that's always been his motto. He hasn't wavered on that at all."

Jared often talked about Tyler Ulis, a five-foot-ten guard who played at the University of Kentucky and then for the Phoenix Suns. Ulis was his evidence—his definitive proof—that someone his size could make it to the modern NBA. Because size was by far the biggest knock on Harper as a prospect—in many cases, the *only* knock. His speed and athleticism were absurd. His basketball IQ was extremely advanced. His talent was undeniable.

At Pebblebrook, he starred alongside future NBA guard Collin Sexton. The two would stay behind after practice to play one-on-one. Harper prevailed in a majority of those battles, according to Coach Washington. They would play to 10, beginning with only one dribble allowed. Then they would go to two dribbles, then three dribbles, then unlimited dribbles, then back to one dribble. Sexton was a year younger and still learning the moves that Harper had already mastered. Washington described the games, which tended to be quite chippy:

> Collin would say, "Hey, let's go to three dribbles." Because with three or four dribbles, Collin's going to try to get to the basket. And Jared knew he could be creative off of one or two dribbles—*really* creative. He would one dribble, pound, pull you, step off, he'd do all kinds of crazy stuff. And that's when Collin was learning how to do all that. And Jared was just killing him, toying with him.
>
> Finally, Collin won a game and oh my God, when Collin won that game, you would have thought he had won a championship. People don't understand how much Jared helped Collin to become the player Collin has become, because when Collin came to us, in order for him to score, he would take one hundred dribbles. Jared would tell him all the time, "You don't need that. One dribble. You should be able to score off of one dribble. You should be able to get to the cup off of one dribble. You should be able to get to your jump shot off of one dribble." And Collin would lose his mind—he couldn't do it at first. So they'd go two dribbles. Then they'd go back to one dribble. It would just go on and on.

And on and on and on, often past midnight, to the point where they had to be dragged out by their parents.

Despite standing merely five feet ten by his senior year, Harper had become a top-100 national recruit and earned a scholarship to Auburn University—an SEC school, just like the University of Kentucky, where Tyler Ulis played. During his junior season with the Tigers, he helped lead the team on an improbable run to the 2019 Final Four, averaging 16.2 points and 5.8 assists in the NCAA Tournament. They beat a loaded Kentucky squad, featuring

Tyler Herro, Immanuel Quickley, P. J. Washington, and Keldon Johnson, in the Elite Eight, with Harper scoring 12 points in overtime alone.

After that, it was time for the plan to finally reach its pinnacle. Like Cheatham, Harper declared for the 2019 NBA Draft. And like Cheatham, he didn't end up getting picked. His size—he measured five feet eleven with shoes on at the NBA Draft Combine, which was the second shortest height recorded that year—continued to be a major impediment.

From there, he and Zylan embarked on similar journeys. Zylan got his brief chance with the Pelicans; Jared got brief chances with the Phoenix Suns and the New York Knicks. As of 2021, however, he had logged just twenty-four total minutes on an NBA court, fifteen less than he played in that Elite Eight clash with Kentucky alone. His belief in himself, unsurprisingly, hadn't wavered, though it was frustrating how much remained out of his control. He could vary his approach and keep improving his game, but he couldn't change his height. Only ten players under six feet—Harper included—had appeared in an NBA game during the 2020–21 season.

"My thing is that he gets a chance," Patrick said. "That's it. Now if he gets a chance and it doesn't work out, I can live with it. But give him a chance."

"It's just trying to control what I can control," Harper added. "I know I'm an NBA player. And I know there are people out there that understand and know. But it just takes that one team that's really going to pull the trigger and be, like, you know what, we're going to give him a real shot. And I feel like that's all I need."

• • •

As the summer of 2021 began, Hill, Young, Cheatham, and Harper all found themselves in the same precarious position: on the outside of the NBA, fighting to make it in. Chasing a dream. It meant that their disparate paths, from Israel to China to the United States, were about to converge in a single place. A place nobody wants to be.

A place called the G League.

1. WHAT'S THE G LEAGUE?

Growing up on the South Side of Chicago, Illinois, Renaldo Major was convinced that he would one day be a professional baseball player. He wore number 30 and was the centerfielder for the Meyering Park Mets, a local youth team. He was good too. *Really* good. Good enough to be singled out by coaches as a potential future star, even though he was just in elementary school. For a brief time, Major thought he was destined to become the next Ken Griffey Jr.

That all changed at a family barbeque in May of 1991—right around Renaldo's ninth birthday. His uncles were all huddled around a small television, watching the Chicago Bulls game. Little Renaldo wedged his way into the crowd. He stared curiously at the screen. He didn't know much about basketball, but the announcer kept repeating the same name, over and over again: *Michael Jordan. Michael Jordan. Michael Jordan.*

"Who's Michael Jordan?" Renaldo finally asked.

Michael Jordan—the eventual five-time NBA MVP and six-time NBA champion, widely considered the greatest basketball player to ever walk the earth—would soon become Renaldo's hero. More than that, Jordan would completely change the direction of Renaldo's life. The Bulls legend grew to be so famous and so idolized that it became almost cliché to say, "Michael Jordan inspired me to become a basketball player." But Michael Jordan inspired Renaldo Major to become a basketball player, without a doubt.

Not long after that family gathering, Major quit baseball forever—no more centerfield, no more Meyering Park Mets, no more worshiping Ken Griffey Jr. Instead, basketball became his obsession—the sort of obsession that drowns out everything else in the world. Major's life was basketball. And soon, his dream was to make it to the NBA. "They say don't put all your eggs in one basket, but I kind of did that," he said. "I wanted nothing but the NBA. I had my mindset stuck on the NBA. NBA or nothing. NBA or nothing."

Though rail thin, Renaldo had the physical tools for basketball. He was tall, long-armed, fast, and athletic—just like his father, Ronald, had been. His go-to move was a little midrange jumper, catching the ball around the foul line and rising over smaller defenders. Renaldo became a good player at Carver High School, but not *that good*. Not the kind of player who dreams of making it to the NBA. Not the kind of player who puts all his eggs in one basket.

Still, despite a high school career that caused about as much splash as a rock tossed in the ocean, he fully, albeit foolishly, believed that basketball was his purpose. So much so that he neglected schoolwork—he had to scramble in the last few months of his senior year just to graduate from Carver—and any semblance of a social life.

"I was weird in high school. I had no friends," he remembered with a laugh. "It's funny—I didn't want to pay attention to anything else. All I wanted to do was just play basketball."

His confidence was admirable, sure, but also delusional. He was a zero-star recruit in a pre–social media era. Even at six feet seven with solid skills, how was Major going to get noticed? How was he going to make it to the pros? What miracle path existed? And here's the thing: Major didn't just dream of a life in the NBA, he prepared for it as if it were inevitable. As a teenager, he would practice talking to imaginary reporters.

"What were your thoughts on your performance today, Renaldo?"

"I did well. I could've gotten my teammates more involved, and I could've played better defense."

"Walk us through that play down the stretch."

"Well, I tried to turn baseline and uh—"

Stop. Jordan never said "uh."

So Major would start over, rehearsing lines about a nonexistent play for a nonexistent team in a nonexistent game—sometimes for over an hour. "I knew I was going to be a basketball player. I knew I was going to make the NBA," he said. "I was put on earth to be an NBA player. I always envisioned that. I just knew it was going to come." He just didn't know *how*.

Major graduated from Carver in June of 2000 without any college scholarship offers. He had no thoughts of going to school strictly for an education. Sulking at home all summer, his father ultimately presented him with two options: get a job or enlist in the army. In other words, it was time for Renaldo Major to face reality. To move on.

• • •

Right around the same time, then NBA commissioner David Stern held his annual state-of-the-game press conference during the 2000 NBA Finals. Among the topics addressed was the formation of a new minor league for the NBA. The National Basketball Development League (NBDL) would begin play for the 2001–2 season, Stern announced. Players had to be at least twenty years old to participate in the league, with one noteworthy exception: players under twenty who had been drafted and subsequently released by an NBA team were also eligible.

At the turn of the century, teenagers were flooding into the NBA like it was Daytona Beach on spring break. An increasing number of players were entering the NBA with little or no college experience (in the 2001 NBA Draft, for example, three of the top four picks came straight out of high school). Of course, not all of them were ready for the big stage—not yet. Dwain Price, longtime writer for the *Fort Worth Star-Telegram*, presented the dilemma: "How does the league improve while at the same time develop young players into veteran professionals?" he wrote in June of 2000. "And what happens to the young players who don't make it?"[1]

Those players couldn't return to college basketball, having forfeited their eligibility. Minor leagues like the Continental Basketball Association (CBA) and the International Basketball League (IBL) were options, as was going overseas. A lot of players ended up just buried on an NBA bench somewhere, waiting for an opportunity. Many faded into irrelevance.

Enter the NBDL. The league would be all about development. Development of young players, coaches, referees, managers, executives, PR reps—*everyone*. The goal was to foster a system that functioned similarly to Triple-A baseball. Organizations such as the CBA and IBL served as pipelines to the NBA, yet it was critical, in Stern's view, to build something more closely intertwined— where players could move freely up and down.

"I think [the NBDL] can be a real good thing. I certainly know that in the time I've been coaching in the league, I've seen all kinds of players that aren't quite ready and have no place to go," then Seattle SuperSonics coach Paul Westphal told the *Star Tribune*. "And sometimes they're on a roster, and they need more playing time. Hopefully this developmental league will address a lot of the people that have fallen through the cracks."[2]

• • •

Ronald Major, Renaldo's dad, liked to reference a specific passage when talking to his son about the future, written by noted author Carlos Castaneda in *Journey to Ixtlan: The Lessons of Don Juan*, as a quote from don Juan:

> "There is something you ought to be aware of by now," don Juan said. "I call it the cubic centimeter of chance. All of us, whether or not we are warriors, have a cubic centimeter of chance that pops out in front of our eyes from time to time. The difference between an average man and a warrior is that the warrior is aware of this, and one of his tasks is to be alert, deliberately waiting, so that when his cubic centimeter pops out he has the necessary speed, the prowess to pick it up.
>
> "Chance, good luck, personal power, or whatever you may call it, is a peculiar state of affairs. It is like a very small stick that comes out in front of us and invites us to pluck it. Usually we are too busy, or too preoccupied, or just too stupid and lazy to realize that that is our cubic centimeter of luck. A warrior, on the other hand, is always alert and tight and has the spring, the gumption necessary to grab it."[3]

Ronald encouraged Renaldo to be a warrior—to be ready for his cubic centimeter of chance. And Renaldo listened. He was a fan of Castaneda's passage. He trusted its message, so he remained alert, deliberately waiting. And

What's the G League?

time and time again, when all hope seemed lost, a door suddenly opened up for him. It happened first at the end of his high school career, when Renaldo had no scholarship offers. Just as he was considering a future in the army, the phone rang. A small community college in Levelland, Texas (South Plains), had heard about Major and was willing to give him a shot. His dream was alive.

Major didn't hesitate. He went down to Levelland, worked furiously on improving his game, and dominated the competition right away. "Sometimes you see someone or something happens and you think, *I got a real prospect here*," said Steve Green, who coached Major at South Plains. "There was something about him. He was kind of like a praying mantis—all arms and legs and skinny—but he had a beautiful jump shot."

Green's star player eventually transferred to a bigger program at Fresno State, but when he finished college in 2004, all hope seemed lost again. Though Major went to several camps throughout the summer, not a single professional team expressed interest in signing him. He accepted a job at a Ford manufacturing plant in Chicago and was just about to start when the phone rang. It was Coach Duane Ticknor from the Gary Steelheads, a team in the Continental Basketball Association, inviting Major to try out for their 2004–5 squad—another cubic centimeter.

That was all Renaldo needed. He beat out seven other players to make the Steelheads' final roster and used that season as a stepping-stone to keep chasing his dream.

• • •

The NBDL had kicked off in mid-November 2001 with eight teams owned by the NBA: Asheville (NC) Altitude, Columbus (GA) Riverdragons, Fayetteville (NC) Patriots, Greenville (SC) Groove, Huntsville (AL) Flight, Mobile (AL) Revelers, North Charleston (SC) Lowgators, and Roanoke (VA) Dazzle. They were all based out of the Southeast in cities with modest populations. That was part of Commissioner Stern's vision—to bring basketball to more remote locations, helping to grow the game at the grassroots level.

The first few seasons were rocky. Introducing a new league, especially a minor league, was a huge undertaking. A challenge that required patience. Triple-A had been around since 1946. Before then, Double-A had been the highest classification of Minor League Baseball since 1912. It would take time for the NBDL to build trust with the people and institutions essential to its success: players, coaches, executives, fans, media companies, television networks.

From the very beginning, the primary goal of the league was a one-to-one affiliation model, where one NBDL team would exist for every NBA team—a true minor league farm system. That way, the NBDL would be relied upon heavily, and its importance to the NBA would be undeniable.

With that goal in mind, the league made some tweaks in 2005. First, it rebranded from the National Basketball Development League to the NBA Development League. Distinct NBA affiliations were also established—each D-League team was shared among multiple NBA teams. Rules about sending players down to the D-League were instituted. NBA teams could assign guys with less than two years of experience a maximum of three times throughout a season.

By the 2006–7 season, none of the original eight teams remained, as the D-League had garnered momentum and expanded out of the Southeast. The CBA was slowly dying, and a handful of their teams jumped ship before the inevitable demise. The Dakota Wizards, Sioux Falls Skyforce, and Idaho Stampede all joined the D-League in 2006, along with the American Basketball Association's[4] Bakersfield Jam and three completely new organizations: the Anaheim Arsenal, Colorado 14ers, and Los Angeles D-Fenders. There were now a total of twelve teams, divided up among the NBA (Bakersfield, for example, was affiliated with five NBA teams at once). New policies also allowed NBA franchises to own and operate D-League franchises—an option that the Los Angeles Lakers took advantage of with the D-Fenders.

Amid this period of growth and transformation, Renaldo Major, then twenty-four years old and playing in the United States Basketball League (another small pro league that would cease operations in 2008), entered the D-League. He was selected in the fourth round of the 2006 D-League Draft by the Dakota Wizards. At long last, the NBA was right within reach. Major was one step away from his dream.

Life in the D-League was far from glamorous, however. The NBA—an association of million-dollar contracts and billion-dollar TV deals—might have

What's the G League?

been one step away, but it felt like another universe. Players in the D-League were earning between $12,000 and $25,000 during the 2006–7 season. Players in the NBA were earning between $412,000 and $21 million that same year. "I thank the Lord that the D-League allowed us to play, but the resources weren't as good," Major said. "It was tough. The checks you got would be gone in like two weeks because most people had families and kids to take care of."

Teams flew commercial—not private. If bussing to away games was an option (meaning the distance wasn't *completely* absurd), then they took busses. Some road trips lasted more than ten hours. Hotels were, at best, Holiday Inns, and sometimes motels with stained red carpets crawling with bugs. Cities that hosted teams were remote and unexciting—no Miami, no New York, no Chicago. Per diems were enough to buy fast food or stock up on cheap options from a local grocery store. Games had crowds in the hundreds—not thousands.

At home, everyone had a roommate. The Wizards shared two beat-up vans—which, according to Major's teammate Richard Hendrix, "looked like the Mystery Machine off of Scooby Doo"—to navigate around town. The gas tanks always hovered around *E*, as none of the players wanted to pay the full cost of filling them up. When it snowed—not a rare occurrence in Bismarck—players had to get up early to shovel the driveway. One morning, the guys headed out for practice, only to find one of their vans stuck on a sheet of ice. "We're trying to push it down the driveway, but we can't get any footing," remembered Rod Benson, another of Major's teammates. "So it's literally ten of us moving this car like a quarter inch every five minutes. We were an hour late to practice."

Still, Major was thrilled to be a part of the D-League. He knew that several guys in his position had been called up to the NBA in previous years, including Chris "Birdman" Andersen, Rafer Alston, Ime Udoka, Smush Parker, and Will Bynum. He would be next.

I was put on Earth to be an NBA player. I just knew it was going to come.

Just being in the D-League was extra motivation. Major could finally see the finish line, which turned his marathon of a journey into an all-out sprint. He wasted no time with the Wizards, immediately proving to be one of the most dynamic forwards in the entire D-League and leading his team to victory after victory. Dakota entered the 2007 D-League Winter Showcase—an annual scouting event attended by representatives from every NBA team—with a 13-3 record, the best in the league. And Major was the Wizards' best player.

The Showcase, held in Sioux Falls, South Dakota, that year, was a vital opportunity to impress NBA higher-ups and decision-makers. Major had no sense, though, that any of those bigwigs were interested *in him*. He didn't have an agent or any communication with people in NBA circles. There was no social media, no constant stream of rumors and reports. Major was just focused on basketball, which is why what happened next, at the Sheraton Sioux Falls, came as such a surprise.

Major was finished for the day. In Dakota's only game, a 95–94 win over the Albuquerque Thunderbirds, he had scored a team-high 23 points on 7 of 14 shooting. Now it was evening, and he was prepared to crash. As he plodded through the hallway to his hotel room, his phone rang. He picked it up. On the other end was Chris Alpert, the D-League's vice president of basketball operations.

"Are you sitting down?" Alpert asked.

"Should I?"

"Yeah, I think you should."

Major got to his room and plopped down on the side of the bed, a bit fearful. What was this about? Had he done something wrong? Was he in trouble with the league? He still didn't suspect what Alpert quickly blurted out: the Golden State Warriors were calling him up. Renaldo Major was going to the NBA.

"Honestly, I kind of blacked out. I didn't see that coming at all. I didn't see that—that was—" Major struggled to find the words. "I bowed twenty-five to thirty times, just thanking the Lord. *Thank you, Lord. Thank you, Lord!* Then I called my dad and told him, like, 'Yeah, pops, I got called up to the NBA.' And he just instantly started crying. 'You did it, son! There's gonna be a Major name on the back of an NBA jersey. I know it was tough, and it was a long road for you, but you did it.' And I just sat there and cried."

Ronald was one of the few people who truly understood what Renaldo was feeling—how thrilled and excited and relieved his son was. The transaction barely made the news—it got a line or two in select newspapers—but it meant everything to Renaldo. This was the moment he had waited for his whole life, the moment he had dreamed of sharing with his father since he first watched Michael Jordan play basketball more than a decade earlier. It was the moment Stern had envisioned when he established the D-League in 2001.

Short-handed due to injuries, the Warriors signed Major to a ten-day contract, for which he was paid nearly double what he received for the full D-League season. He played in the team's very next game—an away game against the Los Angeles Clippers.

"I remember at the start of the game, I was sitting on the bench, and it still seemed surreal," Major said, smiling wide. "I'm, like, *I'm really in the NBA. I just kept saying that to myself. I'm really in the NBA. Wow.* I just kept telling God, *This is only you. Only you could make this happen. This wasn't me; it was you.* No lie, I can say it now, but I'm on the bench thinking, like, *Sam Cassell! Elton Brand!*"

Major was in awe of his peers. As he sat there, mesmerized, Warriors head coach Don Nelson suddenly called his name. Renaldo sprung to his feet and sprinted to the scorer's table. In his haste, he forgot to remove his warm-up shirt and had to be reminded by Nelson.

Waiting at the table to check in, Major tried to calm his nerves. *Just breathe,* he thought. *Breathe, Renaldo. You've been doing this your whole life. Breathe.* "I swear I thought I was about to pass out," he would later describe. "I was so excited that I couldn't breathe."

He missed his first few shot attempts—in hindsight, it's amazing that he didn't shoot them into the stands with his adrenaline pumping as it was—but eventually got on the board with a baseline dunk. He logged twenty-seven total minutes, finishing with 5 points, 2 rebounds, and 2 steals in a 115–109 loss.

Ten days came and went in a blink. Major didn't get another opportunity to play. His contract expired, and it was time to head back to the D-League. *No big deal,* he thought. *I'll be back.* It was certainly reasonable thinking. Major was just twenty-four years old, on the rise, and clearly on the radar of NBA teams now. And his stock would rise even more when he returned to Dakota and guided the Wizards to the 2007 D-League championship, averaging 18 points, 5.5 rebounds, 4.5 assists, and 4.5 steals in the playoffs.

Everything was about to change though. Major went to training camp for the Denver Nuggets in 2007, where he first had to pass a routine physical. During that appointment, team physicians discovered that Renaldo had an irregular heartbeat, the product of a loose aortic valve. Left untreated, the condition could be extremely dangerous. Major would require open-heart surgery right away.

On October 18, 2007, doctors at Stroger Hospital in Chicago successfully performed the procedure, leaving a nine-inch scar across Renaldo's chest. The recovery process would be long and grueling. Ronald was right by his son's side the entire time, waking up at 6:00 a.m. every morning to check on him. Renaldo missed the entire 2007–8 season but was progressing toward a return and feeling hopeful for the future. Then, in May 2008, two days before Renaldo's twenty-sixth birthday, his father suffered an unexpected stroke and died.

"I went through a dark phase," Renaldo said. "I didn't really want to play basketball anymore." He had just overcome an incredible hardship, then this—something even more devastating and inconceivable. Basketball was the last thing on his mind. He was broken, physically and emotionally. In that state, he couldn't imagine doing anything.

As the summer crawled by, and the next D-League season approached, Major's will to play gradually returned. He wouldn't stop. He *couldn't* stop. Ronald would have wanted him to keep going. He rejoined the Wizards in October 2008, got back in tip-top shape, and began his race to the NBA again. Only this time, that race would never reach its finish line.

Age was not on Major's side. The NBA sought younger players, not veterans. Teams invested in potential—what might become, not necessarily what was. Renaldo was still a solid big man, but he wasn't getting any better. He had reached his ceiling, and his ceiling wasn't quite good enough.

Major never got another call-up. He never appeared in another NBA game. He remained in the D-League for nine more seasons, 356 more games, 10,040 more minutes played, eventually setting a number of league records (most points, field goals, free throws, steals, and win shares) that still stand today. Though it wasn't the plan, the D-League became Renaldo's home. His career. His fate.

Thus, Major saw and experienced the growth of the league firsthand. More fans started to pay attention, especially as games became more accessible on television and online. More teams, spread out across the United States, joined almost every year—the total rose to sixteen by 2011–12, then to twenty-two by 2016–17, Renaldo's final season. More teams meant more one-to-one affiliations with the NBA—a major reason that the number of call-ups and assignments continued to climb. Major was one of twenty-two call-ups in his first D-League season; in 2016–17, there were fifty-one call-ups. Throughout Major's decade in the D-League, some big names came through on their way to successful NBA careers: players Jeremy Lin, Hassan Whiteside, Seth Curry, Danny Green, Shaun Livingston, Spencer Dinwiddie, and Quinn Cook and coaches Dave Joerger, Quin Snyder, Taylor Jenkins, Nick Nurse, and Luke Walton.

When Major entered the NBA's minor league system, it was transitioning from the NBDL to the D-League. When he retired, it was about to transition from the D-League to the G League, a byproduct of a new groundbreaking partnership with the sports-drink company Gatorade.

The real question many wondered was, why did Major stay that long? Practically no other players did. They all, including Major, received numerous offers from organizations overseas, where they stood to make significantly more money. D-League salaries had increased over the years, but only slightly. Major never took home more than $30,000 a season. A team in China was prepared to pay him $30,000 a month after his return from heart surgery.

He stayed, in part, for the competition. Every game, every practice, in the D-League was war. The talent level was far higher than anywhere else Major could have played. D-Leaguers couldn't afford to mess around or take days off—they were fighting for their dreams, jockeying for a few select spots each year. That kind of competition brought the best out of Major. Like his hero, Jordan, it was why he loved the game.

Even with that ruthless competition, a unique camaraderie was in the D-League—a sense of brotherhood. Everyone shared the exact same goal. There was something about being in it *together*, about going through the arduous grind of a season *together*, that felt special. It was a feeling that couldn't possibly be replicated somewhere else.

And, of course, Renaldo was chasing his dream. Logic says he should have jumped at one of those contracts overseas. Logic says only around 450 players are in the NBA at a given time, making it one of the most exclusive and far-fetched jobs to obtain in the world. But logic tends to fade away when you're chasing a dream. Overseas, the path to his dream was hard to envision. In the D-League, it was *right there*.

NBA or nothing. NBA or nothing.

For Major, no amount of money was worth more than a shot at his dream, so he never gave up on its pursuit. He always believed that it might happen— that a cubic centimeter of chance might pop out again. And if it did, he would have the spring, the gumption, necessary to grab it.

2. IT'S NICE TO HAVE YOU IN BIRMINGHAM

According to Roman mythology, the goddess Juno took one look at her son Vulcan and was so appalled by his appearance that she hurled him from the top of a cliff. Vulcan tumbled to the sea below—from the mountain's peak to the valley's bottom—where he was discovered by nymphs and raised in caverns. Those caverns provided him with all the resources he needed to become an expert blacksmith. Vulcan dedicated his time to perfecting the art of forge, eventually becoming so masterful that the other gods desired his services. Out of iron, copper, gold, silver, and other materials, he crafted some of the most beautiful and influential items in Roman lore.

A colossal statue of Vulcan sits atop Red Mountain in Birmingham, Alabama. It is the largest cast-iron statue in the world, standing fifty-six feet tall and weighing 101,200 pounds. You can take a winding staircase to an observation deck near the head of the structure, where much of the city—the Magic City, as it's known—is visible below: Sloss Furnaces, which first went into blast in April 1882 and produced the pig iron that facilitated Birmingham's rise; the Sixteenth Street Baptist Church, which became a symbol of the modern civil rights movement after it was the site of a Ku Klux Klan bombing that tragically killed four young girls; Regions Field, home of the Birmingham Barons, a Minor League Baseball team dating back to 1885; Railroad Park, a nineteen-acre green space in the heart of downtown, hailed as "Birmingham's

Living Room"; John's City Diner, a local fixture serving Southern staples, with its mural that pays homage to an old city slogan: "It's Nice to Have You in Birmingham."

Vulcan presides over all of it, reaching his spear high toward the sky. He is the most iconic emblem of the city, meant to reflect its roots in the iron and steel industries and Birmingham's rapid ascent into a boom town. One of the messages of Vulcan's tale—and, thus, of the city of Birmingham—is highlighted on the official website for the statue: "Legends aren't born, they're forged."[1]

• • •

In 2021 Birmingham became the proud new home of a G League franchise. After two decades of growth, the NBA's minor league had just about reached its longstanding goal. Three new teams were welcomed for the 2021–22 season—the Birmingham Squadron, Motor City Cruise, and Mexico City Capitanes—bringing the total number to thirty, twenty-eight of which were single-affiliates of an NBA parent club.

Three years prior, in October 2018, the NBA's New Orleans Pelicans announced that they had acquired the right to own and operate a G League organization in Birmingham. A lot of work was yet to be done, including the massive renovation of Legacy Arena, which would host the team's home games. In the meantime, the franchise would begin play in Erie, Pennsylvania, as the Erie BayHawks.

"We know this has been a lengthy process, but we wanted to ensure that we found the best partner for this endeavor, as we are fully invested in our team and building basketball in the Gulf South," Pelicans president Dennis Lauscha said in a press release. "We've done our due diligence and researched markets across the region, and no one matched the interest and investment that the City of Birmingham will provide."[2]

Basketball in Alabama? It didn't sound quite right. Alabama is a football state—the biggest football state in all of America. According to 2021 Google Trends data, Alabama was the most popular state for the search terms "football" and "college football."[3] When University of Alabama coach Nick Saban first joined the football program in 2007, ninety-two thousand fans came to watch the team's intrasquad scrimmage.

Ninety-two thousand.

At an *intrasquad scrimmage.*

"They say college football is religion in the Deep South, but it's not," *Sports Illustrated's* Rick Bragg wrote in 2007. "Only religion is religion. Anyone who has seen an old man rise from his baptism, his soul all on fire, knows as much, though it is easy to see how people might get confused. But if football was a faith anywhere, it would be here on the Black Warrior River in Tuscaloosa, Ala."[4]

At the center of this football-crazed universe is the contentious rivalry between the University of Alabama (UA) and Auburn University (AU), the two major colleges in the state. Every Alabaman inherits a side. There can be no wavering—no straddling the line or rooting for both schools. It's crimson and white or orange and blue, "Roll Tide!" or "War Eagle!" In a land where football is nearly religion, the Iron Bowl—the annual meeting between the two foes, which was played at Birmingham's Legion Field for many years and derives its nickname from the influence of the steel industry in the city—is one of the most anticipated days of the year.

Of course, there is the infamous story of the late Harvey Updyke, a die-hard Alabama fan who poisoned the eighty-year-old oak trees at Auburn, situated at a popular site for fans to gather following big victories. The incident took place during the 2010–11 college football season, and Updyke called into the Paul Finebaum radio show to proudly admit what he had done.

"The weekend after the Iron Bowl, I went to Auburn because I lived thirty miles away, and I poisoned the two Toomer's trees," Updyke told Finebaum without a trace of remorse in his tone. "I put Spike 80DF in 'em. They're not dead yet, but they definitely will die."

"Is it against the law to poison a tree?" Finebaum asked.

"Do you think I care?" Updyke responded. "I really don't. Roll damn Tide!"[5]

Updyke later pleaded guilty to the crime, serving more than seventy days in jail and being ordered to pay $800,000 in restitution.

• • •

Nonetheless, there are other popular sports in Birmingham. The city has several minor league sports teams: the Barons of Double-A Minor League

Baseball, Bulls of the Southern Professional Hockey League, Stallions of the United States Football League, Legion FC of the United Soccer League, and now, of course, the Squadron of the G League.

Like all NBA franchises, the Pelicans sought to have their affiliate close to home. Movement back and forth from the G League was increasing every year (with the exception of seasons affected by COVID), so proximity—ideally driving distance—made life significantly easier. Sure, pro basketball hadn't existed in Alabama for more than fifteen years, but there was clearly a craving for it. The basketball programs at UA and AU were on the rise and had become more than just a footnote in the legendary rivalry. Birmingham regularly ranked among the highest-rated local markets for nationally televised NBA games.

Situated in central Alabama, the Magic City is about a two-hour drive from Atlanta (home of the Hawks), a four-hour drive from Memphis (home of the Grizzlies), and a five-hour drive from New Orleans (home of the Pelicans). No NBA team dominates, or even controls in any discernible way, the area. The region has some Hawks fans, some Grizzlies fans, some Pelicans fans. Many Alabamans just follow their favorite NBA players, rooting for whatever team has LeBron James or Kevin Durant or the last star to come out of UA or AU. Birmingham is a significant basketball market that has never really been claimed; it is a basketball city without a basketball team.

Until now. The hope in New Orleans is that all those people, all those nomadic fans searching for a home, will fall in love with the Squadron—and, in turn, fall in love with the Pelicans.

Step one—make them fall in love with the Squadron—wouldn't be so easy, however. Yes, Alabamans had an interest in the NBA. But minor league basketball? The G League? Most of them had never even heard of it.

• • •

"I've never been afraid to fail. You're not always going to be successful. I think I'm strong enough as a person to accept failure. But I can't accept not trying." Renaldo Major's hero, the great Michael Jordan, uttered those words back in 1994, as he was prepared to make a career change—quite a famous career change, actually. The NBA's best player, then a nine-time All-Star, three-time MVP, and three-time champion, had retired from basketball and decided to give baseball a shot. He had left Chicago and arrived in the much smaller, much quieter city of Birmingham, where he joined the Birmingham Barons, a Minor League affiliate of the Chicago White Sox.

It was, unsurprisingly, a strange transition to observe. Jordan was on top of the world. He was untouchable. His greatness on a basketball court was as predictable as the sun rising each morning. And then, suddenly, he was in Birmingham, in the Minor Leagues, making $850 a month and trying to work his way to the MLB. You had to see it to believe it.

So people flocked to Birmingham. The Barons were thrown into the national spotlight, featured on the front page of major papers like *USA Today* and the *Wall Street Journal*, and on television programs like the *NBC Evening News* with Tom Brokaw. Games at Hoover Metropolitan Stadium ("the Met")—fifteen miles outside the downtown area—became the hottest ticket in town.

When Jordan made his debut on April 8, 1994, fans started lining up outside the Met more than two-and-a-half hours before the gates opened. The final attendance was recorded at 10,359, less than the 14,000 some were expecting, but way more than the 4,075 the Barons had averaged the season prior.[6] One hundred thirty members of the media were there, including representatives from as far away as Tokyo. The crowd roared anytime Jordan did *anything*. He even received an ovation after striking out in the fourth inning.

"The fans weren't at the Met to see him play baseball," Paul Finebaum, then a columnist for the *Birmingham Post-Herald*, wrote. "They just wanted to see him, period."[7]

That's how it was all season. Baseball was the sideshow; Jordan was the main attraction. He single-handedly gave a Minor League organization, which still bused to away games (as far as twelve hours to Orlando) and stayed at La Quinta Inns, a brief taste of Major League limelight. According to the *Post-Herald*, "More than 500 journalists from the United States and eight foreign nations covered Jordan's Birmingham odyssey, and the Barons shattered single-game and season attendance records during his stay."[8]

Jordan batted .202 with 3 home runs and 51 RBI in 127 games that season, before opting to return to the NBA in 1995. He never got a call-up to the MLB—but at least he tried.

• • •

For the Squadron, there would be no Michael Jordan. No one remotely close. Selling tickets and filling seats would not be so simple.

Every player in the G League was a former college star, but none of them possessed the fame to attract a significant fan base on their own. Plus, in the minors, rosters changed drastically every season—sometimes *completely*. While Birmingham was keeping the same coaching staff from Erie, it would have zero returning players.

The franchise had elaborate plans to embed itself in the community. It would host events around the city, introducing its brand, staff, and players to the people directly. It would build relationships with local organizations, support local businesses, and partner with local staples like Saw's BBQ restaurant. All of that would help, no question. But there's really no trick to capturing the hearts of Alabama sports fans. Ask locals, and they will tell you. Want to build a fan base in the region?

Win.

Win some more.

Keep winning.

Don't stop winning.

As Paul "Bear" Bryant, legendary head coach of the Alabama football team from 1958 to 1982, once said, "Winning isn't everything, but it beats anything that comes in second." The people of Alabama worship football in large part because the college football programs in the area have been so dominant. *Dominant* actually undersells it. They have been nearly unconquerable, claiming twenty combined national championships.

Constructing a good G League team, with the potential to succeed right away, was easier said than done. As of mid-September 2021, the Squadron knew a handful of names that were likely to end up on the final roster. The front office had executed a trade to get Zylan Cheatham and a 2021 second-round pick from the Iowa Wolves, giving up the returning rights to guard Tony

Carr and 2021 first- and third-round picks. Cheatham would spend time with the Pelicans during NBA training camp, along with a few other exhibit-ten players, including Malcolm Hill, Jared Harper, twenty-three-year-old big man James Banks III, and rookie sharpshooter John Petty Jr., all of whom were expected to eventually land in Birmingham.[9] Two-way players Jose Alvarado and Daulton Hommes also seemed like safe bets to be periodically transferred to the G League throughout the season.[10]

The group was solid but far from a sure thing to win a lot of games, at least on paper. Squadron decision-makers weren't focused solely on stockpiling talent, though. It was about building the *right* roster, finding the *right* fits. In that regard, they felt optimistic about the guys already in the mix. But there was far more work to do.

3. TRYOUTS

The morning of September 18, 2021—a Saturday—inspired little activity in Birmingham. A light rain fell. The sky was a depressing shade of gray. Wind howled ominously through the deserted streets. On the outskirts of downtown, however, sixty G League hopefuls had convened at Bill Harris Arena for the first ever Birmingham Squadron open tryout.

Tryouts are a longstanding tradition in the G League. Anyone over the age of eighteen is eligible to participate, as long as he pays the organization's entry fee, which typically ranges from $150 to $250. G League teams are permitted to invite up to five players from their local tryouts to preseason training camp. Although a majority of the Squadron roster would be assembled in other ways, the stakes of this Saturday-morning event were still significant. Many notable players had emerged from tryouts in the past, going on to successful careers not just in the G League but also at the highest level.

• • •

Ron Howard was a standout guard at Valparaiso University, a midmajor school in the Missouri Valley Conference. After going undrafted in 2006, he struggled to find other opportunities to play professionally. He was twenty-five years old and prepared to move on from basketball forever. Money was tight, and his wife, Reesha, had just given birth to a baby girl.

"I had decided that basketball was done. It wasn't for me. I knew I could play, but it just wasn't working out. It's not for everybody," Howard said. "I had to pull my degree out and start getting the résumé together."

Howard started applying for jobs—desk jobs and normal nine-to-fives. As he awaited responses, a friend encouraged him to try out for a new D-League team launching in Fort Wayne, Indiana—just a three-hour drive from Ron's hometown of Chicago—called the Mad Ants. Howard agreed to go, but showed up an hour late by mistake, not realizing that Fort Wayne was in the eastern time zone. Still, he performed well enough to be invited to day two of the tryouts. Only one problem—Howard didn't know that there *was* a day two. He didn't have a change of clothes, didn't have money for a hotel room, didn't have friends in Fort Wayne. Seeing no other option, he raced the 160 miles back to Chicago, got roughly three hours of sleep, and drove all the way back to Fort Wayne while it was still dark outside. And somehow, he managed to play well *again*.

The Mad Ants went on to pick Howard in the seventh round of the 2007 D-League Draft. "I was a nobody," he said, thinking back. "I didn't have a name. I was just nobody." Today, in the city of Fort Wayne, Howard is better known as "Mr. Mad Ant." His number 19 jersey hangs from the rafters of the Allen County War Memorial Coliseum, where the Mad Ants play their home games. He was with the organization from its inaugural tryout in 2007 to its first D-League championship in 2014, claiming an MVP trophy, three All-Star nods, and two Jason Collier Sportsmanship Awards over that span. Before Renaldo Major, Howard briefly held the D-League's all-time scoring record. Upon retiring, he accepted a job—a desk job, finally—as the community development manager for the Mad Ants.

Several years later, Jonathon Simmons, a high-flying six-foot-six guard out of the University of Houston, found himself in a similar predicament. After going undrafted in 2012, he had no desire to walk away from basketball but needed a job to support his four daughters. He was skilled at cutting hair, which he did for friends on occasion, so he contemplated getting his barber's license. Before making the career change, though, he traveled to Concordia University in Austin, Texas, and paid the $150 registration fee to try out for the Austin Toros, the affiliate of the San Antonio Spurs. Simmons clearly stood out among the players in attendance. According to Austin's head coach Ken McDonald, the talent level at the tryout ranged from "guys that I can beat one-on-one to guys like Jon."[1]

Simmons was invited to training camp and eventually made the Toros' final roster. He spent the next two seasons in the D-League, improving and expanding his game. During the summer of 2015, he earned a two-year deal with the Spurs, where he became a steady contributor off the bench. His play in San Antonio led to a bigger contract offer from the Orlando Magic in 2017, worth $20 million. Prior to the Toros' tryout, Simmons had been borrowing money to pay for his children's diapers.

More recently, forward Juan Toscano-Anderson made the Santa Cruz Warriors after attending an open tryout in 2018. "He was the last guy to make our team," remembered Kevin Danna, longtime play-by-play announcer for Santa Cruz. "He takes the court, he's smart, he knows how to play, and he plays his ass off. He was a bench guy for us that year but he was, like, *the* reason we were winning games, in my opinion. Juan Toscano-Anderson was like the heart and soul of that team."

Less than three years later, Toscano-Anderson would sign a standard, multiyear NBA contract with the Golden State Warriors, the team he rooted for as a kid growing up in East Oakland. "I'm super excited, obviously for myself to be on the team and continue to play basketball, but this is a life-changing contract," he said, upon making the deal official, "a life-changing signature."[2]

That's precisely what tryouts offered: a potential life-changing opportunity, a glimmer of hope, a chance to resurface after falling through the cracks. As Mr. Mad Ant liked to say, "When a door shuts, try to see if the window is open."

• • •

Of the sixty players gathered at Bill Harris Arena, some were residents of Birmingham; others had flown in from overseas. Their levels of experience varied greatly: high school, college, pros. A few guys openly admitted that they had never played in an organized capacity. They ranged in height from five feet nine to six feet ten and in age from nineteen to sixty-two years old. Yes—*sixty-two years old.*

When Kelvin Davis first picked up a basketball, the three-point line didn't exist, the NBA was televised once a week, box scores were printed only in newspapers, and players wore shorts the size of boxer briefs.

Davis was born in 1959 and raised in the small town of Evergreen, Alabama, about 170 miles south of Birmingham. He grew up in a very different Alabama, one defined by racial injustice, conflict, and violence. Birmingham was regarded as the most segregated city in America during the civil rights movement, often referred to as "Bombingham" due to the number of racially motivated bombings in the area from the late 1940s to the mid-1960s. In 1963 Birmingham's Sixteenth Street Baptist Church, a predominately Black congregation, was bombed by the Ku Klux Klan, leaving four young girls dead. Outrage over the attack helped galvanize the struggle to end segregation across the United States.

Davis, who is Black, experienced racism on a daily basis as a child. He sat on a different side of the bus than the white kids, used different facilities, entered buildings through different doorways. Basketball was his refuge. He became a star at Evergreen High School and later played at Alabama State University. Though he always hoped to turn professional, that opportunity did not present itself until two decades later. At the ripe age of forty-seven, Davis was invited to try out for the Atlanta Vision of the American Basketball Association (ABA) after a chance encounter at an Atlanta Hawks game. In preparation, his training regimen looked like this:

1. Stretch
2. Five-mile run
3. Wind sprints
4. Push-ups
5. Sit-ups
6. Curls
7. Bench press
8. Basketball

Out of a pool of 150 people, Davis, a dad of five, somehow made the Vision's fifteen-man roster. Local news was all over the story. "The oldest rookie" declared one headline. "LeBron James and Kelvin Davis should do a Nike commercial together because this weekend, WE WERE ALL WITNESSES!" Vision owner Quentin Townsend said after the team's tryout.[3]

On weekdays, Davis, who also had a job as a paint contractor, got up at 3:30 a.m. to drive to Suwanee for 6:00 a.m. practice. His first pro basketball paycheck, which was mostly based on incentives, was for $42.09. "Of course, the other teams think it's a stunt," Townsend told the *Atlanta Journal-Constitution* in February 2007. "It's not. He's earned his spot on the team. He's legitimate. He's following his dream."

"My goal is to put that NBA uniform on and walk in that arena and watch America just go nuts because of this old guy who's done something that's never been done before in history," Davis said to the paper. "I don't care if it's for a day. Just sign me to a contract. Let me do that because I have the faith to believe that anything that I go after is going to happen."[4]

Davis spent two full seasons in the ABA before retiring at the age of fifty— well, not *really* retiring. Twelve years later, when he learned of the Squadron's open tryout, he began training again. His faith remained strong. His dream hadn't faded. The oldest rookie was ready to return, never mind that his children were old enough to register for the tryout themselves.

Squadron head coach Ryan Pannone admired Davis. Both are true basketball junkies. Pannone's passion for the game is so pure that it comes across almost childlike. His enthusiasm is comparable to that of popular television character Ted Lasso, played by Jason Sudeikis in the Emmy-award-winning series of the same name. When players left puddles of sweat on the floor, it was Coach Pannone who raced over, towel in hand, eager to clean up the scene. Before placing an order at a nearby Starbucks, Pannone wandered Bill Harris Arena like a waiter working a section, checking to see if anyone else wanted coffee, then checking again, then checking one more time, then cracking a joke when someone inevitably ordered a complicated beverage like a grande caramel ribbon crunch frappuccino with almond milk and two shots of espresso.

Like Lasso, Pannone is a father, with brown eyes and scruffy facial hair. He is quick with a corny dad joke and prone to breaking into monologues, loaded with wisdom and life lessons. Pannone and Lasso have a few consequential differences, however. The latter admittedly knows nothing about the sport he is hired to coach. Pannone, on the other hand, knows an *obsessive* amount about basketball.

By the time he took over the Squadron, Pannone had been coaching for almost two decades, starting at Oldsmar Christian School—a high school in Florida—at the age of eighteen and continuing there while simultaneously managing the men's basketball team at the University of South Florida, coaching an AAU program, interning for well-known trainer David Thorpe, and taking classes. ("The school part is debatable," he later said with a laugh.) From the beginning, Pannone was determined to make a career in coaching work, regardless of the sacrifices.

"There's never been a thought, *It isn't going to work out for me.* It's going to work out, one way or another, some way, shape, or form," he said, before jokingly adding: "A lot of people give you advice, like, 'Always have an option B.' And that's good for smart people. But if you're stupid, there is no option B. You're either going to make it or be homeless. So for me, at some point, *I'm going to make it.*"

With some freedom to recruit the players he wanted, Pannone built Oldsmar Christian into a powerhouse. His sole focus became helping his players reach the college level. The team was playing close to two hundred games a year, entering leagues in every season. Pannone crafted the schedule himself and pursued the best competition. If a top-ranked school was within a fifteen-hour drive, Oldsmar would make the trip.

Pannone created an email database of every Division I, Division II, Division III, National Association of Intercollegiate Athletics (NAIA), and junior college (JUCO) school in the country. He made highlight tapes for all his players. He took them to elite camps, where they would have exposure to college coaches and scouts. The team had mandatory study hall and SAT/ACT tutoring with Pannone's wife, Sarah. Any player who had under a 2.3 core GPA was required to take summer school. Pannone preached structure, accountability, and discipline.

"I made it very clear how we were going to be," he said. "If guys didn't want that, they usually transferred out in the summer. But we had very few guys transfer out." On the contrary, kids started transferring *in* to play for Pannone.

A handful of them even lived at his house. Without financial support from Oldsmar, the team fundraised on its own.

That type of dedication and persistence has defined Pannone's entire coaching journey. No matter what, he was going to *make it work*. When he sought to join a staff overseas, he went on Eurobasket.com, a website that covers international basketball, and combed for every American coach he could find. Then he contacted each of them, either by phone, email, or Facebook. Joe Whelton, who was coaching in the Chinese Basketball Association, responded, and Pannone soon became an assistant for the Foshan Long Lions. Since then, he has coached in the NBA Summer League, South Korea, Germany, Slovakia, Israel, and the G League, taking pay cuts to chase the best openings. His dream, like everyone else in the G, is to make it to the NBA.

"My whole career mentality is money is not going to be the reason why I don't take a job," he said. "If you look at all those jobs, my mentality was, once I got in, I would be able to prove my own value. And it's like I tell coaches all the time, it doesn't say on your résumé what your salary was. It says what your *position* was."

Though he seldom raises his voice, Pannone does have a sterner side to him, at least compared to the overly positive, it's-all-sunshine-and-rainbows Ted Lasso. Pannone is always honest, even if that means being a little harsh. He addressed the group to kick off the tryout, telling them, in blunt terms, that the Squadron had a "no asshole policy." The team was planning to invite a couple of players to training camp and could guarantee that none of them, regardless of talent, size, or athleticism, would be an asshole.

What was Pannone looking for exactly? "A guy that defends, is unselfish, has a high IQ, and makes the right play," he told reporters. "I hate selfishness. I hate selfishness in any part of the game. I'm looking for guys that make the right play, that know how to play, that defend at a high level, and that compete"—and that aren't, under any circumstances, assholes.

Pannone was far more concerned with a player's character than his ability—as he often said, "Everything is easier with high-character people." So, priority number one was to identify those people. Pannone would watch film of prospective players and study details such as temperament on the bench, reaction to bad foul calls, body language, cheering for teammates.

If he noticed sulking or complaining, he would save the clip and send it to Squadron general manager Marc Chasanoff. "See this?" he would say. "This is what we don't want." During the tryout, Squadron coaches knew to look out for that type of behavior. A crappy jump shot was a red flag, but it paled in comparison to a crappy attitude.

Players were immediately divided into six teams. They were taught a few standard offensive sets, which allowed Pannone to weed out the low-basketball-IQ bunch—as he assured the group, those who couldn't remember the plays would be eliminated from contention—before scrimmages began. Games consisted of four ten-minute quarters. Squadron assistant coaches handled the substitutions for each team. The basketball was predictably sloppy. Fouls were *hard fouls*. Turnovers were *ugly turnovers*. Loose balls led to near-rugby scrums. The pace was unrelenting: back and forth, back and forth, back and forth. There were no long, drawn-out, methodical possessions like in an NBA game—just constant attacking. At one point, a player was sprinting back on defense, abruptly stopped, hunched over as if pummeled in the stomach by some invisible force, gazed up with an expression that said, *uh oh*, and vomited right in the middle of the court. He wasn't the only person to get sick; thankfully, the others all made it to a trash can.

Aside from the fact that he wore glasses—not protective goggles a la Kareem Abdul-Jabbar, one of his idols, but *real glasses*—Kelvin Davis didn't stand out much. Given that he qualified for the senior discount at the movies, that was a huge win. Davis kept up with the fast pace, grabbed a few rebounds, moved the ball on offense, stayed in front of his man on defense. During one possession, he recognized an opponent barreling toward the rim, slid into the paint, set his feet, and took a charge. The collision prompted audible gasps from the sideline, but Davis just popped up, flexed his muscles a bit, and let out a loud scream.

Teammates called him "Unc"—short for "Uncle." One of those teammates was six-foot-one guard Xavier Moon, an Alabama native and the nephew of former NBA forward Jamario Moon. Xavier was twenty-seven years old and a three-time MVP and two-time champion in the Canadian Elite Basketball League (CEBL). Over the preceding weeks, he had tried out for three other G League teams.

Moon was dominant without forcing the action. In games that frequently spiraled into chaos, his poise stuck out like Davis' thick glasses. He was under control, even when zipping past everyone else on the court, and could stop on a dime for pull-up jumpers. He checked all the boxes: unselfish—check; talented—check; lightning quick—check; athletic—check; high character—check. The question was less, "Is this guy good enough to play in the G League?" and more, "Could this guy be good enough to play in the NBA?"

Moon had bought out of a contract in Italy to uncover the answer to that question. "That's my dream," he said of the NBA. "This is it. I gotta take this opportunity while it's on the table." He gave himself a C+ for his performance in the Squadron tryout. Privately, Birmingham's coaches were far more generous with their assessments.

• • •

Two players from the tryout wound up accepting invitations to training camp: Dylan Smith, a six-foot-five guard from nearby Mobile, Alabama, and Nate Bradley, a six-foot-four guard from Rochester, New York. The Squadron wanted Xavier Moon, of course. But so did the Agua Caliente Clippers, the G League affiliate of the Los Angeles Clippers. Moon worried that being so close to his hometown of Goodwater—about an hour drive from Birmingham—could present distractions. He ultimately agreed to join Agua Caliente instead, relocating to the serene, distraction-free city of Ontario, California.

Although he didn't make the Squadron, Kelvin Davis succeeded at his larger mission. By participating in the tryout, "Unc" hoped to inspire others. He recognized that to be his life calling, touring as a motivational speaker and offering private coaching to young athletes. Whenever he spoke, he stressed the same message: never give up on your dreams, regardless of the obstacles you face.

"There are times when you'll have to push yourself beyond boundaries and self-limitation," Davis wrote in his autobiography, *The Oldest Rookie*. "Whatever your passion is, you must go after it with everything you have—might and soul. Nothing will come easy in life, but you must be proactive in your pursuit of your dreams. Hurdles were put on the racetrack to be jumped over."[5]

4. DRAFT DAY

Marc Chasanoff took a quick glance at his contact sheet, found the number he was looking for, and dialed it right away. As always, he was moving in fast forward.

"Hello," a voice answered.

"Hey, is this Maurice?" Chasanoff asked.

"No, this is Joe."

Shit.

In his haste, Chasanoff had dialed the wrong number. He meant to call Joe Young's agent, retired NBA forward Maurice Evans. Instead he called Joe Young. Chasanoff—an experienced basketball executive and former scout who had been with the Pelicans organization for twelve seasons—was hoping to gather some intel about where Young was expected to be picked in the upcoming G League Draft. Evans was the person to ask about that—not Young. But Young was the one on the line, and Chasanoff figured, *Oh well, let's roll with it.*

"Hey, Joe, this is Marc Chasanoff, general manager for the Birmingham Squadron. I was actually trying to reach out to your agent."

Chasanoff was forthright about his goal: to find out Young's range for the 2021 Draft. Birmingham was *very* interested in Young—he was the number-one target on its draft board—but at the moment, the team was not in a position to get him. Not even close. The Squadron had traded their first-round pick to Iowa for Zylan Cheatham. As of this phone call, roughly twenty-four hours before the draft, Birmingham held the number forty-seven pick and the number fifty pick. Young would be long gone by then. His flights would be booked to whatever city was lucky enough to draft him.

What Young—a six-foot-two sharpshooting guard formerly with the Indiana Pacers—brought to the table was, in many ways, obvious. Only a handful of players in the 2021 G League Draft pool had touched an NBA court before. Young had logged over one thousand minutes in the NBA, scored 20 points in an NBA game, and gone head-to-head with NBA All-Stars like Paul George and Jeff Teague every day in practice.

Since his career first took off at Yates High School in Houston, Texas, Young had been an explosive scorer, later nicknamed "Joey Buckets." It was in his blood—his father, Michael Young, was an unstoppable offensive player during his own pro career, once leading the entire Italian League in scoring. Joe could pull up from deep, finish over taller defenders at the rim, and regularly destroy teams with his midrange jumper. His speed and handles enabled him to create something out of nothing on any possession. As a senior at Yates, he carried his squad to a perfect 34-0 record, averaging 27 points per game and winning Gatorade Texas Boys Basketball Player of the Year. He spent two seasons at Michael's alma mater—the University of Houston—and then transferred to Oregon, where he registered 1,388 total points, the highest mark over a two-year span in program history. The Indiana Pacers selected him with the forty-third pick in the 2015 NBA Draft, and while he didn't get much of an opportunity in NBA games, he would often dominate in practices.

"If he wanted to take anybody off the dribble, he could," said Dan Burke, an assistant coach for the Pacers from 1997 to 2020 who is currently on the Philadelphia 76ers' staff. "There were some practices where it was like, *Jeez, can anybody guard this guy?* That three would be going, and you'd push up on him, and he'd go by you. If you didn't help, he'd finish. If you did help, he started finding guys."

"Joe was crazy. He was one of the best guys I've ever played against as far as practice," former Pacers teammate Thaddeus Young told *The Athletic*. "He didn't get very much burn in games. But in practice, you could not stop his ass. If we were here and doing five-on-five, he would score 30. I swear to God. He's an NBA player."[1]

An NBA player, maybe. But not a player in the NBA.

Indiana declined to pick up the team option on Young's contract in 2018, which led him to sign a seven-figure deal with the Nanjing Tongxi Monkey Kings of the Chinese Basketball Association (CBA). In China, opponents really "could not stop his ass." Young was one of the top players on the entire continent for the next three seasons, putting up some of the craziest numbers in CBA history. He won the league's scoring title in his second year with an average of 38.3 points per game. The buzz about him grew in the United States, especially when he scored 48 or more in *seven* straight outings, including a legendary 74-point performance (the third highest scoring output in league history). Joe's CBA highlight tapes were almost comical—in many of them, he looked like a high schooler competing against a bunch of tall third graders. He could do whatever he wanted, whenever he wanted.

Birmingham needed a guy like that. A proven talent capable of creating offense and making things happen. The sort of player who gets nicknamed "Joey Buckets." The team's current roster, while solid, didn't have many go-to scoring options. It lacked firepower, another give-me-the-ball-and-get-out-of-the-way type of star. Yes, the roster was loaded with high-character people. But character alone wasn't going to win games. They needed a Joe Young.

There were some question marks about Young, however, or at least reasons to dig deeper. His reputation around the NBA was slightly tarnished. In the business of basketball, narratives about players—whether accurate or misguided—spread like rumors in an elementary school cafeteria:

Did you hear that Alex still pees the bed? Can you believe that? How insane! Alex is a bed-wetter!

Did you hear that Alex got into three fistfights in the locker room? Can you believe that? How insane! Alex is a locker room problem!

In the NBA, narratives circulate *fast*. Reputations stick with the permanence of tattoos. Labels follow players everywhere. When front offices gather intel, they do their best to sift through all the narratives—to get closer and closer to the truth about a player. The bad narratives obviously vary in severity. Some warrant nothing but shrugs; others are deemed unforgivable. And of course, the more talented a player, the more teams are willing to tolerate. NBA superstars can get away with *a lot*. But players on the fringe? They can't get away with anything.

Consider Rod Benson, a dominant force in the D-League between 2006 and 2010. The six-foot-ten undrafted forward led the entire league in rebounding during the 2007–08 season and averaged 14.1 points and 9.7 boards in 2009–10. Off the court, Benson liked to blog about his experience in the minors—a hobby that, as he soon discovered, deeply troubled NBA teams. In the eyes of executives, he became "the writer." *Might he present distractions? Expose locker room secrets? Spend too much time punching keys instead of practicing free-throws?* The label was enough to prevent Benson from ever getting an opportunity in the NBA. "My biggest crime was writing about my Myspace messages and that I thought Steak 'n Shake was delicious," said Benson, who had an extremely successful career overseas and is now a columnist for SFGATE. "The thing I couldn't change was that I was already known as a writer before I got good enough as a basketball player."

One of his college teammates at the University of California, Berkeley, was later hired by the Atlanta Hawks. He reached out to Benson after his first day on the job. "I just had a meeting, and I know exactly why you're not in the NBA now," the friend told Benson. "You're never going to be in. After what we just talked about on my first day, there's literally no way."

Like Benson, Joe Young was a player on the fringe. His slightly tarnished reputation was built on minor mistakes, primarily the lack of maturity he showed as a young professional and an obliviousness for how the NBA business sometimes operates. He did nothing that would deter other franchises from expressing interest, say, he had been a top-twenty pick in the 2015 NBA Draft, as opposed to the forty-third pick. During his three seasons with the Pacers, Young wasn't the subject of negative headlines. He never got suspended by the organization. He wasn't racking up fines or showing up late or getting into fistfights. What tarnished his narrative was much subtler—things that fans and reporters didn't necessarily know about: how he sometimes carried himself, his attitude toward certain decisions, his private dealings with coaches and executives.

Rookies, especially second-round picks, are expected to behave in a certain way, to embody a certain humbleness. When a player hasn't yet earned his stripes in the NBA, he is supposed to act accordingly. That means abandoning any ego, accepting a lesser role without question, and conducting himself in a manner that communicates, *I am thankful and ecstatic to be here*, and not, *I want and deserve more.*

Young joined an already talented Indiana Pacers roster on the rise. He was buried on the depth chart behind more established guards: George Hill, Monta Ellis, Rodney Stuckey (and later, All-Star Jeff Teague, Aaron Brooks, and Lance Stephenson). The face of the franchise was Paul George, a dynamic forward just entering the prime of his career. By some strange coincidence, a day after Young was drafted by the Pacers, he found out that George was in fact his fifth cousin. Relatives started calling Joe's mom, Tina, to ask if she had any idea about her son's relationship to Paul. The connection, as official paperwork confirmed, dated back to twin sisters who were slaves in Opelousas, Louisiana, during the 1800s. According to family research, Young's maternal fourth great-grandmother, Olympe Donato, was the twin sister of George's paternal fourth great-grandmother, Merice Donato.

The cousins ended up hanging out a lot—perhaps too much, at least from the perspective of others within the Pacers organization. Young emulated the team's superstar in many ways. He acted similarly, purchased similar things, drove similar cars. He wore flashy jewelry and designer clothing. He starred in multiple Gatorade commercials alongside George. But Young wasn't like George—not when it came to their status in the NBA. One was a second-round pick on a rookie contract; the other was one of the league's top players, making $17 million a year.

Does spending recklessly and rocking expensive jewelry actually matter when it comes to basketball? Does it affect one's ability to put a ball in a hoop? Of course not. But it can rub people the wrong way. It can be taken as a sign of immaturity, as a foreshadowing of bigger problems to come. Picture a freshman swaggering through the halls of his high school, clutching a Versace backpack and wearing large Gucci shades. Harmless? Yes. But what would the teachers think?

"Those things—they piss people off [in the NBA]," Pannone explained. "Then it becomes water-cooler talk. Then it just spreads. It's all narratives.

What does buying a bunch of stuff have to do with winning basketball games? It really doesn't."

"I think he wanted some of that lifestyle, and he got caught up in that— 'Yeah, I want to be like Paul [George],'" Burke said. "You just can't have that same lifestyle. You gotta be a little more down [to the] level where you're at."

"Paul would include Joe in little things—little deals and commercials and all that stuff. Once you're a rookie and you're [involved] in these things, you're like, *Oh, I made it*, kind of thing," Squadron assistant coach Perry Huang added. "So you can start kind of acting a fool. That's basically what happened with Joe. He just acted bigger than his paycheck, basically. When you start acting like that, whether it's fair or not, a lot of NBA personnel don't like guys who are boisterous like that that haven't made it. There's this flamboyant personality that sometimes you have to tone down."

Here's how Korey Harris, one of Young's assistant coaches in Beijing, framed the dilemma:

We grew up on a certain era of basketball where our stars were a little more brash. It was before social media. It was before a lot of this stuff was accepted. Now you can come flossy to the game and be wearing a hundred chains and your drip be crazy, and that's cool. They'll throw it up on an NBA affiliated Instagram page because that's what everybody's into. But when we were kids, [NBA commissioner] David Stern was telling everybody, "You gotta put on a suit." And then certain guys bucked the trend. I think Joe has some of that—it's not like he's trying to rebel; he just wants to be able to express himself. Some teams view that as a question mark. Like, hey, can he buy in? Can he be on board with the way that our organization asks our players to move? Can we invest money in him and know that he's going to be reliable—like, we're not going to have any type of negative press?

It didn't help that Young was a tad bullish when it *did* come to basketball. Confidence is a good thing for a player to have, as long as it is held in check. If not, it can easily be construed as arrogance. Confidence also cannot interfere with a player's patience. In the NBA, players have to wait for their turn. Newcomers are expected to do so patiently, without ruffling any feathers and with an understanding that the NBA is a business. That's particularly true for newcomers who were drafted in the second round and should have minimal expectations when it comes to playing time.

"I think his frustrations ran over. We say it a lot, maybe too much, but a lot of kids want stuff now," said Burke. "They want fast. Really, you can't blame them. In the world of sports, that window is pretty short. So you can't blame them on that aspect too. Part of being a pro is not just collecting a check; it's not just coming in for workouts; it's not just getting on the bus on time. All of that is important, but I think one hard aspect that these kids fail to grasp—there's a certain hierarchy. There really is."

That hierarchy is built on a number of factors, not just talent: experience, trust, versatility, fit, need. In a billion-dollar business like the NBA, money is obviously a factor too. The bigger a player's contract, the bigger a team's investment in that player. And the bigger a team's investment, the more it seeks in return. Translation—the players who are paid more are likely to get a greater opportunity to prove themselves on the court.

Young didn't have a full grasp of these concepts. He didn't see the big picture. As a rookie, he appeared in just forty-one games, averaging 9.4 minutes per contest. As a sophomore, he saw action in just thirty-three games, averaging 4.1 minutes. Young was training hard, taking the right steps, following the rules, performing well at practice. So why wasn't he playing more?

"I think it got ahead of him, where he thought, you guys owe me some playing time," Burke added. "Sorry, that's just not how it works. When you start having to manage guys toward the end of the bench on that every day, that kind of grows. It affects the team. I'm guessing Joe probably has some regrets on that. It's like all of us; I would have been a better kid if I was a parent first. But it's not a right or wrong, it's just part of the learning and the timing of a roster and the fit of a roster. Joe was just on the outside all the time looking in, as far as rotation."

"It was just an unfortunate chain of events in terms of his fit," said reporter Zach Pearson, who has been covering the Pacers for various outlets since Young's stint with the team. "He was super well liked by the fan base because of his hustle, and he was just fun to watch when he had those good flashes." Pearson recalled two life-sized cardboard cutouts being in the team store at

Bankers Life Fieldhouse: one of big man Myles Turner, a lottery pick seen as a future centerpiece, and one of Joe Young.

Although he was putting in a staggering amount of individual work, it didn't help that Young was constantly posting about it on social media. Whether intentional or not, it screamed "look at me" and "acknowledge this," which didn't sit well with Indiana's coaches.

People around Young did little to encourage patience. On the contrary, they often fed Young's ego. His confidence never diminished; it grew and grew. "I'm thinking the best players play, because I felt like I was the best person in the gym," he later said. Much of that belief centered on his ability to light it up on offense. Young wasn't as impactful on the other side of the ball, which contributed to his lack of minutes too.

"At a young age, entering the NBA, he wanted to play a lot more than what he actually played," Michael Young, Joe's father, said. "And his representation would tell him, 'Hey, just go talk to the coach.' I don't think he got the best advice there. And I don't think he did anything wrong. I don't think there's anything wrong with somebody wanting to play."

"I think [Pacers head coach] Nate McMillan was more of a no-nonsense guy," explained Pearson. "Joe's a second-round pick, he's hungry, he wants to get out there and prove himself. And McMillan was just a this-is-how-we're-going-to-do-it type of coach. *If you have qualms about it, I'm sorry.* He was doing it his way. And Joe maybe thought he had more that he could show and do."

Young would meet with the coaching staff or with general manager Kevin Pritchard and president of basketball operations Larry Bird. They all preached the same message: *Be patient, your time is coming.* But Joe didn't always react to that well. He was overly confident and overly ambitious. When his minutes fluctuated or decreased, he became noticeably frustrated; he stopped working as hard; he didn't bring the energy and enthusiasm that was expected of role players and benchwarmers. His attitude resonated poorly, especially for someone in his position.

"It was my maturity," Young later said. "I knew that I was good enough to play on the court, but did I have the mindset and the mentality to cheer my teammates on, like they would do for me if I was out there? I didn't have it. I would be over there mad. Like, what am I mad for? I was young."

He was periodically assigned to Indiana's D-League affiliate, the Fort Wayne Mad Ants. Young looked at those transfers as a demotion, not as an opportunity to grow and develop. His actions reflected that perspective. The Pacers assigned him to the Mad Ants for the 2017 D-League Showcase in Ontario, Canada—a decision that did not excite Young. Still, it offered him the chance to make a good impression on representatives from every NBA team. Young did not take advantage.

He started Fort Wayne's first game and seemed uninterested, hogging the ball and launching some questionable shots outside the flow of the offense. The Mad Ants came into the Showcase with a 15-7 record, one of the best in the D-League. But with Young, their most skilled playmaker, struggling—17 points on just 6 of 15 shooting in thirty-three minutes—and the rest of the guys providing little assistance, they got blown out, 102–78, by the 9-13 Windy City Bulls.

Before their second game, a matchup with the 17-9 Maine Red Claws, Young was told that he would not be in the starting lineup. Suddenly, during the team's shootaround, he was feeling banged up and not compelled to play much. He ended up logging fifteen minutes off the bench, scoring 4 points on 2 of 7 shooting from the field. His poor showing that weekend stuck out prominently. Given that he was an NBA assignment player, Young was supposed to *dominate* the D-League competition.

Perhaps Joe's greatest blunder, and the one that left the largest stain on his reputation, was telling the Pacers organization that he did not want to be assigned to the Mad Ants again. The implication, of course, was that the D-League was beneath him—that he deserved to be at the NBA level, contributing for the Pacers. "Who was I to say that?" Young later reflected. "I had to be honest with myself. I should've gone down there, did my job, and gotten better." Instead he stayed with the Pacers for a little while longer and then was let go.

"He just wanted to play, and I think it was taken the wrong way," Michael Young said about his son. "When you watched your dad do something for a living and you wanted to do it, it's your childhood dream, you get there, you want to play—not in the G League, with the other team. There's a little bit more pressure on kids when you have a dad that was a pro. And sometimes it can get taken the wrong way."

Right or wrong, it all became part of Joe Young's narrative. But there was, of course, more to the story. Sure, Young was immature and naive in his early twenties, fresh out of college and suddenly *very* wealthy. Now the situation was different. Young was twenty-nine-years old, married with two kids. Three years in China had given him ample time to reflect and grow. He was desperate to get back to the NBA—to rewrite his narrative. The mere fact that he was prepared to enter the G League just a handful of years after refusing to go there was evidence that he had changed.

"If I could get that back, I would change the narrative to how I act now," Young said. "I would just act like how I am as a father to my kids. I can't be childish. I gotta make sure I show them how to live life, how to respect life, how to respect yourself, and how to become successful at a high level."

After doing their homework on Young, Birmingham had no overwhelming concerns about his character; otherwise, the team would have stayed away. Did he make some mistakes as a young professional? Yes. So did most people in the world. Any hesitation about pursuing Young was completely dispelled when Chasanoff (accidentally) got to speak with him the day before the G League Draft.

Without being asked or prodded, Young was candid about his past mistakes, about how he should have handled things differently with the Pacers. He took accountability for his actions. He talked about his family and what it meant to be back home, especially with his wife expecting their third child. He assured Chasanoff that he was ready to be a leader, play the game the right way, and show people a new and improved Joe Young. "I just need one more chance," he said.

Birmingham wanted to provide that chance. Chasanoff, specifically, wanted to provide that chance. "Look, we're picking at forty-seven and fifty-three," he told Young at the end of the call. "You're not going to be there where we are. But if there's a way I can get up to get you, you're the type of guy that I would want to have with our group. No matter what happens tomorrow, I wish you nothing but the best this year. But if I find a way to trade up, trust me, you're the guy we would want."

The conversation lasted only ten minutes, but it sold Chasanoff. Had Young denied his prior mistakes, it would have left a sour impression. Instead he was honest, remorseful, mature.

"It was just one of those conversations where you had a good feeling," Chasanoff later said. "I just had a good feeling with him. And we knew the player. We knew the opportunity we had with the roster. It was more of a gut feeling." Chasanoff called Pannone shortly after hanging up with Young.

"How'd it go with Joe's agent?" Pannone asked.

"Yeah, I talked to Joe for a while instead," Chasanoff replied, chuckling. Then his tone became more serious. "If we have an opportunity to get him," he added, "we're going to do it."

• • •

By the morning of the 2021 Draft, however, Squadron decision-makers weren't convinced such an opportunity would arise.

Headquarters for the event was a cozy, windowless conference room in the Squadron's ninth-floor office suite in downtown Birmingham. The building overlooked the newly constructed Protective Stadium, where the University of Alabama at Birmingham (UAB) football team played its home games. A single table took up much of the room and was covered with miscellaneous items: laptops, printed lists of the draft pool, coffee cups, water bottles, takeout boxes from Zoë's Kitchen, and a corded conference phone. Seated around the table, in addition to Pannone and Chasanoff, were associate general manager Billy Campbell, associate head coach T. J. Saint, assistant coaches Mery Andrade and Perry Huang, strength and conditioning coach Jordan Kincaide, athletic trainer Gilchrist Schmidt, player-development coach Andrew Warren, and basketball operations associate and equipment manager Dillon McGowan.

Against the far wall rested a giant whiteboard containing all the notes and insights relevant to the draft. The full order was written on the left side. Across the middle, available players had been divided into four tiers, organized by columns. More material followed on the right, such as potential trade opportunities (which easily could have read "potential opportunities to get

Joe Young"), team needs (bigs, creators, shooting), a projected starting lineup based on the current roster (Jared Harper, John Petty Jr., Malcolm Hill, Zylan Cheatham, James Banks III), and Birmingham's picks in the 2022–23 Draft, which could be valuable trade assets.

It was a quiet Saturday morning at the office. Almost eerily quiet. At times, the only noise stemmed from nine floors below, where UAB students flooded the closed-off streets, tailgating for a football game in the afternoon. Their excited shrieks were not-so-subtle reminders that while professional basketball was coming to Birmingham, this was still very much a football town.

Those assembled discussed the team's primary targets, shared intel, continued to work the phones to explore trade options, and debated between specific players. Most of the staff was familiar with the G League draft process already. There was one new wrinkle to consider this year: the question of coronavirus vaccination status. Unvaccinated players were allowed to participate in the G League but, based on the policies in place, would miss a bulk of training camp. The turnaround was immediate—the draft was on a Saturday, and training camp was set to begin that Monday. Those who were unvaccinated (or vaccinated within the past two weeks) had to pass five days of testing before taking the court. So even if they were coronavirus free, they would have to sit out half of camp. For obvious reasons, teams were wary of selecting those players.

Joe Young was vaccinated. He remained the Squadron's top target—in their Tier 1, alongside another former NBA guard, Brandon Knight, as well as Gabe York and Tyler Hagedorn. The trades that were "in play" for the Squadron, which were scribbled on the whiteboard, would land them a pick in the early twenties. Surely that would be too late. If the team's assessments were correct, Young would be picked far higher.

There was pressure, still, to do *something*. Moving up to the first round could get Birmingham a solid player, even if that player wasn't Young. The vibe in the room didn't match that pressure. It was calm and laid-back—more like a casual Monday morning meeting than what the term *war room* implies. Coach Pannone was, by nature, a master at defusing tension. He could tell someone not to worry without actually saying not to worry, just by making some sly remark. When the staff discussed players with possible "weed issues,"

Pannone joked, "Would it help if we opened a dispensary at the facility?" He ended one debate with McGowan by saying, teasingly, "You can play devil's advocate if you want. . . . I just don't listen to stupidity." He was constantly being sarcastic, to the point where he often had to clarify when he was being serious, not the other way around. "I'm never serious until I'm serious," he said—sarcastically.

The draft, which started at 1:00 p.m. eastern time, was far different from the large-scale, elaborate spectacle that the NBA Draft has become. No packed arena, no fans, no media circus, no ESPN coverage. Representatives from every team did not convene at one specific location. Players did not wear fancy suits, sit in a fancy green room, and walk across a fancy stage to shake the commissioner's hand. In the G League, the draft was conducted via conference call. Following along was difficult, even for the players involved in the draft. Most found out their futures via social media or just sat by the phone, waiting for it to ring.

So no, the G League Draft didn't have the allure of the NBA Draft. It lacked all the glitz and glamor or any sense of being momentous. For many, though, the emotions were similar. This might not have been a realization of the NBA dream, but it was a meaningful step in that direction.

G League president Shareef Abdur-Rahim and David Wagner, associate vice president, player operations team leader, helped to kick off the event. "Today signifies the commitment of players to pursue a journey to the NBA," Abdur-Rahim said. He and Wagner took roll call before outlining the draft rules. Each team would have two minutes to make its selection and was asked to do so in a precise manner: *Birmingham is ready to select. With the X pick, the Birmingham Squadron select—*

The Delaware Blue Coats—which had expressed interest in Young—were on the clock first. Squadron brass anxiously awaited their decision, preparing to hear Young's name called and having any far-fetched hopes of getting their guy shattered.

Delaware is ready to select. With the first pick in the 2021 G League Draft, the Delaware Blue Coats select . . . Shamorie Ponds.

Shamorie Ponds? It was a complete surprise to everyone in the Squadron war room. Ponds, a skilled six-foot point guard, was a former star at St. John's

University, but he was far down on Birmingham's draft board. None of their intel suggested Ponds might be the first pick.

There was no time to pass judgment, however; the clock was ticking. The next pick would be made in less than two minutes. Chasanoff and Campbell continued to make calls, trying to trade up into the first round. Hagedorn, an elite shooting big man, went second to the College Park Skyhawks. Then guard Gabe York was picked by the Fort Wayne Mad Ants. Brandon Knight was taken sixth by the Sioux Falls Skyforce. Everyone in Birmingham's Tier 1 was gone within fifteen minutes—except for Joe Young.

Zaire Wade, the son of former NBA superstar Dwyane Wade, was grabbed with the tenth pick by the Salt Lake City Stars. Former Indiana Pacer and teammate of Joe Young, Lance Stephenson, was gone at number thirteen to the Grand Rapids Gold. One spot later, the Greensboro Swarm selected guard LiAngelo Ball, the brother of Lonzo and LaMelo Ball. The Iowa Wolves used the nineteenth pick, which they got from the Squadron in the trade for Zylan Cheatham, to take Ruot Monyyong, a forward who played at Arkansas–Little Rock.

All the while, Young remained on the board. The longer he sat there, the more aggressive Chasanoff and Campbell became in pursuing trades. Finally, they found a deal. Just before the Stockton Kings were up at number twenty-one, they agreed to send the pick to Birmingham in exchange for the returning rights to guard Devearl Ramsey and a second-round selection in the 2022–23 Draft.[2] Details about the trade would be conveyed later, but it was set in stone. The pick belonged to Birmingham. And the pick was—

Stockton is ready to select. With the twenty-first pick in the 2021 G League Draft, the Stockton Kings select . . . Joe Young.

There were some fist pumps and high-fives in the Squadron war room, but not the type of celebratory reaction one might expect. The draft was moving so fast that everyone had to stay focused. Celebrations could wait until afterward—well, maybe not that long.

As the first round ended, what had just transpired began to sink in with Pannone. For a meager price, Birmingham had landed the player it coveted the most in the draft. "We just got our fucking number one. We just got our fucking number one!" Pannone repeated, smiling. "I feel like we're not celebrating enough!"

At home in Houston, Young was celebrating with his family. "It was big for us, just to get another opportunity," he said. It represented a new beginning—hopefully a blank slate. Soon, Young would receive a call from Pannone, congratulating him and welcoming him to the Squadron. The conversation went similarly to the one shared between Young and Chasanoff.

"Joe, what makes you want to play in the G League?" Pannone asked. "Why do you want this? What's your goal?"

Once again, Young was open about his mistakes, about the negative reputation he had developed, about his desire for one last crack at the NBA. "He just opened up the floodgates," Pannone later explained. "He was super honest."

Young also expressed a willingness to fill whatever role the team needed. By now, he knew what NBA scouts were looking for and the importance of certain intangibles—being a leader, bringing positive energy, keeping the right mentality—to NBA coaches.

"Look, I don't care about your past," Pannone told Young. "I don't care about your age. I care about who you are today. If I were to be judged off of who I was at twenty, twenty-one, twenty-two, twenty-three years old, I wouldn't have the job that I have today, like most of us. Everyone's got the right to grow up."

5. TRAINING CAMP

It was Monday, October 25, less than forty-eight hours after the G League Draft, and the entire Squadron organization had gathered in the Skylight Lounge at the Lumen Apartments in downtown Birmingham. This was the team's first official meeting, and the staff sought to set a clear foundation for the season. Associate general manager Billy Campbell helped to break the ice.

"How many people in this room want to make it to the NBA?" he asked the group. Everyone raised a hand. Not just the thirteen players—*everyone*. Gilchrist Schmidt, head athletic trainer, raised his hand. Dillon McGowan, basketball operations associate and equipment manager, raised his hand. Mery Andrade, assistant coach and former WNBA player, raised her hand. Every single member of the Squadron organization for the 2021–22 season, Campbell highlighted, shared the exact same goal.

"And who is willing to make the necessary sacrifices to make it to the NBA?" Campbell followed up. Once again, everyone raised a hand.

"Okay, so, everyone in this room is now willing to be held to the standards required and do the things that we feel can help get you to the NBA."

If anyone knew the standards required to get there, it was Campbell. A veteran in the business, he had worked with the NBA's Washington Wizards as a basketball operations assistant and coaches' assistant for four years (2006–10), as well as with the main G League office (2012–16). He had seen many guys make it and many more squander their opportunities. Now it was his job to ensure that Squadron players didn't do the latter.

Associate head coach T. J. Saint, who had previously served as a video coordinator for the NBA's Detroit Pistons (2014–18), addressed the team next. The main focus of his speech was establishing a *Squadron identity*. He opened with a short PowerPoint slide that posed three questions, written in all caps:

WHO ARE YOU?

WHAT DO YOU DO?

HOW DO YOU DO IT?

Saint then underscored a quote from Chinese general Sun Tzu, author of *The Art of War*: "Every battle is won before it's ever fought."

On the court, part of the Squadron identity would be a hard-nosed, disciplined, physical defense. Saint, the team's defensive coordinator, outlined his expectations. Certain lapses, he explained, would result in an automatic substitution, such as not sprinting back to protect the paint and failing to contest shots. These were his nonnegotiables. Mess up, sit down—end of discussion.

Pannone, who would lead the offense, spoke after Saint and began by going through a long list of team standards, all essential to building the Squadron's desired identity:

Be a good person.

It is a league full of excuses—don't have them.

Hold yourself accountable and be accountable.

Be honest.

Be respectful.

Be grateful—no complaining.

Be helpful.

Change your mindset from "I have to" to "I get to."

Be professional—reputation is everything!!!

Early is on time, respect the time of others, be early to everything!!!—being late is a sign of arrogance.

Communicate and early communication.

No ego—"Get over yourself."— Gregg Popovich
Embrace the suckiness.
Show appreciation—please and thank you.

A majority of the rules were applicable to any team at any level of basketball. Some were more G League-specific: not making excuses in a league full of them, shedding all egos, embracing the "suckiness," changing one's mindset from "I have to" to "I get to":

I *have to* fly commercial in the G League.
I *get to* fly commercial in the G League.

Pannone recognized that an integral part of his job was teaching his players how to be professionals. Those who came from top college programs were used to a comfortable lifestyle. Big staffs catered to their every need. Facilities were top notch. Teams flew private, stayed in five-star hotels, ate gourmet food, had police escorts. Any young adult entering the real world has a lot to learn, but the transition from a powerhouse university like Kentucky or Duke to the G League can be especially jarring.

In 2010 Grizzlies seven-footer Hasheem Thabeet was assigned to the D-League's Dakota Wizards. As the former number two overall pick out of the University of Connecticut (UConn), he was the highest draft pick ever sent to the minors by an NBA team. During one road trip, the Wizards were getting ready to play a game when the twenty-three-year-old Thabeet realized he didn't have his shoes—they had been left at the previous stop on their trip. At UConn, as with the Grizzlies, someone on staff packed up all the shoes, usually bringing multiple options for each player. With the Dakota Wizards, players were responsible for their own belongings. It would have been easy enough for Thabeet to borrow shoes or hustle to a local mall, except that he wore a whopping size 18. There was no way, under the time constraints, that the team was going to be able to find a pair that big. So Thabeet had to miss the Wizards' next game. Reason—*no shoes*. Since the D-League attracted so little media attention, his absence was able to fly under the radar.

That type of stuff just happened in the minors—players forgot things, showed up late, missed buses, acted immaturely, made foolish mistakes on the court. In 2015 Iowa Energy teammates Jarnell Stokes and Kalin Lucas were both ejected from a game for fighting . . . each other. Lucas was, according to announcers on the broadcast, "bloodied up a little bit" by Stokes. A year later, Houston Rockets forward Montrezl Harrell was on assignment with the Rio Grande Valley Vipers when he pushed a referee to the ground during an altercation. He was subsequently suspended for five games. The G League was where such behavior was corralled. Like any first job, it was where a bunch of twentysomethings learned to grow up. And those who didn't, didn't make it.

Longtime D-Leaguer Mo Charlo remembered when big man Hassan Whiteside got assigned to his team—the Reno Bighorns—from the Sacramento Kings during the 2010–11 season. Whiteside thought he was above it, not buying in or listening to Reno's head coach Eric Musselman (now the head coach at the University of Arkansas). After practice ended, Musselman put a single chair in the middle of the locker room and told everyone to leave except Whiteside. Charlo stayed close to the door and listened as Musselman ripped into his seven-foot center. "He just went crazy," Charlo recalled with a laugh. "I was in there cracking up, like, *Oh, shit!* That was kind of the wake-up call that I think Hassan needed." Whiteside would learn to mature, eventually earning a four-year, $98 million max contract from the Miami Heat.

To ensure accountability as Musselman did, the Squadron imposed fines for various slipups. Pannone ran through the catalog of infractions. Being late to a team function would cost a player $50; failing to promptly report an injury, illness, or condition—$100; missing player programs—$250; displaying improper bench conduct or team insubordination—up to $500; suspension—2 percent of a player's salary. Considering standard G League contracts were valued at just $37,000 for the 2021–22 season, those penalties weren't as trivial as they sound. When NBA superstars doled out $25,000 or $50,000 for an offense, they were actually relinquishing a smaller percentage of their paychecks than a G Leaguer coughing up a fifty-dollar bill.

With those particulars out of the way, Pannone detailed his offense. More than anything, it was a system predicated on unselfishness. In Pannone's mind, being unselfish was the best way to win basketball games *and* to impress scouts. There were other key elements to his system, many of which were based on analytics (pushing the pace, not settling for midrange shots, attacking the rim, making the extra pass). Selfishness, though, would cause the entire machine to break down. And besides, NBA coaches weren't looking for ball-dominant, one-on-one players, Pannone assured his team. They already had those guys.

The numbers backed Pannone's argument. He compared tracking data from NBA stars to former G Leaguers. While reigning NBA MVP Nikola Jokic averaged 101 touches per game, guard Gary Payton II, who was called up from the Raptors 905 to the Golden State Warriors in 2020, averaged just 6.3 touches. While Dallas Mavericks superstar Luka Doncic possessed the ball for an average of 6.02 seconds per touch, Miami Heat sharpshooter Duncan Robinson averaged just 1.56 seconds. While three-time scoring champion James Harden averaged 4.96 dribbles per touch, Oklahoma City Thunder wing Lu Dort averaged just 1.36. And so on. NBA front offices weren't combing the G League for the next Nikola Jokic, Luka Doncic, or James Harden. They didn't covet isolation players with score-first mentalities. And neither did Pannone.

In 2020 assistant coach Perry Huang had done an independent study of NBA call-ups. He found that very few of the top G League scorers were making it to the NBA. During the 2016–17 season only three of the thirty-eight total call-ups ranked in the top fifteen in scoring; in 2017–18, five of the fifty-one; in 2018–19, three of the forty-eight; and in 2019–20, four of the thirty-nine. Huang's research confirmed what he and Pannone already knew—there was no scoring one's way out of the G League. As Huang wrote in a presentation sharing his findings, NBA teams were searching more for consummate professionals and mistake-free role players than flashy bucket-getters.

In theory, that was a good thing; it made life simpler. Jobs were whittled down, responsibilities were fewer, burdens were lighter. A player once asked to fill every role was now instructed to focus on just one or two things. Dominate the boards and protect the rim; facilitate the offense and knock down threes. Much easier, right?

Wrong. The main obstacle was ego. Players wanted bigger roles, more responsibilities, heavier burdens. One of the toughest challenges facing any G League staff was to convince a bunch of former stars to become something *less*, to sacrifice *more*, to accept that if they sought to move up the ladder instead of down, they would never be stars again.

"A big reason guys get stuck in the G League is because they don't realize the position they're trying out for," Chicago Bulls guard Alex Caruso, who played 106 games in the G League from 2016 to 2019, said on *The Old Man and the Three* podcast. "It's like going to a job interview thinking you're going to be the CFO of the company, and they're looking for someone to clean the bathrooms."[1]

"One thing I realized is that so many guys get in their own way and can't get out of the way of whatever it is, whether it be their egos or a lack of willingness to accept a role," said Duncan Robinson, who spent part of the 2018–19 season with the Sioux Falls Skyforce. "I think the examples of guys who have played in the G League and gone on to have success in the NBA, more often than not, it's people who are level-headed around *This is where I fit in and this is how I'm going to have an impact at the NBA level*. Alex Caruso is a great example."

The blueprint to reach the NBA, as Pannone told his team during that first meeting, was to do a *specific* job exceptionally well. Pannone even shared his definition of the phrase *do your job*, which he would repeat many times in the months to come: "It means complete your assignments, execute to the best of your ability, and trust that your teammates will do the same. To become a championship team, everyone must be bought into their role and do their job."

• • •

Training camp for the Squadron was held at Birmingham-Southern College (BSC), a private university three miles west of the city's downtown. For a team of this caliber, the conditions were laughable. It was like placing a bunch of PhD candidates in eighth grade biology. The Bill Burch Gymnasium wasn't even the main gym at BSC, which, for reasons described by coaches as a "sensitive subject," was not regularly made available. This gym was on the second floor of a weathered, red-brick building, indistinguishable from any of the other buildings on the school's campus. It was dimly lit, and stained gray paint was peeling from the walls. Thick layers of dust had gathered in the corners and crevices. Light streaked in through the tall windows behind each basket, making the rims barely visible from certain angles. A busted scoreboard hung over one sideline, stuck on the same score, with the same time remaining.

Coaches had moved some equipment in—a stationary bike, training tables, water coolers—to give the space a slightly more professional feel, but in reality, this was a below-average high school gym packed with former and future NBA players. Nothing fit, both literally and figuratively. Their bodies seemed too big for the space, their talent too advanced for such an amateurish environment. When someone dunked, especially Cheatham, the basket shook so violently that it appeared on the verge of collapsing.

The first practice was at 6:30 p.m. on the evening of October 25. Coaches had little control over the scheduling. This wasn't the Squadron's facility; it was one of forty-five buildings on the 192-acre Birmingham-Southern campus. A new team facility was in the works for the 2022–23 season, but for now, a lot just depended on the school. Pannone was presented with available time slots and simply took advantage of what he could get. "That's the G League," he said, when asked about the arrangement. It was a common refrain used throughout the minors.

Can't choose your gym time? That's the G League. Filming practice on an iPhone to save $100? That's the G League. Stuck in a middle seat on a flight to South Dakota? That's the G League. Chick-fil-A breakfasts and Chipotle dinners? That's the G League. Four games in six nights? That's the G League.

"Be prepared for the unpreparable," Pannone said about life in the G. "The reality is that for most of these guys, everything is worse. If you're coming from a Division I school, how we travel is worse; what we eat is worse; our facilities are worse; our gear is worse. But being in the G League is about guys who love to hoop. You have to be easygoing. You have to be able to go with the flow."

Most of Birmingham's players were from highly regarded Division I programs. It was an interesting array of characters, all of whom had signed in the G League and then been acquired by the team—a process that allows players to be called up to *any* NBA franchise, not just direct affiliates. University of Alabama guard John Petty Jr., Montana guard Sayeed Pridgett, and Georgia Tech center James Banks III were recent college graduates. Zylan Cheatham (Arizona State), Jared Harper (Auburn), Malcolm Hill (Illinois), Tra Holder (Arizona State), and Riley LaChance (Vanderbilt) were all in their mid-twenties, having competed overseas or in the minors for a handful of seasons.

And Joe Young (Oregon) and Ra'Shad James (Iona) were seasoned veterans, probably closer to the end of their careers than the beginning.

Some G League organizations focused solely on acquiring young talent. The reasoning was sound; by loading up on young players, they increased their odds of uncovering a few hidden gems with plenty of time to develop. Guys like Young and James were more likely to have reached their full potential already. There was less mystery behind them—teams had a better idea of what they were getting. But with a rookie like Petty, the picture that executives could paint in their heads was intoxicating. The sky was the limit.

Birmingham's front office had followed that approach in its first year (2019–20), when the franchise was located in Erie, Pennsylvania. But it backfired—big time. Entering the season with six rookies messed up the development process. Chemistry and structure were lacking. The buy-in was minimal. Losses mounted. Before the season was shut down due to COVID, the team had the third-worst record in the league (13-30). From that point forward, the staff's approach changed. "We learned, year one, we can't come in with six rookies," Chasanoff said. "It's just not going to be a successful process. So, we wanted guys with experience."

Zylan Cheatham was the only player from that woeful first year in Erie back with the organization. And even then, it was a different Zylan Cheatham. By his own admission, the six-foot-eight forward was less engaged as a rookie in 2019. He didn't care as much about the process. He was signed to a two-way contract with the New Orleans Pelicans, splitting his time between the NBA and the minors. Yet Cheatham was only concerned with the NBA, so when he was assigned to Erie, he wasn't always present.

"I wish I would have embraced [the G League] more," he later said about that season. "I think my rookie year, being on a two-way, I was so focused on the fact that I'm potentially on the Pelicans or whatever. I was more focused on being an NBA player, as opposed to just taking it day-by-day and getting better and being ready for whenever my opportunity [came]."

"I think what's tough is when you have a player like that—he's at a big school, he's kind of been propped up on this pedestal a little bit by whatever it is, his circle or his school or his coaches, and then on top of that you're with [the agency] Roc Nation," added Coach Huang, who was also on the staff in Erie. "And you're on a two-way. So yes, in some ways, I don't think anybody laid out how it was supposed to happen. This doesn't just go for Z—I think this goes for a lot of guys. When they get these [two-way] contracts, they think they're already NBA players. When in reality, this is literally just a tryout. It's a tryout for a season."

Cheatham's perspective was more mature now. He was twenty-five years old and fully appreciated that, one, he hadn't truly made it yet, and, two, the G League was a valuable resource—a trampoline that could spring him to the next level. *For good.*

Birmingham had traded for Cheatham over the summer with the hope that he would become one of the team's leaders. Cheatham is, in a word, *engaging.* His natural voice commands attention; low and gravelly, it sounds like it might be booming through a PA system on an airplane. He is the type of person who jumps out of bed every morning, eager for *whatever* lies ahead, bursting with the excitement of a six-year-old who just spotted the ice cream truck. As his close friend and teammate at Arizona State, Rob Edwards, once explained, "If Zylan's just going to the store, he's *hyped* to go to the store."

"I call my brother a 'free spirit,'" Darvis Fletcher, Cheatham's best friend, said. "Because he's going to do him. He's going to be him at all times. He's going to be smiling, laughing, cracking jokes. He's going to be obnoxiously loud, probably blasting music. He's unapologetically him. You gotta love him for it. You don't have a choice—he's going to bring the best energy out of you at all times. It's contagious. You love being around that."

Cheatham regularly switches the style of his hair, often dyeing it red. He rocks large sunglasses and glitzy jewelry, including a hefty "Z-Cheat" chain. He makes rap music in his spare time, which he then dubs over his highlight mixes. He is tremendously confident, but not overconfident. Sure of himself, but not cocky. Comfortable in his own skin.

Others gravitate to Cheatham immediately—always have. Maybe it's the broad smile, or the infectious laugh, or the boundless energy. Whatever it is, it makes him the center of every room he steps into. On day one of training camp, Cheatham danced around to his favorite artist, the rapper Future. He joked with his new teammates. He hollered words of encouragement from the sidelines.

"Get better!"

"Lock in!"

"Keep going!"

None of it felt forced or phony. Cheatham was an effortless leader, popular with seemingly everyone. As Fletcher said, "You love being around that."

Of course, Cheatham hoped he wouldn't be around for that long. He was perhaps the likeliest player on the Squadron to get called up to the NBA. Physically, he possessed all the tools: height (six-foot-eight), strength, speed, agility, athleticism. His skill set had improved considerably during the offseason too. Cheatham was clearly *right there*, right on the precipice of making it. Had it not been for a few unlucky breaks over the preceding years, he might already be in the NBA.

After his rookie season with the Pelicans and BayHawks, which was disrupted by COVID, Cheatham was sent to the Oklahoma City Thunder as part of a blockbuster trade that included big names like Jrue Holiday, Steven Adams, and Eric Bledsoe. The unexpected turn of events was actually good for Cheatham. New Orleans signed him to a three-year contract (first year guaranteed) to make the deal work, which would then be absorbed by Oklahoma City.

"My agent called basically congratulating me," Cheatham remembered. "Like, 'You made it. You went from undrafted, to two-way, to basically getting converted to a three-year, $5 million deal.'" Cheatham would also be reunited with his former Arizona State teammate Luguentz Dort. "And [Lu] was one of the rising stars on the team," he continued, "and they were a young core that to me didn't really have that boisterous dog on the floor that could anchor the defense and bring energy. So I was beyond excited. My whole life changed. Everything changed."

"We was geeked up," said Fletcher. "The chance to play with Lu again—a big thing. To finally be on an NBA team and actually have an opportunity to get on the floor and show what you really can do, it was just crazy. Everybody was having an out of body experience when we heard that news. A lot of people calling and texting, congratulating me like I signed a contract. It was just crazy, like, I can't believe this dude really just signed this deal. This is something we dreamed about and it's about to happen."

This was it—the moment he and Darvis had always imagined back in South Phoenix, training at the South Mountain Community Center. Everything was falling into place. Cheatham would still have to prove himself in training camp, but all signs pointed toward a future in Oklahoma City. The Thunder had expressed interest in him on draft night in 2019; he was asked to pick a jersey number; he did interviews with the media and spoke with head coach Billy Donovan; the team posted a "Welcome to OKC" graphic on its Instagram. "I knew once I got there and got on the floor, there's no way I'm losing my spot," Cheatham said. "I knew that I would've had a chance to show that I'm worth these three years, $5 million."

Opening night of the 2020–21 season was pushed back to December due to the pandemic. Cheatham's flight from Phoenix to Oklahoma City was booked for a Friday, a couple days before training camp was scheduled to begin. During the week prior, he started to feel . . . different. Not sick, but different. He was uncharacteristically lethargic, falling asleep in his car one afternoon while parked in the driveway and taking naps that turned into full eight-hour slumbers. It was strange for anyone to be that tired. For someone like Zylan, whose blood seemed permanently infused with espresso and Red Bull, it was *inconceivable*. Something was obviously wrong. He took a COVID test on Thursday morning, about twenty-four hours before he was supposed to leave for OKC. The results came back soon after: Cheatham was positive.

At the time, confirmed cases were required to quarantine for ten days. The NBA had its own set of strict protocols, on top of the Centers for Disease Control and Prevention (CDC) guidelines. Cheatham would have to return multiple negative tests before reporting to the Thunder. Because of the timing, he would miss a significant chunk of training camp. And so, on December 2, 2020, just a week after the trade with New Orleans had been finalized, Cheatham was waived.

The swing was shocking and abrupt, perhaps the most crushing moment of his career. In the span of a week, his dream had been realized—and then snatched away. "To go from such an emotional high to an emotional low that quick was devastating," Cheatham said.

The first year of his contract ($1.5 million) would still be owed, but the money was a consolation prize. Cheatham was back to square one—back in the G League, where he joined the Iowa Wolves, the affiliate of the Minnesota Timberwolves. His vision of playing alongside Lu Dort, rocking an orange-and-blue Thunder uniform, vanished like a drawing on an Etch A Sketch.

"I'm sure he's probably still thinking about that and the 'what ifs,'" said Edwards, who played with Cheatham and Dort at Arizona State. "But it's a new day. Everybody's path is different. I know he'll find his way back."

• • •

Rain showers were passing through Birmingham all afternoon. In a matter of minutes, the Bill Burch court might be too dangerous to play on. It was day four of training camp and shutting down wasn't an option. But practicing on a slippery floor? That was obviously out of the question.

The rain continued. As expected, droplets began seeping through cracks in the walls, trickling onto the court. Players dug their shoes into the hardwood to test the traction. Nope—this wasn't going to work. There was a scramble to find out if they could relocate to the main gym, briefly interrupting practice. Once McGowan got the go-ahead from the school, the move was both methodical and swift. Guys collected their belongings. Managers packed up all the equipment. Coaches hustled to the other gym and started taping the floor, marking the NBA three-point line. Pannone huddled the team at midcourt.

"This is the fucking G League," he said. "Shit happens. Adjust to it. Don't let it ruin practice."

Behind the scenes, Squadron employees were dealing with bigger problems. The team was supposed to travel to College Park, Georgia, the following evening—a Friday—ahead of its sole preseason game against the College Park Skyhawks on Saturday. The trip was short, only about a two-and-a-half-hour drive down I-20. There was just one issue: the bus company had suddenly canceled. David Lane, the Squadron's general manager of business operations, spent hours calling other options in the Southeast. None of them had drivers available on such short notice. The team already had a twenty-two-passenger van that was used to shuttle guys back and forth from their apartments and the practice facility. It wasn't particularly spacious, especially for a bunch of professional basketball players, but it would have to work. Lane was able to book one other van to transport the coaches. Both vehicles would be driven by members of the Squadron staff. Joseph Hooven, head of public relations, chauffeured the coaches.

The journey was far from ideal—Hooven even had to make an emergency stop due to low tire pressure—but the Squadron reached College Park. The preceding week had been arduous: film at 10:00 a.m. every morning, followed by two-a-days. Coaches had meticulously plotted out the schedule for each practice, down to the precise minute. Drills were fast-paced and intense, with very short breaks in between. There was an emphasis on doing the little things. To the average basketball fan, those things would seem *really* little: getting an early high-hand contest on all three-point shooters, finishing cuts to maintain spacing on offense, being in exactly the right shifts on defense. Success, Pannone preached, was all in the details.

A few players still needed to be cut from the roster, so the preseason matinee against the Skyhawks (affiliated with the Atlanta Hawks) was a crucial opportunity for executives to evaluate. College Park was using the event as a trial run for the season, granting entry to a small number of fans. Hype videos still played on the jumbotron. Arena employees manned food stands that saw but a handful of customers. T-shirt tosses were more like games of catch. Starting lineups and other announcements blared from the arena's sound system, only to be met with awkward silence.

Birmingham played well. Everyone contributed to a wire-to-wire 95–90 victory. Hill set the tone early, knocking down multiple threes and taking a charge that pumped up the bench. After struggling in the first half, Young dominated the third quarter. He was prone to huge scoring outbursts, flashes where it seemed as though he could hurl a ball from the upper deck and it would still find its way into the basket. Squadron fans in attendance were already captivated by him. "Get Joe Young back in the game!" one screamed, as Young was resting in the fourth quarter. "We need some threes!"

The Squadron got enough threes and played well enough defense to come out on top. Pannone liked a lot of what he saw—mainly, the effort and unselfishness. Of course, there was also a lot that he didn't like. The pace was too slow, the spacing too cramped. Pannone wasn't strict, but he *was* constantly nitpicking, searching for every mistake that could possibly be fixed, including his own. In the locker room following the win, he spent much of his speech encouraging the team to watch film of the game later that evening. All of the best players, Pannone stressed, diligently studied film. "Take ownership of your career," he said.

There wasn't much time to fix the mistakes Pannone had identified. Final cuts would be made on Wednesday, and the regular season was set to begin on Friday. Overall, training camp spanned just eleven days.

In the NBA, training camps last three weeks, encompassing multiple preseason games. Since NBA rosters stay relatively consistent, chemistry is easier to build at that level. Systems are easier to implement. Mistakes are easier to fix.

Everything moved a beat faster in the G. The schedule was compressed: fifty total games from November to April, then playoffs. Squadron players had *just* arrived in Birmingham. Many of them were still getting acquainted. Now their opener against the Greensboro Swarm was right around the corner.

"If you look at the NBA level, guys are getting workouts in pretty much all summer," Cheatham reflected one afternoon. "They're linking up. They know who their teammates are going to be for the most part. Despite the rookies and trades, the core pretty much stays together. For us to have pretty much a completely new core—I think we got a little advantage that some of our guys were at [Pelicans] training camp together, and we knew each other a little bit, but that full team chemistry, I mean, you're only as good as your weakest link. To be able to get everybody on board in such a short time is a challenge. But I don't think it's impossible."

6. WINNING MATTERS

Flying out of Birmingham-Shuttlesworth International Airport is tricky. To get to most destinations, travelers must connect through Atlanta, which is forty minutes away by plane and a little over two hours by car. In the G League, teams fly commercial—a stark contrast to the lavish private planes that transport NBA teams, where guys have the space and freedom to lounge, sleep, socialize, gamble, play video games, sing, dance, throw parties—do whatever they want, really.

On Thursday, November 4, the Squadron was on a 12:05 p.m. CT flight out of Birmingham—landing in Atlanta at 2:03 p.m. ET—followed by a 4:37 p.m. flight to Greensboro later that afternoon. All in all, it would be more than six hours of traveling to go just 480 miles, almost the same amount of time it takes to drive that distance.

The trip was not without drama, either. Everyone boarded the flight to Atlanta for an on-time departure. Squadron players and coaches were scattered throughout the thirty-or-so rows. Cheatham and Banks, two guys over six feet eight, quickly relocated to the very back. Empty seats allowed them to sprawl out more, but Banks's long legs were a flight attendant's worst nightmare, spilling out into the aisle.

Passengers were settled in, when suddenly Joe Young was being escorted off the plane. Other members of the Squadron began murmuring, speculating:

"What's happening? Where's Joe going?" Nobody knew. All they knew was that one of their teammates—one of their top players—was no longer on the flight, and the cabin door was now closed. There had been no major disturbance, no commotion. Most people hadn't even noticed.

The pilot's voice came over the PA system; he apologized for the delay. "We have a passenger who just decided to get off the airplane," he said, as if such a strange occurrence wasn't so strange at all.

As it turned out, there hadn't been much of a scene because there hadn't been much of an incident. Masks were still required on planes, and Young wasn't wearing his properly. A flight attendant instructed him to fix it, tapping him rather aggressively on the shoulder. Young responded by telling the attendant not to touch him, then obliged and adjusted his mask. "Do I need to tell the pilot?" the flight attendant asked, clearly offended by Joe's retort. The question was rhetorical. A few minutes later, the attendant returned and ordered Joe to get off the flight. Young didn't protest. He calmly grabbed his things, slipped on his backpack, and walked off.

That was it—no security, no ruckus that might end up on TikTok or TMZ. Young simply wasn't allowed to take Delta Flight 2791 with the rest of the Squadron. The punishment felt too severe—an overreaction to an overreaction—but it made sense given the times. The pandemic was still creating tension in public spaces. Flight attendants were growing increasingly frustrated with passengers who refused to follow mask-wearing policies; passengers were growing increasingly aggressive in their opposition to said policies. Crews were running out of patience, tolerating less and less with each unruly traveler.

For Young, the situation was but a minor inconvenience. With help from the Squadron staff, he found another way to Greensboro, beating the rest of the team there. Coaches weren't worried; they were accustomed to dealing with unexpected travel complications. When they were in Erie, flights were constantly delayed or canceled. On one road trip, they got stuck in a snowstorm and were on the bus for half a day. New rules required teams to fly if the drive would take longer than five hours. To former G Leaguers, that alone sounded like a privilege.

• • •

During the 2008–9 season, the Dakota Wizards were bussing from Bismarck, North Dakota, to Des Moines, Iowa, to take on the Iowa Energy. They left around 10:30 p.m., and two hours into the ten-hour journey, the bus started bouncing. The driver pulled over to investigate the source of the problem. Apparently, something was wrong with the vehicle's axle, the primary suspension system. They were able to continue on, but the bus bounced the entire ride, like a low-rider with hydraulics. No one on the Wizards was able to get a minute of sleep ahead of the game.

A year later, the Reno Bighorns were supposed to fly home from Salt Lake City, but their flight was canceled due to a blizzard. So right after their game against the Utah Flash ended, the Bighorns hopped on a bus to make what was normally an eight-hour drive (given the conditions, it was more like twelve). Players hadn't eaten dinner and were understandably starving. They searched, and searched, and searched for a place to get food off Interstate 80—there was nothing. It wasn't until close to 2:00 a.m. that they found an open McDonald's. Crisis averted—or maybe not.

"Half of us got food poisoning on that bus ride," recalled Rod Benson, a forward on the Bighorns. "It's funny because we had all these girls lined up for when we got back because we had been gone for a while. I remember I was supposed to hang out with this girl, and my stomach was just in excruciating pain. It felt like I was just imploding from the outside in because I ate this McDonald's on this dumbass bus ride."

In 2015 the Bighorns were on a road trip in Texas, scheduled to face the Austin Spurs and the Rio Grande Valley Vipers. Following their game against the Spurs, the Bighorns boarded a coach bus for the five-hour drive to Edinburg, home of the Vipers. Their driver was not actually supposed to work that evening—a mix-up by the company had resulted in her being assigned at the last minute. Within a few hours, it became apparent to everyone onboard that she was far too sleepy to operate a vehicle. The bus started swerving on the highway, so unnervingly that coaches insisted she pull over at a gas station. Even the driver had to admit that she was unfit to soldier on. Rather than be stranded in the middle of Texas, in the middle of the night, one of the Bighorns' staff members took the wheel and drove the team to Edinburg.

Throughout the history of the G League, teams have frequently traveled on game days. Kevin Danna, a longtime play-by-play announcer for the Santa Cruz Warriors who used to travel with the team, recalled the Warriors playing on February 5, 2015, in Bakersfield, California, flying to Boise, Idaho, for a matchup against the Idaho Stampede on February 7, and then *back* to California to face the Los Angeles D-Fenders on February 8. To make matters worse, there was no direct flight from Boise to Los Angeles, so on the morning of the eighth, the Warriors flew to Oakland and then connected on to LA. They arrived in the city around 3:00 p.m. ahead of a 5:00 p.m. tip-off. That's three games and three commercial flights in a seventy-two-hour span.

With teams traveling so hectically and being so understaffed, absurd mishaps were inevitable. One year, the Dakota Wizards flew to Colorado for a game against the 14ers, only to realize that they did not bring enough pairs of shorts. The jerseys were all there, just some of the bottom halves were missing. Getting more shipped out before the game was impossible, so players would have to share. Those on the bench wore nothing but tights and had towels wrapped around their waists. Whenever a player subbed out, he quickly removed his shorts, handed them to his replacement, and received a towel in return. "Only in the D-League," said Wizards guard Maurice Baker, who appeared in that unforgettable game. "If you were going in for that guy, you better get his shorts."

That wasn't the only time the Wizards had to improvise their attire. They once traveled to Oklahoma for a matchup with the Tulsa 66ers and mistakenly checked the bag with all their uniforms. The flight was delayed due to weather, and when they finally arrived, their precious cargo was nowhere to be found. The game was still played as scheduled, but the Wizards had to wear *Tulsa's* practice jerseys. To uninformed fans, it looked like an oddly competitive intrasquad scrimmage.

• • •

By 2021 those nightmare scenarios were far less likely to arise, though some crises could always be expected. Pannone used his long travel days to analyze film. Not just of the Squadron—of teams all over the world. He binged basketball games like they were episodes of *Stranger Things*, getting lost in the various clips and completely losing track of time. Sometimes so many clips were open on his computer that it looked like a glitch—just endless windows stacked one on top of the other. Pannone would shuffle through them on fast forward, his eyes scanning for anything worth saving: a good set, a botched assignment, someone not hustling or closing out.

During the two-and-a-half-hour layover in Atlanta, players ate the food available to them: Chick-fil-A, P. F. Chang's, snacks from Hudson News. Coaches did their best to encourage healthy eating habits, but it was tough to enforce any rules. The Squadron didn't have the budget for a team chef, and per diems on the road were modest.

Atlanta Hawks center Clint Capela, who hails from Switzerland and was formerly with the Houston Rockets, wasn't even introduced to U.S. fast food restaurants until he was assigned to the Rio Grande Valley Vipers. "It kind of helped me discover about the not fancy side of the U.S. We used to eat at Denny's, Applebee's, Chili's," Capela said of life in the D-League. "I would have never known those places if I would've never gotten assigned to the D-League."

When he was with the Vipers, Capela found it refreshing to be at a regular airport again, not taking off from some private runway. Troy Daniels, who was Capela's teammate on the Rockets, played for the Vipers the season prior and remembered players racing to the gate to see who could get an exit-row seat.

In roughly twenty-four hours, the Squadron would be engaged in a physical, fast-paced, competitive game in front of NBA scouts. Right now, they were just a bunch of hungry travelers, munching on Chinese food and chicken sandwiches, navigating the chaotic crowd at Hartsfield-Jackson International.

• • •

The primary goal of every player in the minors is not a secret. Make it to the NBA. Earn a call-up. *Get out.*

Naturally, that feeds the popular misconception that winning doesn't matter in the G. Why would the final score of the Squadron-Swarm game matter to a bunch of guys whose sights are set on the NBA? Given the choice between a call-up and a G League championship, none of them would choose the latter.

But that doesn't mean winning is inconsequential. In fact, it means the opposite. Successful G League teams attract more attention from NBA front offices. The thinking is simple: *If you can't impact winning in the G, how are you going to impact winning in the NBA?* Scouts are drawn to guys who play the right way, not who chase stats. Who are unselfish, not who try to be heroes. Being on a winning team is perhaps the best way to get noticed by the people upstairs. Those with significant G League experience attest to that.

"What I've noticed is that with the teams that win, everybody's lives usually get better on those teams," said Anthony Vereen, who played 127 games in the G League and became an assistant coach for the Santa Cruz Warriors. Vereen won a championship as a player in 2016. "Everybody can't make it to the NBA, but usually you have a better chance of playing at a higher level than you would have without winning in the G League. Nobody wants somebody that doesn't impact winning. I tell these guys, your stats look better when you win."

"It for sure mattered to me," said Maurice Baker, Vereen's teammate on Santa Cruz. Baker played 357 games in the G, third most in league history, and was called up to the NBA twice. "If you're winning, that's when the people start noticing you and looking at you. On a losing team, a guy could average 30; he's going to be the last guy they look at."

"For me, winning a championship is paramount," Scotty Hopson, a long-time G Leaguer, said. "I think putting your best foot forward and trying to win a championship is how you get the most out of the experience. I can attest to this, too, especially when you're younger—your goals to win might not coincide with your goals to get to the league, to get to an NBA contract. That's not just the fans thinking that; players are *feeling* that. But I think the goals need to be in line, because if you focus on winning and playing good basketball, that's only going to help your performance."

"Any individual player that doesn't care about winning, I think that the game, at the professional level, has a way of weeding those guys out," Ron Howard, or "Mr. Mad Ant," added. "Anyone that doesn't care about winning, they won't have a long career. And if they do, they won't be playing anywhere that we've heard of. That's why we play—to win. No one just wants to lose. Losing sucks."

Howard's final point should be obvious, though it sometimes goes overlooked. Even if winning had no bearing on a player's chances of getting a call-up (which it does), *no one just wants to lose.*

•••

The first twelve games of the G League season would determine the seedings for a mini-tournament (the Showcase Cup) at the Winter Showcase, an annual scouting event to be held in Las Vegas from December 19 to 22. Teams were divided into four regional pods. The team with the best winning percentage in each pod, along with the next four top teams across the G League, would have a chance to claim the Showcase championship and the $100,000 cash prize that came with it. Every team would compete in Vegas, but only a handful would be in the running for the title.

The road to the Showcase began opening night: November 5, 2021. Tickets for the game could be purchased for less than $15. Hot dogs were being sold for $1, cans of Natural Light for $2. The Greensboro Swarm Fieldhouse—a small venue even by minor league standards—would eventually be near capacity, with just over seventeen hundred people filling the bleachers. One of those seventeen hundred was LaVar Ball, father of NBA players Lonzo Ball and LaMelo Ball and G Leaguer LiAngelo Ball, who came off the bench for the Swarm.

Tucked beneath the bleachers, hidden from the crowd, was the visiting locker room, where the Squadron convened thirty-eight minutes before tip-off. Ten players were currently with the team; Dylan Smith and Nate Bradley, the two players from tryouts, had been cut at the end of training camp. The starting lineup was Jared Harper, Joe Young, Malcolm Hill, John Petty Jr., and Zylan Cheatham.

Coach Saint kicked off the pregame speeches. Up on the television screen was the Squadron's logo: a blue star with hits of red, gold, and white. The top and bottom two points of the star mirrored the spear of the Vulcan statue. A pair of wings stretched out within the star, meant to embody the unity, precision, and power of a squadron, or a group of pelicans on the hunt together.

Saint encouraged the team to look at the logo and consider the broader significance of this moment. This was the official start of a brand-new organization, representing a proud city that hadn't experienced professional basketball in more than fifteen years. As Saint emphasized, it was an opportunity to establish a "Squadron way," to lay the first foundational bricks of the Squadron identity.

"*You* set the tone," he said, pointing to the logo. "*You* write the script."

On this night, it was Harper who set the tone. A minute into the game, he recorded the first points in Squadron history: a step-back three-pointer from several feet behind the arc. It was a bad sign for the Swarm, particularly point guard Jalen Crutcher, who was tasked with guarding Harper.

The onslaught continued: driving layup, midrange fadeaway, corner three. The way Harper maneuvered at his size, weaving through defenders at high speeds, was like a figure skater gliding around cones—fast yet smooth, arduous yet effortless, a blur.

Harper was fearless too. He had been playing against older competition—bigger and stronger athletes—since elementary school. Now the men patrolling the paint were seven-footers, fourteen-or-so inches taller than Harper, but he attacked them without hesitation. As Erica Harper, Jared's mom, always says about her son, "It's like no one told him that he was small."

Along with Cheatham, Harper was one of Birmingham's leaders. Both were well liked, though their styles were the complete opposite. Cheatham was boisterous and animated—the type to give speeches, break huddles, and participate in film sessions. Harper led more by example. He was quiet, rarely speaking up in the locker room and usually hoping to avoid interviews with the media. The court was where he did most of his talking. He directed players where to go, called audibles like a quarterback, displayed a sense of poise that permeated the entire team. His knowledge of the playbook—and basketball overall—was remarkable; he knew what every position on the floor was supposed to do on a given play, not just his own.

"A lot of kids are around basketball, but they don't become students of the game," said Desmond Eastmond, who ran the AAU program that Jared joined growing up. "Jared was one of the ones who was a student of the game. That's what allowed him to excel early." Eastmond would go on to coach *against* Harper at the high school level. By then, he knew the only strategy that might succeed at slowing down the Pebblebrook star: send a double team right away. "Our job was to get the ball out of his hands and make somebody else beat us," Eastmond explained. "We couldn't defend him one-on-one."

Bruce Pearl, Harper's head coach at Auburn University, used to call him the Tom Brady to his Bill Belichick. "It's my way of giving Jared credit for having a high basketball IQ," Pearl told the *Montgomery Advertiser*. "There will be times when I'll have something called, and he will have already had a play called, and I'll defer to him. It's sort of out of respect."[1]

As defenses adjusted, Harper adjusted *quicker*, always staying one step ahead. In private film sessions with Squadron coaches, he often pointed out things that they hadn't even noticed. Years after he graduated, Harper would get calls from his former coaches at Pebblebrook: "Hey, Jared, we're at practice, and we forgot how to run this play. Any chance you remember?" And Harper would walk them through it, like he was standing right there.

During the state championship game his senior year, Harper suffered a concussion in the third quarter. He drove hard to the basket, elevated for a layup, and was clotheslined in midair, landing directly on his head. To this day, his memory of what happened next is murky. He was in a complete daze; at one point, Pebblebrook switched to a zone defense, and Harper picked up a man.

Basketball was second nature, though. Even in a daze, Harper's body knew where to be—knew the motions to perform—because of all his training. Pebblebrook trailed Westlake High School by five points in the final minute of the game. Harper hit a floater to cut the lead to three. After Westlake's Chuma Okeke, a future NBA player, missed a pair of free throws, Harper nailed an improbable three-pointer with two defenders in his face to force overtime. Though Pebblebrook went on to lose, the only person in the building who could forget such a heroic effort was . . . Harper himself.

Unlike Cheatham, Harper scarcely—if ever—showed emotion on the floor. His expression remained blank, focused. He approached basketball like a grandmaster hunched over a chess board, reading the action, planning out his next moves.

This was Harper's third consecutive season in the G League. He spent his first year, 2019–20, with the Northern Arizona Suns—the affiliate of the Phoenix Suns—and recorded 20.2 points and 5.5 assists per game. In 2020–21, the league's bubble season, he played with the Westchester Knicks and averaged 21.3 points and 7 assists, being named to the All-NBA G League First Team. The Knicks faced the Erie BayHawks, coached by Pannone, in the last game of the regular season. Erie was hoping to secure the top seed in the playoffs, but Harper erupted for a career-high 35 points to lead Westchester to a 130–124 victory. When the season ended and Squadron decision-makers began preparing for the 2021–22 campaign, they immediately went after Harper. *If you can't beat him*, they figured, *then sign him.*

By now, Harper was accustomed to G League competition—the bruising, up-tempo style of play. From the opening tip against Greensboro, he controlled the game for the Squadron. He scored or assisted on the team's first six baskets. At halftime, he had 20 of their 59 total points, as Birmingham held a double-digit advantage. He got help in the second half: Young came alive, finishing with 30 points and the best plus-minus (+22) in the game; Cheatham and Petty played stifling defense; Ra'Shad James, Riley LaChance, and James Banks III all contributed off the bench. Harper shined brightest, however, matching his career-best of 35 points and adding 6 assists (with just 2 turnovers) in thirty-four minutes. Birmingham secured the 128–117 victory. The tone had been set.

Pannone and Chasanoff found each other in the hallway outside the locker room. "Thanks for trading for Joe Young," Pannone cracked, as the two embraced. Then he jokingly hollered to a nearby reporter, "Jared Harper saved our asses!"

Despite his big night, Harper received far less media attention than the well-known LiAngelo Ball, who notched 22 points for the Swarm. Not that it mattered to Harper. He believed, as every G Leaguer must, that *somebody* was watching, be it a scout, coach, or executive. Players in the minors had to approach every game like they were walking into a job interview. One exceptional performance could put them on the radar of an NBA team; one dud could result in their name being crossed off a list. Those were the stakes.

"The thing about Jared is, he's an NBA player," Pannone said following the game. "He's so much different than what I thought. He's so smart—and not that I didn't think he was smart—but he's *so smart* and thinks the game, and he's ahead in how he's moving the pieces around. And he scores, but he scores unselfishly. He's an excellent passer, an excellent reader of the game, and willing to give it up. Man, he's so good, and people get so caught up in his height; there are plenty of guards that are six feet four in the NBA that can't do what he can do."

•••

Birmingham played Greensboro again the following night. Back-to-backs against the same opponent are common in the G League. Winning both games, particularly on the road, is uncommon. The game started about as poorly as it could have—the Squadron scored just 16 points in the opening quarter, none of which came in the paint. The team's offensive woes continued into the fourth, when Birmingham fell behind 85–70 with 6:49 remaining.

It was an easy game to concede: an early November back-to-back, down 15 midway through the final quarter, on the heels of a victory the evening prior. But the Squadron were a resilient bunch. Malcolm Hill nailed a three-pointer to give the team some life. On the Swarm's ensuing possession, Young got a steal and dished it to Hill for a wide-open layup. The rally was on.

Birmingham came storming back, getting big buckets from Hill, Young, and guard Tra Holder. Cheatham continued to be a dominant presence on defense; he locked down the Swarm's top offensive weapon, big man Vernon Carey Jr. The former Duke star struggled to deal with Cheatham's hounding pressure, turning the ball over a combined 14 times in the two games. (As Coach Saint later learned, the Charlotte Hornets abandoned their plans to bring Carey up after seeing what Cheatham did to him.)

With 15 seconds remaining, and the Squadron down 94–92, Harper drew a foul and calmly strolled to the free-throw line. He never appeared nervous during a game; on the contrary, he sometimes appeared so relaxed that others perceived him as disengaged. He denied ever *feeling* nervous, too, except maybe the first time he put on an NBA uniform as a member of the Phoenix Suns. The work, Harper would say, erased the nerves. He had prepared for every scenario, studied every scheme, taken every shot before. So what was there to be nervous about?

"I'm very comfortable, whether it's pick-up basketball, a college game, a Final Four, or whatever it could be, I feel like I'm always prepared because it's always basketball," he said. "Basketball has always been basketball for me. It's all the same."

"He would come to the huddle and tell us, 'Calm down. Why are y'all so riled up?'" Coach Washington remembered from Harper's Pebblebrook days.

Winning Matters

"The coaches would be screaming, cursing, showing their emotions. He's like, 'Calm down. Why are y'all making a big fuss? We're okay. We're down right now; y'all relax.' That's what he would be telling us." Washington had a nickname for Harper: "Cool Hand Luke." Others would call him "Vino"— the same nickname as the late Kobe Bryant, one of Harper's favorite all-time players—because he, like wine, got better with age.

Vino now stepped to the line, Swarm fans screaming and clapping to distract him. He dribbled four times, took a deep breath, and nailed the first free throw. Then he repeated the routine and buried the second. Neither touched the rim.

Overtime. Two minutes on the clock.[2]

Just one basket was scored during the extra period: a three-pointer from the right wing by . . . Jared Harper. He finished with a game-high 27 points, and Birmingham stole the victory, 97–94, to sweep its first road trip. It was a gutsy display, a statement from the guys.

Winning matters.

The first chapter of the Birmingham Squadron had thus been written. Its brief synopsis—"Jared Harper saved our asses."

7. THE MARSHMALLOW EXPERIMENT

Immediately upon arriving in Frisco, Texas, Squadron players dropped their bags at the Staybridge Suites and got back on the bus. Young had planned a team dinner at a nearby Benihana. It was the second big dinner that Young, who was embracing his role as a veteran leader, had organized. During training camp, he had arranged for the team to have a private room at Ruth's Chris Steak House, picking up the tab of over $2,200.

On the way to Benihana, he made an announcement: "Order whatever you want when we get there. Don't worry about it, I got it."

"Oh, you didn't have to say that," Cheatham responded, chuckling.

Young wore a black hoodie, juxtaposed with a few glistening chains, and a pair of fuzzy slippers with the word "CHILL" on one foot and "OUT" on the other. It was an outfit emblematic of his personality: bold, self-assured, laid-back, goofy. Off the court, he seemed to always be giggling, always bearing a wide and toothy smile. "He's a big kid in some ways," described Korey Harris, one of Young's assistant coaches on the Beijing Royal Fighters. When he was in China, Young purchased a pet rabbit at a local market, which became a hit with his teammates. Because, well, why not? Life wasn't meant to be taken so seriously. Only basketball was.

"He's one of the goofiest and most personable guys on the team," said Jordan Kincaide, head strength and conditioning coach for the Squadron.

"He's one of those guys who can talk to anybody. He's always got a smile on his face. He's always going to try to make you laugh. He's just fun to be around. That's the best way to describe him."

"He's *so* funny," said Squadron teammate John Petty Jr. "But his approach to the game is always serious. He's always locked in."

As the meal at Benihana was going on, and people were slowly being put to sleep by a combination of teriyaki chicken and yum yum sauce, Young checked in with Kincaide. He wanted to confirm their workout time for the following morning: 5:45 a.m.

It was mid-November, just shy of a month since the start of training camp. Young had built a habit of working out early in the morning, before most of his teammates were even awake. He called it "The Breakfast Club." On this night in Frisco, Kincaide pushed back a bit. For one, the next day was a game day. And two, on account of the leisurely service at Benihana, it was already past 10:00 p.m. Neither of them knew it then, but the gym at the three-star Staybridge Suites was also a disaster: a cramped space with several missing dumbbells, a few barely functioning strength machines, and two broken treadmills.

"We can't let anyone beat us," Young said, pleading his case. Anyone referred to . . . *anyone*, not just players on the Squadron. Young couldn't bear the thought of another G Leaguer, somewhere out there, outworking him.

One could question Young's maturity at times throughout his career but never his work ethic. He was in shape for every season, and it showed in his frenetic style of play. "His passion and scrappiness stood out right away," said Dan Burke, former assistant coach for the Pacers. During the 2015 NBA Summer League, Burke had a nickname for Young: "Scrat," like the squirrel from the movie *Ice Age*, who was forever on the hunt for acorns. Young was a source of perpetual energy on the floor, pursuing the basketball like Scrat pursuing his acorns.

"He was a worker," said Steve Gansey, who coached Young on the Fort Wayne Mad Ants. "The dude always wanted to be in the gym. He busted his ass in every workout that I saw him do. The dude always gave 110 percent, and I always respected him for that. When I think of Joe, I think, *This guy is going to try to win every sprint.*"

In their first conversation, Young told Kincaide that he had recently gone to Birmingham's Life Time gym at 4:30 a.m. Kincaide was eager to work with Young, but at 4:30 a.m.? That was insane. *Too insane.* They compromised at 5:45 a.m., and "The Breakfast Club" was born.

The Club mostly met at the Lumen apartment complex, where the fitness center was open twenty-four hours. Kincaide would show up right at 5:45 and Young would already be there, running a couple miles on the treadmill to warm up. Given the minutes Young was playing at twenty-nine years old, Kincaide designed workouts that were quick and effective. Young would do three sets of six different exercises—a twenty-five-minute rotation—and then stretch. Practice at Birmingham-Southern would start at 10:00 a.m., and Young liked to get there early to shoot around. Fueled by energy drinks (his favorite was Monster), he rarely looked, or played, like someone who had woken up before the sunrise.

"You say athletes are built different, but Joe is, like, *seriously* built different," said Kincaide. "He's a machine."

Kincaide kept a monthly log of all the players' workouts—a way to hold guys accountable. He charted everything on a table entitled Squadron Strength, ranking players based on a point system that factored in the number of treatments, correctives, Breakfast Club lifts, practice lifts, pregame lifts, postgame lifts, and conditioning workouts. Young would finish first in November, tied with center James Banks III.

"He's one of the hardest working people I've ever seen on the basketball court," Harris said. "Before a game, after a game, getting up for morning workouts. Sometimes you have to tell him to stop because he'll almost hurt himself, because he's overdoing it and wearing the tread on his tires."

Many players came to the G League without the right work habits, lacking the commitment necessary to reach the NBA. Joe Young was not one of those players. For others, the challenge was often seeing the bigger picture. The G League was a *grind*—players had to chip away, day by day, at a goal that tended to feel incredibly distant, sometimes insurmountable. But only the ones who kept chipping had a chance to earn a call-up.

Squadron assistant coach Mery Andrade—a former professional player, whose inspiring journey took her from humble beginnings in Lisbon, Portugal, all the way to the WNBA—would later encourage Banks to consider the marshmallow experiment. In the study, which was originally conducted by psychologist Walter Mischel, children were offered a choice between a single marshmallow right away or waiting to be rewarded with a second marshmallow after fifteen minutes. It was a test of instant versus delayed gratification. Those who exhibited patience and discipline—who saw the bigger picture—ended up with more gratification. "You want to go out, you want to eat whatever you want, you don't feel like watching film—those things have consequences," Andrade told Banks. "They will affect your success." If the Squadron Strength chart was any indication, Banks understood.

So did Young, who would never let a lazy work ethic affect his success. He was confident, too, that it would only take a handful of games in the G League for him to get called up—that the highest form of gratification, in this case, wouldn't be so delayed.

• • •

The 2-0 Squadron were in Frisco for a back-to-back against the 2-0 Texas Legends, the affiliate of the Dallas Mavericks. After their morning shootaround at the Comerica Center, Birmingham got a visit from veteran NBA forward Anthony Tolliver. Saint had coached Tolliver, a six-foot-eight sharpshooter out of Creighton, on the Detroit Pistons. Tolliver was also a former minor leaguer—he appeared in three G League seasons from 2007 to 2010 before sticking in the NBA for over a decade, earning $35 million in contracts.

In the visiting locker room, Tolliver addressed the team. "My story was definitely unique," he began. "I didn't get drafted. I came from a small school, so no one was expecting me to make it to the league. I was the only person probably on the planet that thought I was going to make it to the league, but that's all you really need sometimes."

Tolliver was never a flashy player; his game was more appreciated by the basketball savants than the casual spectators. He didn't put up massive numbers during his four years at Creighton, averaging 13.4 points and 6.7 rebounds as a senior in 2006–7. Most notably, Tolliver wasn't known as a three-point shooter in college—he attempted just 63 total threes in 124 games. He went to training camp with the Cleveland Cavaliers in 2007, and head coach Mike

Brown told him straight up: Tolliver had all the intangibles a coach could want—he defended, hustled, took charges, communicated, sacrificed his body. If he just became a great perimeter shooter, Brown said, then he would be around the NBA for a long, long time. That was the message Tolliver received—as he was being cut from the Cavaliers.

It changed everything. He started working on his shot relentlessly, trusting that his path to the NBA was through that precise role: do the intangibles and knock down threes. Tolliver didn't try to model his game after the dominant forwards at the time, such as Kevin Garnett or Tim Duncan. Instead, he looked at the role player Robert Horry, a seven-time NBA champion from the Rockets, Lakers, and Spurs, for inspiration. Tolliver knew that he could do what Horry, a three-point marksman and versatile defender, did.

"Everybody here has been really good at basketball probably your whole life," he said to the Squadron. "Probably the best player on your team. Probably could get busy, get 30 a game, whatever. That's all good. But teams in the league don't really need players to score 30 a game anymore. They got those. They got two of those, maybe three of those. They need guys who are gonna knock down shots, have great attitudes, move the ball, be unselfish, play great on defense, and not make a bunch of mistakes."

So that's exactly what Tolliver had focused on becoming. He recognized how the NBA was evolving and adjusted his game accordingly.

"You're here for a reason, so continue to do those things that got you here," he added. "But realize that the best path to the league is through a role. Wherever you go, whatever team you get called up to, you're not going to be 'the man.' You gotta get that in your head. Maybe you look at somebody in the league and say, *He's about my height, about my athleticism, about my length. I can probably do that job.* What is he doing? Go perfect that. Because clearly he's doing something that got him to the league, right? Clearly he's doing something that made him stick around for ten-plus years. That's how I developed my skill set."

Tolliver bounced around to eleven different NBA teams in thirteen years, but someone was *always* interested in his skill set. He developed a niche and perfected it, hitting almost 900 threes over those thirteen years. It wasn't smooth sailing, though, and Tolliver didn't want it to sound that way. The road tested him both mentally and physically. The beginning of his journey was a roller coaster; he was with G League teams in Iowa and Idaho, went overseas to Germany and Turkey, got cut by numerous NBA organizations. Tolliver just stayed the course, patient and disciplined.

"If you're here, that means there's a chance," he said. "There's a possibility of you getting *there*. But the thing is, it's going to take a whole lot of discipline and a whole lot of being humble. You gotta humble yourself." The message wasn't new—Squadron coaches had been preaching it since day one—but it struck a different chord coming from Tolliver, a player who had been in their position and *made it out.*

"I want to emphasize and make sure you guys really home in on what you can do to help this team win," Tolliver continued. "When you win, you get noticed, you get *paid*—all of that."

Cheatham sat near the front, nodding along, muttering "facts" under his breath. He could see himself in Tolliver: same height, same position, on similar paths. After playing more of an inside game in college, Cheatham had been working on expanding his range to the three-point line. He understood, as Tolliver did in 2007, that NBA teams wanted big men who could hit threes efficiently—role players who could space the floor for their stars.

When Tolliver opened it up for questions, Cheatham was the first to chime in. "What kept you professional even when things got tough?" he asked. "How did you maintain being professional?"

Being professional "is a choice," Tolliver stressed. He had chosen every single day of his career to be a pro. That meant putting in the work, taking care of his body, knowing the playbook, watching extra film, maintaining a positive attitude—even when he wasn't getting an opportunity to play. "I said this to myself probably every day for fourteen years: *How many people would kill to be where I am? How many people would kill to even be in the G League?* Y'all have to realize how blessed you are to even be here," Tolliver went on. "And if you don't understand that, you'll never appreciate where you are, and you'll never appreciate where you're gonna be if you ever get there."

He turned to face Joe Young. "I know that you've been to the league," he said. The two had met several times in the NBA. In fact, one of Young's best games as a rookie came against Tolliver's Pistons, when he scored 8 points on 3 of 3 shooting off the bench. Tolliver nailed five three-pointers in that same contest.

"I know you appreciate [the NBA] now, right?"

Young nodded.

"That's exactly what happened to me," Tolliver responded. "Being in training camp my first year, experiencing the league even for a month and then going to the D-League, I was like, *Yo, I gotta work!* That's what it really comes down to, man. You just gotta make a decision to be a pro. There's no getting around that. Because it's not always going to go your way. There's no doubt about that."

• • •

Picture the scene at a first grader's birthday party, or an understaffed day-care center, or a crowded Chuck E. Cheese, and then place a basketball court, with professional athletes, right smack in the middle of it. That's the Comerica Center on game days.

Play zones were set up behind each basket. Kids twirled hula hoops, jumped on mini trampolines, scribbled on poster boards, learned how to spin basketballs on their tiny fingers, bounced around inflatable houses—all while the Squadron and Legends played a basketball game less than twenty feet away.

Some G League organizations focus solely on player development (PD), unconcerned with running a profitable business. NBA parent clubs view those organizations—and the expenses they incur—as a price worth paying to help their players improve. Other G League teams, like the Legends, concentrate on PD *and* business. Building a successful business in the minors is a huge challenge *even if* an organization chooses to make it a priority. Due to the transient nature of rosters, marketing players is difficult. Plus, the G League can't sell stars in the same way the NBA does—because the G League doesn't have stars.

The Texas Legends drew the most fans in the G League by offering a unique game experience, albeit somewhat bizarre. In the past, coaches had expressed frustration with the shenanigans happening around the court. But the business staff didn't waver; their approach was working.

"For the most part, they're committed to making money at all costs," said Billy Campbell, who served as director of basketball operations for the Legends before joining the Squadron staff. "And sometimes that comes at the cost of the basketball experience. It's all about fan experience, and that's what sells. Their goal is to sell a family experience. Their goal is that no matter what happens on the court, you're going to enjoy the experience you had while you were there, and that's going to make you want to come back and spend money."

Birmingham aspired to be like Texas—to establish a strong PD program and an effective business. Back in the Magic City, the sales team was hard at work preparing for the home opener in a few weeks, when Legacy Arena's $125 million renovation would finally be complete. Creating an enjoyable, family-fun atmosphere was crucial. So, too, was something out of the staff's control: having a winning team.

To that end, the Squadron faltered, losing both games to the Legends in ugly fashion. Ahead of the second matchup, Dallas assigned two NBA players: center Moses Brown and guard Josh Green. Both practiced with the Mavericks in the morning and then made the short drive to Frisco to join the Legends—an advantage of having such a nearby affiliate. Squadron coaches discovered the news just hours before the game and started to rethink their strategy. They shared scouting reports of Brown and Green with the players.

"Should we start James?" Saint asked in the coaches' group chat at 3:52 p.m., an hour before the bus was set to leave for the arena, referencing Banks.

"Malcolm or Z sits?" Huang responded.

"Idk. Just a thought to put out there. We could go opposite and start Petty to go super small."

Tick-tock.

Tick-tock.

Tick-tock.

Time was not on their side. Decisions and adjustments had to be made fast in the G—rosters changed daily, and teams were not required to disclose who was playing for them until an hour before tip-off.

Amid the many transactions, organizations sometimes forgot to activate their players. It happened to Cheatham when he was on a two-way contract with the Pelicans and got transferred down to the Erie BayHawks. After going through warm-ups, Cheatham was informed that he couldn't play. Someone on staff had neglected to officially activate him—a process as simple as pushing a button on a computer.

Birmingham was fortunate to have a little more time to prepare for the new-look Legends. Coach Pannone ended up sticking with the same starting lineup. Cheatham, the tallest of the bunch, was dominated by the seven-foot-two Brown, who notched 23 points, 15 rebounds, and 3 blocks to lead Texas to a 117–102 victory. Green also pitched in 20 points, 7 rebounds, and 5 assists.

More than five thousand people attended each game. Mavericks head coach Jason Kidd and general manager Nico Harrison were in the building for game two, along with several of their players, including All-Star Luka Doncic. Also present were scouts for the Denver Nuggets and Indiana Pacers. Campbell was aware beforehand that the scouts would be there and asked Saint whether they should inform the players. It might, Campbell reasoned, motivate them further. Saint didn't see it as necessary. "There are always going to be scouts at our games," he responded. Drawing attention to their presence would suggest it was an anomaly.

At the Squadron's next film session, Pannone criticized his team's effort in the back-to-back defeats. He showed clips of players not sprinting back on defense and turning their backs to the ball in transition. Saint went through more humiliating footage—lapses on defense, mental mistakes, "nonnegotiables," guys jogging instead of running. (He would later come up with a nickname for the last of those gaffes, calling it the "Sammy Sosa," a reference to the baseball slugger's signature slow trot after belting a home run.)

"Imagine you're Jason Kidd, sitting courtside, evaluating," Pannone said. "What do you see? Who do you want to pay a million dollars to here?"

Campbell suddenly chimed in from the back of the locker room. He was always present at film sessions but seldom spoke. When he did, though, his words held weight. "*Everything* you put on tape matters," he said. It was all bound to get analyzed, dissected, blown up, broken down. As Campbell stressed, people were *always* watching, not just the big names like Jason Kidd and Nico Harrison who were front and center: the scouts hidden in nooks around the arena, the coaches who would study the film—the same film they were currently panning—later on.

So every play *did* matter. All the my-bad and whoops moments would get noticed. In the G League, not sprinting back on defense could be the difference between someone liking you and dismissing you, between a call-up and a season in the minors, between millions and $37,000.

8. NOVEMBER 17, 2021

It was warm enough to roll down the windows as Cheatham cruised on Arkadelphia Road toward Birmingham-Southern. He wore a black-and-gold Versace robe that draped down to his knees, and he sang along to the booming car stereo. He looked, and felt, like royalty. And why shouldn't he? It was November 17, 2021, his twenty-sixth birthday. He was healthy and inching closer to his NBA dream. He was thankful to be in this position—to have made it this far—given everything he had been through.

Even after escaping South Phoenix, Cheatham was often reminded of the perils he had circumvented. As a senior at Arizona State University, he was arriving home from dinner one night when his father called with tragic news. Cheatham's younger brother, twenty-two-year-old Wanyaa Stewart, had been shot and was in critical condition. Cheatham raced to the hospital, but Stewart did not survive.

The two had been close growing up, playing Pokémon and sports together. They had similar personalities: loud, witty, good-humored. Cheatham moved away during high school; Stewart stayed behind and was swept into a dangerous lifestyle. Still, Stewart was always rooting for his big brother to make it, always encouraging him to keep going. The news of his passing left Cheatham heartbroken. "I just remember him not being Z," said Darvis Fletcher, Cheatham's best friend. "He was quiet. He just didn't seem like himself."

Basketball was Zylan's escape, his safe place. Arizona State head coach Bobby Hurley told him to take all the time he needed, but Cheatham showed up to practice the next day. "That's what I did because being out on the floor, being around my guys, being in a position to get better in that hour, hour and a half, two hours or whenever we are out on the floor, it offers me a time to just take my mind off everything and just focus on the game I love," Cheatham told reporters. "It's almost like people go to the beach or read books. My happy place is on the court."[1]

Over the past few years, Zylan had been quietly coping with another heartache: his mom, Carolyn, was battling cancer. He and Carolyn were extremely close; for much of his childhood, it was just the two of them. She looked out for him through all the tough times, ensuring he always had something to eat, even if it was just a Hot Pocket or Hamburger Helper. Every day, Zylan watched her get up and go to work—first at Bank of America and later at Humana—no matter her exhaustion. It allowed him to be a kid, to pursue basketball and not worry so much about their circumstances. He wanted to make it to the NBA *for her*, to be able to buy her a new house and give her a new life and repay her for all the sacrifices she had made for him.

"She's literally the super woman, like a superhero. To see her going through what she's going through now is just unbelievable," said Zylan. "It just doesn't seem fair to me. She's literally been the best person ever. I just don't understand how something like this could happen."

There were good days and bad days—hopeful moments and painful moments—but Carolyn's condition was gradually deteriorating. It weighed on Zylan, more than he even knew.

After he was waived by the Thunder in 2020, Cheatham was invited to join the Minnesota Timberwolves for part of their training camp, with the expectation that he would play for their G League affiliate. Cheatham reported to Minnesota around the same time that his mom was scheduled to have an important doctor's appointment back in Phoenix. Before taking the floor, he was required to pass a routine physical exam. Cheatham failed his stress echocardiogram, a test of how well one's heart and blood vessels are working under stress. He continued to take the test every day—and continued to fail. As a result, Cheatham wasn't allowed to do any physical activity and was stuck in his hotel room. Waiting. Praying. Trying to relax. It was only after his mom's appointment was done—and went well—that he started to feel better and finally passed the test. The irony was that Cheatham's stresses tended to fade away *on the court*, not holed up in some hotel.

At practice for the Squadron, regardless of what he was shouldering away from basketball, Cheatham was always upbeat. On his birthday, he was even bouncier than usual. This wasn't Z; it was "Versace Z." Imagine a little kid on the blacktop, finally freed for recess, releasing all of his pent-up emotions at once. Now add thirty inches to his height and 150 pounds to his frame. That was Versace Z.

During full-court five-on-five action, the trash talk began. Most of the time—this day included—Cheatham went after Banks. The two were typically matched up against each other, and Banks made for an easy target. He was the second youngest player on the team at twenty-three years old, still adjusting to the pace and physicality of the pro level. His kindhearted nature was at odds with how the coaches wanted him to play. They didn't want their six-foot-ten, 250-pound center to be Mr. Nice Guy. They wanted Banks to be a beast, bullying his way to the rim and dominating the glass. They wanted him to be like Cheatham.

"I am a nice guy—it's not conducive to being a beast," Banks said. "You gotta flip that switch. When the shit talking comes out, that's when the nice guy goes out the door, for real."

Well, the shit talking was out, and the nice guy was headed for the door. Cheatham attacked Banks relentlessly, as if the tiny BSC gym was filled with scouts. He got to the paint and finished strong. He drilled a few shots from the perimeter. Banks wasn't backing down, but he wasn't quite matching Cheatham's production either. And Cheatham's energy? That was *always* unmatchable. If Cheatham was there, it was impossible to be the loudest person in the room.

The buzzer sounded: water break, two minutes.

"Coach him up, Mery! He needs it!" Cheatham hollered, as Coach Andrade was walking Banks through some defensive adjustments. Andrade was a standout defender herself during an illustrious playing career.

The clash continued. Coach Pannone had a unique scoring system for scrimmages—midrange baskets were worth nothing, unless they came with fewer than four seconds on the shot clock; assists were an extra point; turnovers were minus a point. Nonetheless, whenever they were keeping score, things tended to get chippy. And Cheatham tended to be one of the culprits.

Nearing the end of practice, Zylan grabbed a defensive rebound, drove the length of the court, leapt toward the rim, and, at the last second, decided to kick the ball out. He contorted slightly in the air to create a passing lane but was moving too fast to align his feet for a normal landing. His body was off-center. His weight was shifted. One leg hit the ground first, planting at a weird angle and buckling beneath him. Cheatham went tumbling to the floor, his six-foot-eight body crashing with a *thud*. He immediately clutched his knee.

Then he screamed: a piercing sound that caused the rest of the gym—the rest of BSC, it seemed—to fall silent. Rolling around on the baseline, he continued to groan in agony. Gilchrist Schmidt, head athletic trainer, sprinted to his aid. Players fanned out, staring down at Cheatham with expressions of profound concern. It didn't look good.

It didn't feel good either. Cheatham was sure that his season was over. In that moment, with the intensity and acuteness of the pain, his mind went to the darkest place possible. *I'm done. No more basketball. No more NBA.* Any sort of serious injury would change everything. Even a nagging one that slowed him down *just a bit* could deter NBA teams from taking a chance on him. Cheatham already carried some swelling in his knee from prior—thankfully minor—injuries. This one, however, didn't feel minor.

Practice was called. Coach Pannone assembled the team. Usually they spoke for a bit in the huddle, breaking down the day's work and relaying any important announcements. This time, they just put their hands in the middle and faintly mumbled, "1, 2, 3, family."

Cheatham was helped to the trainer's table in the corner of the gym. He sprawled out, resting a hand on his knee, replaying the last few minutes in his mind. *Why did I do that? What was I thinking? How could I have been so reckless?* Schmidt examined the area and ran through a series of preliminary questions, just to get a sense for what they could be dealing with. "Where's the pain?" he asked. Zylan pointed a bit higher than the back of his knee, more on his hamstring. *Phew*, Schmidt thought. *Not an ACL*. His initial impression was that the area got, in layman's terms, overstretched. Like, *really* overstretched. Because of Cheatham's preexistent swelling, a freak landing like that, where the knee bent so sharply, would be excruciating.

"When you have really no space in your knee—when you're bending your knee, you already feel more pressure in it because you have a little bit of fluid in it—and then it gets cranked down on like that, it's going to feel like, *I just jacked something up*," Schmidt explained.

Schmidt was hopeful that it was nothing serious, as he informed the coaches. Of course, nothing could be ruled out until an MRI was conducted, which would be arranged right away. Cheatham was less optimistic. Based on what he was feeling, he was preparing for the worst. Next steps were beginning to be outlined when McGowan, the team's equipment manager and basketball operations associate, emerged from a side door carrying a birthday cake.

Despite the giant cloud hanging overhead, everyone gathered around the trainer's table. McGowan held the cake in front of Cheatham and the team performed perhaps the gloomiest rendition of "Happy Birthday" in the history of birthdays: "Happy birthday to you. Happy birthday to you. Happy birthday, dear Zylan. Happy birthday to you."

Cheatham wore a smile the entire time. But beneath it, deep down, he was panicking. If this was as bad as he thought it was, it wouldn't be a happy birthday at all.

• • •

"You think this is doable?" Hill asked, turning to face Pannone. It was late afternoon now, several hours after practice had ended, and several hours before Cheatham would limp his way to Topgolf for a birthday celebration. Hill and the Squadron coaches had gathered in the Skylight Lounge, reclining on cozy couches as radio hits played softly in the background.

Hill didn't doubt that it was doable himself—of course not. He just sought confirmation, to gauge for sure whether Pannone and the rest of the staff truly believed what they were telling him: that if he adhered to the player development (PD) plan laid out before him, he could make it to the NBA.

And so he looked Pannone in the eyes, measured his expression carefully, and waited for a response. "T.J., what were you saying about Malcolm the other day?" Coach hollered.

"I said a lot of things," Saint answered, smiling. He was hardly brief. A few days prior, he had told Pannone that he thought Malcolm had a real shot to be called up to the NBA during the 2021–22 season. Hill's defense would appeal to NBA scouts, Saint reasoned. He just had to shoot at least 40 percent from three-point range—which, as of this meeting, he was not doing.

"Do *you* think it's doable?" Pannone asked, flipping the question on Hill.

"Yes," he replied, without hesitation.

Forty-five minutes earlier, Hill had entered the room unsure of what to expect. He wore shorts and a white T-shirt with the words "God's Plan" printed in big letters across his chest. He had picked up a late lunch from Chipotle (his first meal of the day) but told the coaches that he would wait to eat until the meeting was over. This—whatever it was exactly—deserved his full attention.

Coach Huang, who worked most closely with Hill throughout the season, had put together the plan and was leading the presentation. This type of thing wasn't a given in the G League—the Squadron staff went above and beyond to ensure that each player understood his individual roadmap to the NBA. They would leave no stone unturned when it came to development, lest a player miss out on a potential million-dollar opportunity because of their negligence. Thus, the attention to detail in Huang's plan, down to the intricate design of the PowerPoint slides, was striking.

It began with a rundown of Hill's numbers from his past two seasons overseas, ignoring his complicated stint in the Israeli Basketball Premier League. There were the basics—his points, assists, rebounds, and turnovers per game, along with his shooting percentages. Having meticulously pored through all of Hill's footage, Huang was able to chart more specific metrics as well. In a table entitled "Shooting Breakdown," he had separated Hill's shots into five categories: rim finishes, paint shots, overall 3s, catch & shoot 3s, and off-the-dribble 3s. Those categories were further divided into four subcategories, based on *how* Hill took each shot exactly.

For example, the table indicated that Hill shot 27 of 43, or 63 percent, at the rim. Of those rim finishes, he was 2 of 2 when he used his left hand and

25 of 41 when he used his right hand. He was also 16 of 23 when he jumped off of two feet and 9 of 18 when he jumped off of one. All this data was put to use—Huang pointed out, for instance, that players tended to elevate quicker when they jumped off of one foot, which would be a necessary adjustment for Hill should he reach the NBA.

Hill nodded along as the presentation continued, his eyes bouncing back and forth between Huang and the large television screen. His three main development goals, according to the coaches, were to increase his three-point efficiency, become an All-Defensive player, and be contagious with his energy. Huang challenged Hill to impart his good habits—his *routines*—to the rest of the team.

Though just twenty-six years old, Hill had the approach and demeanor of a vet. He was one of the most disciplined players on the Squadron, perhaps *too* disciplined. Coaches sometimes worried that he was doing too much. Even Pelicans center Jaxson Hayes, who was with Hill during training camp, admitted, "I ain't never seen somebody like that."

Hill had been uniquely motivated since childhood. Growing up in Fairview Heights, Illinois, he never tried to fit in or follow others. He enjoyed anime (still does) and video games (not so much anymore) but never let those interests interfere with the pursuit of his goals—one of which, of course, was to make it to the NBA.

After getting so far ahead in school, Hill skipped the second grade. The move concerned his father, Malcolm Sr., a former Division II basketball player at the University of Missouri-St. Louis and longtime coach, who knew how much an extra year could do for his son's athletic development. "So we doubled our amount of work during workouts because we were trying to make that year up," he said. "And Malcolm didn't mind doing the work."

As he got older, Hill maintained that intense mindset. He was a big Kobe Bryant fan—his dog was even named after the late Lakers legend—and tried his best to emulate the "Mamba Mentality." Hill's stepbrother, Clayton Hughes, remembered him running several miles a day in middle school and constantly going to the gym. "Some people just know that they are destined to be great," Hughes said. "Malcolm has always been that way."

"What really helped him separate from the rest of the competition was that he was never afraid to work," Malcolm Sr. said. "If I said, 'Hey, let's go to the gym and work on this,' there was never any pushback from him. Never. Not one time. He always wanted to improve his game."

"He would work above and beyond the expectation," added Machanda Hill, Malcolm's mom. "So, the expectation would be that you show up for practice and you go home. Even at an early age, and he still does this now, he would show up to practice early before everyone else, just to get shots up. Or he would stay after practice late to get shots up. Or we would come home and he would go outside and work on his ball handling or go to the local park and shoot free throws or run the track."

That discipline carried Hill to the University of Illinois. Then it carried him to a professional career overseas. When he was in Jerusalem during the pandemic, he took his approach to another level. He became, in his words, "locked into life." Not just locked into *basketball*, as he had been previously. *Locked into everything.* He embraced a holistic plan of attack. No more video games after practice. No more junk food. Every decision he made, every action he took, every thought he had—it would all influence what transpired on the court.

Hill liked to start his days in Birmingham around 6:30 a.m. with meditation, prayers, breathing exercises, and yoga. He would walk around barefoot on the grass at Railroad Park, across the street from the Lumen Apartments, to electrically reconnect with the earth—a practice that frequently made him the target of jokes.

Hill's personality doesn't exactly fit his intense lifestyle. He's incredibly approachable, soft-spoken, polite—not the least bit intimidating. The sort of person to ask strangers about their days and express genuine interest in their responses. Whenever he goes back to Belleville East High School, he takes the time to visit his old teachers. "All the teachers loved Malcolm," said Abel Schrader, who coached Hill as a senior at Belleville East. Schrader loved him too, as did Ray Hoffman, Hill's coach before Schrader. "Just an unbelievably kind kid, and his family is the same," added Hoffman. It was no different in Birmingham. *Everybody* loved Malcolm. They loved his attitude, his humbleness, and, yes, even his strange idiosyncrasies.

The only person Malcolm Hill is ever harsh to is Malcolm Hill. And that's often. "Come on, Malcolm!" he will murmur under his breath during work-outs. "Let's go, Malcolm! Why are you missing shots, Malcolm? What are you doing, Malcolm?" He has never bought into the idea of natural talent; in his view, talent is built from hard work. *Legends aren't born, they're forged.*

So the mild-mannered Hill is always seeking ways to improve. He reads books about becoming a better man. He writes blog posts, reflecting on his current situation and encouraging subscribers to develop their own routines. "I want everyone who reads this to know and understand that anything is possible," he once wrote. "I dare you to challenge yourself. Write down a goal and read it every day, multiple times a day."

That was precisely what Hill had done. At the beginning of the year, while still in Jerusalem, he had written down a goal: *Make the NBA by the end of 2021.* He believed in it, even though few others did.

"I believe in believing," he explained. "I think that's just a part of the journey through life. You don't really know how things are going to shake out, but if you just walk with that faith—true faith—then things will turn out in your favor. You just have to keep going long enough to see it turn out that way."

The Pelicans had followed Hill since his days at Illinois. Even when he was glued to the bench in Israel, New Orleans was still intrigued by his potential. Pannone had previously coached Hapoel Jerusalem and understood that Hill's situation there was tricky. Yarone Arbel, an international scout for the Pelicans, organized a lunch meeting with Malcolm. The two ended up talking for close to four hours—about Hill's journey, his overseas experience, his distinct approach. Arbel was struck by Hill's professionalism, especially amid such a frustrating phase of his career.

Malcolm was subsequently invited to join the Pelicans for the 2021 NBA Summer League. After training camp, he landed in Birmingham with the Squadron. How far he had come since writing that far-fetched goal down in his journal was extraordinary. In his eyes, it was all because of his daily routines that he was now on the doorstep of the NBA.

He hadn't made it yet, though. There was just over a month left to achieve his goal, and Hill remained stubborn in its pursuit. He sweated through multiple T-shirts a day. He never went out or partied, adhered to a strict diet, reduced his phone time, and eliminated other distractions entirely.

"I haven't seen many people from the G League with his type of focus," Huang emphasized. "Because in the G League, guys come to us and they're the misshapen or defective toy—there's something wrong with them, whatever the case may be. And sometimes they have talent, but they're just lacking the focus and work ethic. For him, the way he approaches the game is like an NBA player. His nutrition is right. His recovery is right. His weightlifting schedule is right. His sleep schedule is right—on and on and on."

"Malcolm is not one of those people who can just wake up and do something different," Hughes reaffirmed. "There's a routine to everything he does. He probably has a routine for the way he brushes his teeth."

Hill wasn't the most athletic player on the Squadron—not even close. Each week, Kincaide tested the players' vertical jumps; and each week, Hill's ranked right around the middle. He couldn't run the fastest either. Birmingham liked to push the pace and Harper was perhaps the quickest guard in the G League with the ball in his hands. Keeping up wasn't always easy, but Hill gave 100 percent effort on every possession. Most guys didn't have the stamina to do so—Hill did.

During grueling stretches—two-a-days and back-to-backs—he swore he wasn't tired. All that he did in the offseason, he would say, prepared his body for these moments. And he wouldn't allow what limited athleticism he had to be at less than full capacity. "He's in like a '97 Honda Civic, and he's full-on pressing the accelerator, getting the max juice out of it. Literally, the *max juice* out of it," Huang analogized.

Hill's PD plan broke down all of his tendencies, specifying which he should aim to keep and which he should try to abandon. Predictably, the coaches wanted him to stop taking midrange jumpers and focus on shooting threes and attacking the basket. They had a list of new things for Hill to add to his game as well, like expanding his finishing package and becoming a more active cutter.

Huang had gathered film of players in the NBA to analyze. For offense, they studied four-time All-Star DeMar DeRozan's ability to get to the rim, bump guys off, maintain balance, and create enough space to lay the ball in. For defense, they watched former G Leaguer Alex Caruso, noting how he clung to and chased his man all over the court.

"And he's making, what, like, $9 million dollars now, coach?" Pannone said, as the tape rolled.

"He's *getting paid*," Huang responded.

Caruso was one of the G League's best success stories. In August he had signed a four-year, $37 million contract with the Chicago Bulls after morphing into an elite on-ball defender.

The PowerPoint concluded with a screenshot of an unidentified player's career history from Wikipedia. "Do you know whose career this is?" Huang quizzed Hill. Beginning in 2006, the player had gone from the Toronto Raptors, to the Colorado 14ers (D-League), to Hapoel Holon (Israel), to Donetsk (Ukraine), to Bnei HaSharon (Israel), to Aris Thessaloniki (Greece), to Sutor Montegranaro (Italy), to Piratas de Quebradillas (Puerto Rico), and to Brose Baskets (Germany) before finally sticking in the NBA in 2012. Since then, he had spent time with the Suns, Raptors, Rockets, Bucks, and Heat.

It was the long and winding journey of 2021 NBA champion P. J. Tucker.

For Hill, Tucker was an apt comparison. The two were around the same height, had similar builds, and played the same position. Tucker, like Hill, was not exceptionally athletic but was known for his effort and intensity, particularly on defense. He was usually tasked with guarding the opposing team's best player, including, in the previous year's NBA playoffs, former MVP Kevin Durant. Tucker embraced that role. He loved it. He had made a career, and a very comfortable living, off of it.

"Do you know how old P.J. was when he first stuck in the NBA?" Huang asked.

Hill shook his head no.

"Twenty-seven"—a year *older* than Malcolm. It took time for Tucker to both hone his skill set and get recognized by NBA scouts. The process was long and arduous, encompassing enough stamps to fill a passport, but when his opportunity came, Tucker was ready for it. Hill would be too.

Roughly an hour had passed. Hill's Chipotle bag remained untouched on the table. He sat on an L-shaped couch, sandwiched between Pannone and Huang, silently processing the information. He knew he was capable of everything the coaches wanted him to do; he had, in fact, done most of it in spurts before. They weren't asking for much: knock down open three-pointers, zero in on defense, compete with sustained energy, become more of a leader. They didn't want him to handle the ball, orchestrate the offense, or carry a massive scoring load.

In other words, they weren't suggesting that Hill take on a leading role. He would never be the focal point of an offense in the NBA—the primary, go-to option. But he could, if he stuck to the plan, be like P. J. Tucker. And unlike others in the G League, Hill was willing to accept that. He had come to appreciate the value of role players—something that was once hard for him to wrap his head around. Before college, he would watch the NBA and wonder why some guys were even on the court. *How's a player good enough to be in the game if he's averaging just four points?* he would contemplate. *What's the point of having him out there?*

Hill got it now. He could spot all the reasons, all the little things those guys were doing to help their teams win: communicating, rotating on defense, spacing the floor, hustling, boxing out, taking charges. That would be him if he ever got to the NBA. "Getting on an NBA court is the hardest thing to do," he once said. "So if you get thrown out there for doing the little stuff, that just shows how big it is in the grand scheme of things, you know?"

As Coach Pannone put it during the meeting that day, "Do the shit that no one else will do, like cutting. It's so fucking easy. That's how you get noticed."

Doing the little things well enough to reach the NBA wasn't actually "so fucking easy." Pannone knew that, of course. But his point was clear. It was, for Malcolm Hill, certainly doable.

"In the NBA, a lot of guys are just really awesome at being simple," Huang later explained. "They're awesome at simpleness. It's crazy to say that but it's really hard for a lot of people to grasp that. For Malcolm, once we gave him that singular focus, he got it. And hopefully he just keeps it throughout the season. That's gonna be his calling card for his chance to be in the league. And I hope he does it. I really do."

9. THE PANIC BUTTON

Cheatham could exhale. The MRI revealed no serious damage. He had bruised a bit of the cartilage in his knee and strained his hamstring but would not be sidelined for a long period. From Schmidt's perspective, the preexistent swelling in Cheatham's knee may have actually helped prevent a more devastating injury. "It gave it a bunch of cushion, essentially," Schmidt explained. "That's a speculative answer. I don't know it 100 percent, but I would say I think it probably helped more than it hurt in that case."

At practice the ensuing day, players received their booster shots for COVID. A nurse set up shop on the sideline, and guys took booster breaks like water breaks. Cheatham was in street clothes but back to his lighthearted self. He and Pannone shared that trait; it was one of the reasons they got along so well. Before the team left for the day, Pannone showed them the latest addition to his wardrobe: a "Versace" robe. It was a work of art by his two children: a plain white robe with blue tape stuck to the back, spelling out "Versace P." Pannone strutted around the court as if it were a runway, shouting, "Versace P! Versace P!" He encouraged Joseph Hooven, head of public relations, to take his picture and post it on Instagram. Hooven created a "Who wore it best?" poll on the Squadron's account: Versace P or Versace Z?

Of course, Versace P won.

The Squadron spent Thanksgiving Day traveling to McAllen, Texas, for a weekend series against the Rio Grande Valley (RGV) Vipers. The bus departed from Lumen at 7:25 a.m. for an 8:55 a.m. flight out of Birmingham. After landing in Houston, the team had a four-hour layover that prevented them from getting to McAllen until 4:00 p.m. Players and coaches went straight from the airport to Bert Ogden Arena for practice, just as many families around the country were sitting down for an epic meal. The staff would have a Thanksgiving feast of their own later that night—at the Texas staple Whataburger, near the La Quinta hotel.

The Vipers were 6-0, one of only two unbeaten teams left in the G League. Rockets guard Josh Christopher, the number twenty-four pick in the 2021 Draft, was also with them on assignment. It would be a challenging road trip, but Squadron players were well rested and coming off a good week of practice. Plus, Cheatham had been cleared to return.

Birmingham came out on fire, taking a 13–0 lead to start the game. Once the Vipers settled in, the teams exchanged a number of runs. Cheatham's aggressiveness in the paint and Hill's red-hot shooting carried the Squadron. The score was tight until late in the fourth quarter, when RGV went on the final run to secure a 112–105 victory.

It was not the result Birmingham wanted, but there were positives to take away. While still fighting through pain, Zylan was *everywhere*, scoring 28 points and grabbing 19 rebounds. "It's the best I've seen him play," said Squadron color analyst Rick Moody, who previously coached the University of Alabama women's basketball team from 1989 to 2005.

Hill was even more impressive, simply by doing exactly what the coaches had instructed him to do during his player-development meeting: relocate around the perimeter, launch open shots without hesitation, defend at a high level. He buried eight three-pointers and notched five steals, doing a solid job guarding the highly touted Christopher. He became the first G League player since Frank Mason III in February 2020 to register 30-plus points and 5-plus steals in a single game.

Before game two of the series, the team had a day in McAllen to practice, recuperate, and catch the Iron Bowl—the annual matchup between the University of Alabama (UA) and Auburn University (AU) on the football field. Petty, a proud UA alum, was actually on a visit to Auburn during the historic "Kick Six" game in 2013, when cornerback Chris Davis returned a missed field goal 109 yards for a touchdown to lift the Tigers over the Crimson Tide. Somewhere in the stands at Jordan-Hare Stadium, an awestruck Petty watched as AU's students stormed the field.

This year, Alabama—the number three team in the country—was a clear favorite over unranked Auburn. Petty predicted a 35–14 rout, while Harper, a former Tiger, picked his alma mater to pull off a shocking 31–20 upset. It was closer than both guys anticipated, with Bama eking out the memorable 24–22 victory in quadruple overtime.

The following afternoon, Squadron players arrived at Bert Ogden Arena with a swagger, certain that they were the superior team and ready to prove it.

And then . . .

They got crushed.

This was no thriller, no classic, no clash of titans. Goliath stomped David, and, unlike in the Iron Bowl, David didn't put up much of a fight. Fortunately, there were 85,185 fewer fans in attendance to witness the affair.

The Vipers ran away with it in the third quarter, eventually winning 101–89 to improve to 8-0. Birmingham was careless and sloppy with the ball, turning it over an appalling 22 times. After game-planning how to attack RGV's switching defense, the offensive execution was pathetic. The team was outrebounded (51–33), outhustled, *outplayed*.

It was early in the season, but frustrations were already boiling over. Things were beginning to spiral. Four consecutive losses were enough to push the panic button. The Showcase was less than a month away. Birmingham had played half of its twelve games leading up to the marquee event, where more eyes would be concentrated on the teams with *winning* records. Call-ups were starting to happen and would only increase in the weeks to follow. Cheatham could keep bringing the energy; Hill could keep knocking down threes. But the worry was, if the losses kept mounting, would anyone *care*? Would Alabamans come to cheer them on? Would NBA teams express any interest? Would this season be a waste?

Pannone was obviously frustrated too. He wasn't accustomed to losing—in his eighteen years of coaching, he had experienced just two losing seasons. A lot of that frustration rested with himself. *Perhaps I didn't prepare them correctly*, he pondered. *Maybe the adjustments were too complicated.* Walking to the locker room, he braced for a somber scene. He would have to lift the guys' spirits, motivate them to turn things around.

Or not.

When he entered, the team was already engaged in an honest conversation, so Pannone didn't interrupt. He listened as the players called out each other's flaws. He listened as they took ownership of their mistakes. He listened as they vowed to give more effort, fix the mental lapses, and do the little things right. He listened as back-up shooting guard Riley LaChance, formerly a star at Vanderbilt University, highlighted one of their many blunders: after a timeout, Coach had called "pitch," a play they run close to ten times a game, and the guys had failed to execute it properly. Those types of mistakes only occurred when players weren't focused.

Cheatham was adamant that the better team lost that night—*adamant.* It gnawed at him that they were underachieving, just like it gnawed at Harper, and Young, and Hill, and so on down the line. Nobody was pointing fingers. The losing streak was on them, collectively. And it was on them, collectively, to right the ship. But it had to happen now.

As he listened, Pannone could feel his frustration fading away. In his eighteen years, he had never seen a postgame locker room quite like that one. It brought him comfort. The organization had set out to assemble a roster of high character people, and this, Pannone believed, was proof that they had succeeded.

"It was a pivotal moment," Cheatham later reflected. "It was kind of like a come-to-reality type of moment. It just gave guys a chance to really speak their truths, regroup, and start looking forward—seriously, though. Like, 'Fuck talking about it. Fuck all the hoorahs. Let's really do this.'"

10. THE PRICE OF A DREAM

When Carldell "Squeaky" Johnson arrived at the University of Alabama at Birmingham (UAB) in 2003, he was a nobody. A five-foot-ten point guard originally from New Orleans, Squeaky (the nickname was initially "Squiggy" after a character in the TV show *Laverne & Shirley*, later changed to "Squeaky" because Johnson's steals were squeaky clean) wasn't recruited by any Division I schools out of high school. He went to play at Salt Lake City Community College and eventually caught the eye of UAB head coach Mike Anderson.

UAB, a public university established in 1966, is situated in the heart of downtown Birmingham, just a five-minute drive from Legacy Arena, home of the Squadron. As a member of Conference USA, the UAB basketball team competes in Division I. No, the school isn't known for hoops. And no, the basketball program isn't known for attracting and developing NBA prospects. But for Squeaky Johnson, being at UAB was an injection of confidence. Suddenly the NBA didn't feel like such an impossible goal; it was a summit that Squeaky—just maybe—could reach.

So he began the steady climb. Squeaky was a feisty guard—tenacious on defense, unselfish on offense. After averaging 7.3 points, 6.3 assists, and 2.6 steals in his senior season, he went undrafted in 2006. He bounced around for a year, including stints in Belgium and Mexico, before being selected in the second round of the 2007 D-League Draft by the Austin Toros. He would be taking a considerable pay cut to leave Mexico and join the Toros, but for Squeaky, it was a no-brainer. In his mind, he would go to the D-League, impress scouts, and soon make it to the NBA. "But man, was I in for a rude awakening," he said.

Squeaky was astounded by the level of talent in the D-League. "I remember thinking, *Damn, these guys are really good, and they're not in the NBA*," recalled Johnson. "It made me feel like, *Oh, shit, I gotta work. I'm not as good as I thought I was.*" Throughout that first year with the Toros, Squeaky tried to absorb as much as he could. He started eleven of forty-nine games, showing signs of improvement. Several of his teammates were called up: Marcus Williams, Keith Langford, DerMarr Johnson, Andre Barrett. Squeaky could feel it—the gravitational force of the NBA. Gripping him. *Pulling* him. Now that he was this close, there was no turning back.

Squeaky Johnson *had to* make it.

• • •

Unlike Squeaky Johnson, by the mid-aughts, Richard Hendrix was known all throughout Alabama. He was a four-year starter on the varsity basketball team at Athens High School from 2001 to 2005 and became one of the most decorated prep players in Alabama history, holding the state records for rebounds (1,820) and blocked shots (667). As a senior, Hendrix—a six-foot-eight bruising forward—was named Alabama Mr. Basketball and invited to participate in the 2005 McDonald's All-American Game. He was a top-ten prospect in the nation according to Rivals.com and accepted a scholarship to the University of Alabama over an offer from the University of North Carolina.

In Hendrix's case, the NBA seemed like a sure thing, an inevitability. He even toyed with the idea of entering the NBA Draft out of high school, when he was projected to be a lottery pick, but ultimately decided to honor his commitment to UA. To no one's surprise, he continued to thrive in the competitive SEC. He was named All-Conference as both a sophomore and junior, leading the Crimson Tide in scoring both seasons. Through three years, he averaged 14 points and 8.9 rebounds and fulfilled all his academic requirements to graduate early. There was nothing left to do or prove; it was time to make the leap to the NBA.

Hendrix's draft stock had dropped, in part due to concerns over some injuries. Still, his talent was inarguable, his production undeniable. At the age of twenty-one, Hendrix declared for the 2008 NBA Draft. He worked out for nearly half the NBA teams that summer.

On June 26, 2008, Hendrix patiently waited to discover his fate. With the draft winding down, then–deputy commissioner Adam Silver took the stage and uttered the words that Hendrix had long dreamt of hearing: "With the 49th pick in the 2008 NBA Draft, the Golden State Warriors select . . . Richard Hendrix."

• • •

Squeaky was learning. His experience with the Toros was opening his eyes to what NBA coaches were looking for in the D-League. He was trying to find his way in—knocking on every door, checking every window, investigating every possible entry point. Offers came from overseas (more lucrative contracts than those in the D-League) and Squeaky entertained a few of them, briefly going back to Mexico for a whopping four games. But his mind was dead set on the NBA, and he knew that the D-League gave him the best shot to make it.

So Squeaky was learning. He went to Summer League with the San Antonio Spurs—the parent club for the Toros—in 2009, and during the team's first meeting, they got a visit from legendary head coach Gregg Popovich.

Johnson recalled the story: "Gregg Popovich comes in there and says, 'You know what, I'm not looking for any of you guys to come in and play on our team. All I want is a good locker room guy, somebody who Timmy [Duncan] likes and who Timmy wants to be around the team.' What that meant to me was, be somebody that's just a great team player who people want to be around. At that point, that's when I realized, it's not about your talent, it's about being a good fit."

Squeaky could do that—he could be that good fit for an NBA organization. *I just have to stick it out*, he thought. *I can get there if I stick it out.* That mindset would come at a price, though. Squeaky kept returning to the Toros. He played the full 2007–8 season . . . then the full '08–09 season . . . then the full '09–10 season.

By year three, most D-Leaguers have already abandoned ship, leaving for greener pastures overseas. The contracts in other countries can be *significantly* bigger than in the minors; at one point, Johnson was offered $20,000 a month to play in Japan, more than he earned for an entire D-League season. Like all players on the fringe, Squeaky was forced to confront the same impossible decision every year: take his talents overseas or sign in the D-League.

Chase the money or the dream?

The fact that basketball careers are short-lived—players tend to retire around the age of thirty-two, thirty-six if they're lucky, forty if they're *really* lucky—favored the overseas route. If Squeaky had only a decade or so left to play, shouldn't he make the most of those years financially?

At the same time, he wasn't married and didn't have any kids, which favored the D-League route. If he wasn't desperate for money to support a family, shouldn't he try to achieve his ultimate goal?

Either way, Johnson would be sacrificing. Signing in the D-League meant accepting a diminished role, grinding through an arduous schedule, earning a smaller salary. Signing overseas meant leaving his loved ones behind, having to adapt to a foreign lifestyle, kissing his NBA dream goodbye.

When faced with the decision, Squeaky always tried to think ahead, to consider what his future self might feel looking back. And he just couldn't fathom the idea of abandoning his dream. "I'd rather say I tried and did all I could do and I just didn't make it—I just wasn't good enough—versus me saying I left for some money," he explained. "I'd rather just grind it out and never say woulda, coulda, shoulda."

• • •

Hendrix was hampered by a quad injury when the Warriors opened training camp in 2008. By mid-November, though, he was healthy and confident that his opportunity was imminent. On November 14, 2008, one day before his twenty-second birthday, Hendrix had what he thought was his best practice yet in a Warriors uniform. He scored on the low post, stepped out for mid-range jumpers, blocked a few shots. But right after practice ended, Hendrix received some disheartening news: he was being assigned to the D-League's Bakersfield Jam. It completely blindsided him; even some higher-ups were not made aware of the decision beforehand.

"It just felt like a total demotion," Hendrix said. "You didn't want to be [in Bakersfield] at all. It was a dejected feeling."

Since one-to-one affiliations were not yet established, being with the Jam seemed separate from being with the Warriors. *Distant.* Hendrix no longer felt a part of the organization. And sure enough, just over a month later, the Warriors waived him—despite the fact that he was averaging 13.9 points, 10.9 rebounds, 1.2 blocks, and 1.1 steals for the Jam. His rights were released, ending his stint in Bakersfield, and Hendrix was immediately acquired by the Dakota Wizards. Alongside Renaldo Major, he was a dominant force for the remainder of the 2008–9 D-League season, averaging 14.6 points, 11.5 rebounds, and 1.6 blocks. He led the entire league in total rebounds, double-doubles, and defensive rating and was named to the D-League All-Star team.

There were only twenty-four call-ups that season, a rare drop-off from the previous year. Hendrix wasn't one of them. He went to Summer League in 2009 but received no offers from NBA teams. Thus, it was Hendrix's turn to face the tormenting decision: overseas or D-League.

"I hate to say it, but it's a hard dilemma for many players," Hendrix said, "because, listen, you don't grow up working on your game to try and go play in the D-League, nor do you try to grow to go play overseas. Everybody wants to play in the NBA. And all you think is NBA. And the sad part about it is, the D-League does a tremendous job of marketing to the players that they're one step away and they're the closest step to the NBA.

"After playing the entire year, leading the league in double-doubles, playing Summer League, I had offers to go to the Spanish ACB, which was the best league abroad at that particular time," he continued. "My rationale was, if you played the entire year, and they saw all of that and you didn't get a call-up, what makes you think you're going to get one next year? You're just waiting."

And Hendrix wasn't prepared to wait. He signed a six-figure deal with CB Granada and set off for Spain.

• • •

Of course, the longer Squeaky spent toiling in the D-League, the more pressure mounted. He had taken pay cut after pay cut after pay cut, and for what?

By staying in the D-League, his profile *had* risen. NBA teams were more attuned to his game and what he brought to the table. Still, when he was invited to training camp with the New Orleans Hornets in 2011, the twenty-eight-year-old Johnson was somewhat surprised. He didn't believe that the coaches were truly considering him for a roster spot, but he would *make them* consider him. He treated those few weeks like an Army boot camp: he ate perfectly, went to sleep at the same hour, didn't drink or party or socialize, trained relentlessly.

"Was I the best player overall? No. Was I the best player career-wise? No. But for those two weeks, man, I kicked everybody's ass that was at the guard position," Squeaky later said about that training camp.

Final cuts were staged like a rose ceremony on *The Bachelor*. Four players were gathered in a hotel room: Squeaky, Jerome Dyson, DaJuan Summers, and Trey Johnson. Hornets general manager Dell Demps was there to reveal the team's decisions. It came down to Squeaky and Jerome Dyson, a six-foot-three guard out of UConn, for the last spot. The organization awarded it to Squeaky.

"It still didn't sink in," Squeaky later said. "Like, *Oh shit, I'm in the NBA.*"

Johnson had finally reached the summit, and it was everything he had ever imagined—on and off the court. "Oh my gosh, it's crazy," he told the *Birmingham News* about the perks of being an NBA player in 2011. "You can use your phone on the plane. It's like a four-star restaurant up there. You have seats where you pretty much can lay down. Trust me, I'm enjoying every moment."[1]

During one short road trip, the staff handed out per diems on the team plane: $1,500 in cash, to cover expenses until the Hornets returned home. That was the same amount Johnson had received on his biweekly checks in the D-League. Squeaky watched as four of his teammates immediately used the money to bet on a card game called bourré. "The whole time I'm thinking, *Man, I want to play, but shoot if I lose—I need all of this,*" Squeaky recalled with a laugh. "I pretty much lived off the per diem, honestly."

Not only was Squeaky in the NBA, he was also playing for his hometown New Orleans Hornets, surrounded by friends and family. He remained with the team for about two months before getting waived in February of 2012. Overall, he earned over $168,000 and appeared in 15 games during that stint, averaging 1.8 points and 1.5 assists.

People knew Squeaky Johnson after that. What they didn't know was that every time he stepped on the floor, Johnson was wearing D-League socks beneath his NBA socks—a reminder of all he had been through and sacrificed to get there.

• • •

In Spain, Hendrix did what he had always done: *dominate*. He helped lead CB Granada to the most wins in its club's history and won the ACB Rising Star Award, presented to the best newcomer in the Spanish League. Over the ensuing years, Hendrix would take stabs at getting back to the NBA, going to Summer League and gauging interest from NBA organizations. But he would never chase it in the same way Squeaky did, never signing back in the D-League.

Instead, Hendrix would embark on an incredible journey overseas. He traveled the world through basketball, inking six- and seven-figure deals in Israel, Italy, Russia, Turkey, France, and Japan. He was a two-time Israeli League champion, a EuroCup Finals MVP, a Spanish Super Cup winner. He spent twelve years abroad—immersing himself in different cultures, learning new languages, meeting interesting people, thriving on the court—before moving on to a new career as a broadcaster in 2020.

Based on his international résumé, there is little question that Hendrix had the *ability* to play in the NBA. He just didn't have the *opportunity* right away, and waiting for it to arrive was a risky proposition. A costly proposition.

"You have a responsibility to provide for yourself and for your potential family," said Hendrix. "So that's what you're playing for. You're a professional. You want to be compensated. So compensation was the goal for me, and once I got to a point where it didn't make any sense to come back and try it again, because I had a really good career, then I was content with it."

For every Squeaky Johnson or Renaldo Major, there were numerous others who didn't make it, who sacrificed enormous amounts of money in the pursuit of a dream they never achieved.

Hendrix continued:

> I will go out on a limb and say this—and it's not to be detrimental
> in any way—I understand the logic; I don't agree with the logic.
> Obviously, I have to stand on the type of decision that I made for

myself. I just feel like the rational aspect of it is, like, your body, what you're putting it through, all of those types of things that you have to consider, to look up and after ten years of doing it, to have nothing tangible to show for it—I don't know if it's a decision to make, personally. Like I said, it's life. You let people make the decision they have to make and want to make, and I understand it. But I do think it's sad when I look back and see so many players who have some real skills, and not to say that they wasted it, but they did not maximize financially the opportunities they could have had in their prime years.

It's sad when, as a guy like myself, who played abroad and played with some guys in the D-League and they finally realize, okay, I've tried it for so many years to no luck, and now I gotta go get some money on the back end. And I'm over there established and other people are established, and they are still at the back of the line over there. So you never made any headway in the D-League and you're also not going to make any headway abroad because you started so late. It's sad to me. And I wish that there were better avenues for people to make more swift decisions.

As for his decisions, Hendrix has no regrets. He followed his preferred path and found remarkable success. "But I will say, when you look at guys who had far less ability than you and have achieved far less than you, and you look at them and they have played one [NBA] game, ten games, albeit just for a couple of minutes, there is something that you will have in you, regardless of how well you did overseas and your reputation, for me to say that I never played in the NBA, it does mean something," he acknowledged. On the Wikipedia page for the 2008 NBA Draft, players who have never appeared in an NBA game are highlighted in gray and have a pound symbol next to their names. Every time Hendrix sees that, it stings.

"But you move forward and you say, hey, you got responsibilities as a husband and a father and you handled your business on that aspect," he added. "And it's, like, hey, just swallow it and move on. I wouldn't trade my career. I wouldn't trade it for two games in the NBA to say I made it. I definitely wouldn't do that. But I do wish that I would have had a time that I did play, for sure."

"I'm not going to lie to you, I'm going to keep it 100 percent with you. I didn't make as much money playing that everybody made going overseas," Squeaky admitted.

Even after his brief stint with the Hornets, Johnson returned to the D-League for two more seasons. He had enjoyed a small taste of his dream; now he craved a bigger bite. He signed a free-agent deal with the Atlanta Hawks in 2012, but never stepped foot on an NBA court again. By the end of the road, Squeaky had played 230 games in the minors, the eleventh most in D-League history.

"As a kid, all you want to do is play in the NBA," Johnson said. "And in my career, I probably made the least amount of money out of any ten people you call because I stayed in the D-League so long. But for me, actually making it to the NBA meant more to me than making any amount of money overseas. So ultimately it just depends on the player and what they want overall.

"For guys who could possibly hear this, man, there's nothing like saying you played in the NBA," he went on. "That's going to follow you for the rest of your life. Now that I have a son, that's part of my legacy. Even if I played in the NBA one minute, he could say, 'My dad played in the NBA.' I think the money is great but even now, twelve years later, people still introduce me as, 'That's Squeaky Johnson; he played in the NBA.' I think that's a tag that is priceless. I wouldn't trade that for nothing."

• • •

Every member of the Squadron had confronted the same dilemma. Some were sacrificing more money than others by choosing the G League route. Young, for example, had turned down a $3 million offer in China, signing in the minors for just $37,000. But they all stood to lose *something*. Even those with slim-to-no chances of reaching the NBA were hoping to position themselves for better contracts in 2022.

As the Squadron flew from Texas back to Alabama, the most crucial month of the season approached. And with each day that passed, the stakes were only rising.

The Price of a Dream

11. BASKETBALL IN THE MAGIC CITY

On December 2, 2021, six-foot-six forward Gary Clark was called up from the Mexico City Capitanes to the New Orleans Pelicans. When Cheatham saw the news, he was confused. Hurt. *Frustrated.* He and Clark played the same position. Sure, their games were different, but still—if the Pelicans wanted to upgrade their roster, why hadn't they pursued someone from *their* G League affiliate? If they wanted to call up a dynamic forward, why hadn't that forward been Cheatham?

It was only natural for Cheatham to compare himself to Clark. Every G Leaguer performed a similar exercise whenever a player—perhaps someone with a comparable skill set or comparable physique or comparable stat-line or comparable taste in movies—got called up. In Cheatham's case, this wasn't apples and oranges. He and Clark were both versatile forwards who prided themselves on defense.

No matter. Cheatham couldn't harp on it for too long, lest it distract him from trying to follow in Clark's footsteps. The team was back in Birmingham for its home opener, and the impending three-week stretch ahead of the Showcase was critical. That afternoon, Cheatham went to grab a bite with Young and Petty before the Squadron's first practice at Legacy Arena. They talked about the upcoming game—which, coincidentally enough, was against Clark's Capitanes—and about the significance of bringing professional basketball to Birmingham. Petty was born and raised in Huntsville, Alabama, only one hundred miles north of the city, and played four seasons at UA, so he understood the area's passion for hoops well.

"We were talking, like, 'Look, bro, this is one of the best things that has happened to this state,'" Petty later explained. "It's one of the best things that could happen *for us* to be in the states, in a new city, with a new team, great organization, great people behind you. And we were like, 'We can't go in there and lose the first game. It's the first game ever in this state with this team. We can't go in there and start this whole stretch with losing.'

"It's going to hold weight," Petty continued. "Twenty years later, this is going to be remembered. Like, 'I remember when the Birmingham Squadron first came to Birmingham.'"

The three of them agreed that such a message was worth sharing with the entire team. Cheatham texted Pannone, requesting that the coaches give them fifteen minutes alone on the court that evening for a players-only meeting.

• • •

Legacy Arena was a cut above most other venues in the minors. It presented more of an NBA atmosphere, whereas some G League sites, like the Swarm Fieldhouse in Greensboro, felt more like high school or college. After practicing at the ill-lit Bill Burch Gymnasium, walking into Legacy Arena was like opening a set of blinds in the morning. Beneath the powerful LED lights hanging above, the hardwood floor glistened, its fresh coat of red and blue paint designs popping. Other than contractors, no one had been in the building since before the COVID pandemic. A large-scale renovation had kept the doors closed for several years. The work was finally complete, and the transformation was impressive.

One by one, players filed out of the locker room. "I'm home!" Cheatham shouted, taking in his surroundings: the new hoops (which made the BSC goals seem like peach baskets taped to wooden sticks), the jumbotron, the massive speakers suspended from the rafters, the more than seventeen thousand seats. "Who got the sage?" he asked with a laugh, to which multiple teammates responded, "Malcolm!"

With the coaching staff still in the locker room, the players held their

Basketball in the Magic City

meeting at midcourt. Cheatham conveyed the messages that he, Young, and Petty had discussed over lunch. He encouraged others to participate in the conversation, to share their thoughts on how the team could improve heading into such a meaningful game.

"All it takes is one: one win. One win and then we get on a streak," Cheatham said. "And this shit crazzzzy," he added, marveling again at the ten-story Legacy Arena. "We're here. . . . Might as well take full advantage."

Here was a loaded word. Cheatham meant it in the literal sense—here in Legacy Arena, in the city of Birmingham, in the state of Alabama. He also meant here *in the G League*. It wasn't where any of the players wanted to be, but heck, they might as well take advantage.

• • •

Spirits across the Magic City were exceptionally high as the sun rose on Sunday, December 5. Churchgoers left morning services to discover that some of their prayers had already been answered: the University of Alabama was ranked number one in the college football playoff rankings, one day after beating Georgia in the SEC championship. UA's basketball team had pulled off an upset of its own on Saturday afternoon, taking down number three Gonzaga.

Legacy Arena was ready for its first event in more than two years, and its first professional basketball game since the Houston Rockets and Memphis Grizzlies met in a 2018 exhibition. The top bowl was curtained off, leaving space for roughly eight thousand spectators. Vouchers were taped to a handful of chairs. "You have been chosen as a Squadron winner!" they read. "To redeem your free souvenir, just visit the Squadron Sales & Service table on the concourse near section 132 by the end of the first half."

Upon entry, fans were given white towels stamped with red Squadron logos. Suites were occupied by business partners and distinguished Birmingham residents. John Petty Jr. had his own personal cheering section, made up of twenty friends and family. Patrick and Erica Harper made the short trip from Atlanta to watch Jared, who was also a favorite among the many Auburn alums filling the stands. Clayton Hughes, Malcolm Hill's stepbrother, drove all the way from St. Louis. Kelvin Davis, the sixty-two-year-old from open tryouts, trekked from nearby Huntsville. Former NBA All-Star Gerald Wallace, an

Alabama native, sat courtside, along with Randall Woodfin, the mayor of Birmingham. Scouts from the Indiana Pacers and Cleveland Cavaliers were stationed behind the scorer's table, computers and notepads open.

Considering that many of the 4,972 people in attendance had just a vague idea of what the G League was, the buzz in the building was tremendous. "We've been waiting a long time for this," the PA announcer exclaimed prior to the 6:00 p.m. start. "It's finally time for basketball in the Magic City!"

From the opening tip, the pace of the game reflected the energy of the crowd: excitable and frenetic. Banks won the jump ball. Harper controlled it, raced to the frontcourt, and whipped a pass to an open Hill on the wing. Hill caught it in rhythm and immediately launched a three-pointer. *Swish.*

Eight seconds into the game, Birmingham was on the board. Harper scored shortly after on a midrange fadeaway. Then Cheatham joined in, draining a corner three off a feed from Young and turning to pump up the fans. 8–0, Squadron.

That burst of momentum would fade, however. Abrupt swings are common in the G League, in part due to rule changes that speed up the action and allow points to be scored in a hurry. For example, when G Leaguers are fouled in the act of shooting, they take only one free throw worth the value of *total* free throws that would be allotted under standard NBA rules. So, if Harper gets fouled on a three-pointer, he goes to the line for one free throw—worth *three* points. The innovative rule applies until the final two minutes of the game, when it switches to normal NBA guidelines.

Since its founding in 2001, the G League has been used as a laboratory for the NBA—a testing ground for various ideas that might improve the game. NBA regulations such as the transition take foul, coach's challenge, and 14-second shot clock reset all originated in the G League. Of course, for every successful experiment, one fails to gain any traction. The international goaltending rule—where the ball can be touched as soon as it hits the rim, even if it's above the cylinder—was in place from 2010 to 2015 but never got adopted by the NBA. Others have blurred the line between radical and flat out absurd: in the 2004–5 season, the league tried a rule where three-pointers counted for only two points until the last three minutes of each quarter.

Needless to say, that rule didn't stick, so when Capitanes guard Matt

Mooney nailed a 26-footer to open the second half against the Squadron, it counted for three. Birmingham fell behind by double digits in the period, as the defensive game plan completely crumbled. On one play, Mexico City forward Alfonzo McKinnie grabbed a defensive rebound, dribbled the length of the floor like he was suddenly invisible, found himself right at the Squadron basket, and elevated for a monster dunk. "Coach Pannone was right beside us, and he was not a happy camper when he saw that play," said color commentator Rick Moody.

Spot on, Rick.

There was a clear pattern to the game—when Jared Harper was on the floor, the Squadron played well; when he was on the bench, the Squadron struggled. Unfortunately, Harper couldn't play all forty-eight minutes. He fueled a late run, scoring or assisting on 17 straight Birmingham points—an outburst that prompted a fan sitting courtside to shake his head in amazement and mutter, "That boy's going to the league." Harper finished with 35 points, 8 assists, and a plus-minus of +9, yet the Squadron were defeated *again*, 123–114, thanks to a defense that looked like five guys trying to bring back the Mannequin Challenge. It was the team's fifth straight loss—sixth if you counted the halftime game of musical chairs, where Commander, the Squadron mascot, lost to Juanjolote, the Capitanes mascot.

Storming off the court, Cheatham resembled a cartoon character about to throw a temper tantrum: fists clenched, muscles flexed, face scrunched into a frightening scowl, ears ready to blow smoke. This was supposed to be a night that everyone at Legacy Arena would remember. Instead, back in the locker room, Cheatham and the rest of the Squadron were already eager to forget it.

• • •

"You can't play where you want to go if you're not perceived as somebody who just plays hard as shit," Pannone said.

Once again, the Squadron had lost. And once again, Pannone found himself stressing the same message in the ensuing film session. An embarrassing clip played on the projector screen—after an ugly turnover, no one on the team had hustled back on defense.

"Look at the guys who have made it from here to the NBA," Pannone continued. "Alex Caruso . . . I'm sure everybody saw the quote he had."

Player-development coach Andrew Warren pulled it up on his phone and read it aloud. "The stuff I do is not always glamorous," Caruso, the Chicago Bulls guard and former G Leaguer, had told reporters. "It's stuff that wins basketball games. That's what I love doing—winning."

At 2-5, clearly Squadron players weren't doing the *winning* stuff, like hustling back on defense after an ugly turnover. "It's the little things that win games that truly fucking matter," Pannone said. "You can go down the line of the guys who have made it."

Pannone was right. If you performed such an exercise, you would find a lot of guys just like Caruso—gritty, tough, reliable, blue-collar players: Gary Payton II, Robert Covington, Danny Green, Fred VanVleet, Jonathon Simmons.

Before film ended and practice began, Pannone announced that the Pelicans would be assigning three players for the team's next game (also against the Capitanes): third-year center Jaxson Hayes, rookie forward Trey Murphy III, and undrafted two-way guard Jose Alvarado. "This is the G League," Pannone said. In other words, *this is what you should expect.* "I understand how that impacts some of you individually." Rotations would change. Minutes would decrease for certain players. Hayes and Murphy would be inserted into the starting lineup, replacing Hill and Banks. Alvarado would get extended run off the bench, cutting into Young's playing time.

Some frustration was to be expected in these situations. Assignments often brought tension to G League locker rooms—even more-so in the D-League days, when there were fewer one-to-one affiliations and teams were shared among multiple NBA franchises. Back then, D-League coaches had to earn the trust of various NBA front offices.

"As a D-League team, you had to develop relationships—you may have had two or three NBA teams that worked with you," said Jay Humphries, who coached the Reno Bighorns from 2008 to 2010. "But you had to develop a relationship with the management of the NBA team to make them comfortable. And typically during that time, when a player was brought down to your team, he would play a majority of the minutes, plays were going to be really focused on him and [based on] the conversations that you've had with the coaches, management, general manager of the team that's sending him down about working on the things that he needs to get back."

Even as the D-League evolved into the G League, the expectation remained that assignment players, or two-way players, would receive ample opportunity to shine, regardless of how that impacted others on the roster. It created a strange dynamic. An *awkward* dynamic. "I had a really positive experience in Sioux Falls. To be honest with you, I think part of that was the fact that I was on a two-way," Miami Heat guard Duncan Robinson, who played thirty-three games with the Sioux Falls Skyforce in 2018–19, said. "I think it's a little bit different. Not that I got preferential treatment, but I was kind of in and out, especially toward the second half of the year, and when I was in Sioux Falls and playing with the team, I was featured a lot on offense, plays were run for me, and all that sort of stuff. I'm very aware that I was in a privileged position relative to some of my peers out there."

In some cases, assignment players *did* receive forms of preferential treatment, even when it wasn't requested. "I remember on normal planes, as an NBA player, I would get first class, but the other guys, they would be in eco," said former Houston Rockets center Clint Capela, who was assigned to the Rio Grande Valley Vipers during the 2014–15 season. "Sometimes I felt kind of weird. For some players in the U.S., when they're like top players or whatever, it's normal for them to have special favors. But for me, where I'm from in Europe, usually if we're on the same team, everybody is treated equally. I felt kind of weird to be the only one in first class, the only one with my own [hotel] room, and I remember my per diem was more than everybody else's too."

Capela tried to support his teammates however he could, paying for dinners and passing on insights about the NBA. His mindset on the court, though, was to dominate everyone. "I felt that I had a duty to prove myself, to prove that I deserve to have that kind of sticker on my back that I'm an NBA player, even though I was younger," he said. "I always went hard at practice, made sure to dominate every single time, and to also let the Houston Rockets know that every time I go out there and play, they have to pay attention also. I also felt that I had that duty to be dominant all the time."

That was a mentality shared by most assignment players. Coming from the NBA, those players were *supposed* to be better than everybody else. "I do think that when you're sent down from your NBA team, that is the attitude that you have to have in order to not stay there," Humphries said. "*I don't belong here with these guys.*" Of course, if it leaned more toward cocky than confident and inspired a selfish approach on the floor, that attitude had the potential to spark conflict. Squeaky Johnson even recalled one player who was sent down to the Austin Toros getting into an argument with a coach and shouting, "I make more money than you!" Which, to be fair, was definitely true.

Mix some or all of these aspects together—the mindset of assignment players, the minutes they took from everyday G Leaguers, the preferential treatment they sometimes received—and the results could be . . . interesting. Or, as longtime G Leaguer Scotty Hopson put it with a laugh, "That's a recipe for a disaster." Hopson had experienced both sides of the arrangement; he had been the G Leaguer whose minutes were reduced due to the transfer of an assignment player, and the assignment player who took minutes from a G Leaguer.

"Now when I see somebody not handling it the way I would, I go say something," Hopson explained, referencing the situation from the perspective of a G Leaguer, "because I've been there before and I don't want them to suffer from a lack of humility, you know what I mean? Because it's not that deep—it's not about *you* right now. I would hate to see somebody fail from that as opposed to their performance."

• • •

Coach Huang feared that Hill might struggle with the sudden changes to the Squadron roster, that such a development might be triggering for him. When Hill signed with Hapoel Jerusalem in August 2020, he assumed that a significant role awaited him. Of course, that wasn't the case. When he joined the Pelicans for the 2021 NBA Summer League, he anticipated a real opportunity to showcase his abilities. But that wasn't the case either. Unlike most organizations, the Pelicans had several rostered players competing in Summer League, which made Hill an afterthought. He logged just forty-five total minutes across four games, averaging 4.8 points and 3.3 rebounds.

"Honestly, I thought I was going to make the Pelicans when I showed up to Summer League," he admitted. Instead he barely made the team's box scores.

"He's learned patience," said Hill's father, Malcolm Sr. "When he was with the Pelicans in Summer League, it was a low point for him. He kind of thought he was going to walk in and get all of these minutes. That didn't happen."

Once again it tested Hill's faith—in his routines, in his approach, in himself. Such a discouraging outcome threatened to throw him off course. "The hardest thing about keeping a steady routine," Hill said, "there's three things that you're going to come across. When you have so much success, you're like, *All right, I'm good.* And you stop. Or you come across, *Dang, this didn't work out how I thought it would. Is the stuff I'm doing really working?* Or you come across, *I've been doing this for so long, when am I finally going to catch that big break?* Those are the three obstacles that are probably most common that you see within the journey. And it's easy to fold when you come across those three."

Hill didn't fold in Israel, nor after Summer League. He stayed with his daily routines, even adding more practices. Now another bump in the road—the additions of Hayes, Murphy, and Alvarado, which moved Hill to the bench—could cause him to swerve a bit. Coach Huang wanted to ensure that some swerving didn't result in a crash. "I just knew there was something going on," Huang said. "In his mind, he was basically being benched and not going to play *at all.*"

He pulled Hill aside later that day. "You're too important to this team," he told him. "Why would we bench you like that? You've been playing the minutes. You worked to become our best perimeter defender. You're shooting well. What makes you think we're going to go against our word?"

That calmed Hill. It was the sort of reassuring message he never received in Israel, where communication was lacking. Huang went further; he wanted Hill to understand that similar obstacles were going to keep arising, especially if he reached the NBA. Malcolm needed to start viewing them differently, not as slights but as *challenges.* And once he did, he would emerge from those situations a better player.

"It's not going to be roses all the time," Huang said to Hill. "You're going to be put in situations where it's not fair. This is preparing you for the NBA."

• • •

All it takes is one: one win.

The Squadron finally got one. Having Hayes, Murphy, and Alvarado certainly helped. But with the game knotted at 107–107 with less than 10 seconds remaining, it was Harper who had the ball in his hands, driving hard to his right and finishing a tough lay-up to put the Squadron ahead. Alvarado, an aggressive and pesky six-foot guard, stole the ball on the ensuing possession, and Birmingham was back in the win column.

One win and then we get on a streak.

The three assignment players went back up to the Pelicans (Hill played twenty-five minutes and recorded 3 points while they were in Birmingham), but the Squadron now had momentum. The team had four more games at Legacy Arena before heading to Las Vegas for the Showcase—two against the Lakeland Magic and two against the Memphis Hustle. It won all four by an average margin of 16.5 points.

The key, above all else, was the very complex art of, as the coaches put it, "giving a fuck." Defense was perhaps where "giving a fuck" showed the most; players were competing with intensity on that end, executing Saint's strategy of packing the paint and contesting all threes. The ball zipped around the court on offense, an unselfish display that made Pannone giddy. Everyone had moments. And everyone looked better because the team was winning.

In a 97–88 victory over the Magic, Hill had a near-perfect performance: 24 points (on 9 of 10 shooting from the field and 3 of 3 from behind the arc), 7 rebounds, 4 steals, and 0 turnovers. Cheatham notched 14 points and 18 rebounds that same night and was also shooting above 35 percent from three for the season.

Young's perimeter shooting had been inconsistent, but in a narrow 113–109 win over the Hustle, he buried six three-pointers and led the team with 30 points. Harper remained steady, clearly one of the top guards in the minors. He continued to shoot a high percentage from three and orchestrate the Squadron offense.

As the win streak continued, Campbell's phone was blowing up. His connections in the NBA were calling more and more to inquire about Squadron

Basketball in the Magic City

players. With the Showcase less than a week away, the team was clicking at the perfect moment.

Another factor was beginning to emerge, however. While all this was unfolding, the world at large was facing a new developing crisis, one that would incite the most chaotic and momentous time in the history of minor league sports: the arrival of Omicron.

12. OMICRON

Film went longer than usual on the morning of December 16—*way* longer than usual. The Showcase was a few days away, and there was a lot to cover.

First, the new protocols. An impromptu mandatory meeting for all G League head coaches and athletic trainers had been convened the night before. In a Zoom conference call, league officials had mapped out a revised set of rules for Showcase due to the alarming spread of a new highly contagious coronavirus variant called Omicron. The first confirmed case of Omicron had been detected in the United States about two weeks prior. Research suggested that Omicron was more transmissible than previous variants and could be contracted by fully vaccinated and boosted individuals.

Amid this troubling next phase of the pandemic, the Showcase was going to be run like a bubble. No fans would be permitted to attend. No guests would be allowed in hotel rooms. Masks were to be worn at all times, except when playing. It was strongly recommended that group meals, which could not exceed six people, be eaten outdoors.

"If you are seen at the craps table gambling, or at a bar or nightclub, the repercussions may be getting suspended through Showcase," Pannone said.

"No *may* about it," Campbell chimed in. "They are looking to make examples out of everyone. There's a huge outbreak going on not only in the NBA but also in the G League. If you don't know, Windy City is not going to play at

Showcase. They've had so many positives that they are out of Showcase. So all of the guys who have worked since training camp to get in front of NBA scouts will not be there."

Oof. Just hearing those words made stomachs turn. Showcase undoubtedly presented the best opportunity for G Leaguers to impress NBA scouts. Squadron players couldn't fathom the idea of it being taken away at the last second by something so largely out of their control. The team had undergone testing earlier that morning and fortunately received zero positives. Around the G League, however, the number of cases was climbing. The NBA was in even worse shape. Injury reports were starting to look like CVS receipts, with more and more players being sidelined by COVID each day. Coaches, executives, referees, and broadcast crews were also coming down with the virus.

The spread of Omicron was so rampant that Commissioner Adam Silver found himself scrambling for solutions to avoid a complete NBA shutdown. Should the league postpone games? Expand rosters? Impose stricter guidelines? Test daily? All of these questions were presently being floated. And the situation was trending in the wrong direction—*fast.*

In the meantime, as Silver puzzled his options, there was a silver lining to this period of chaos: an unprecedented number of opportunities were opening up for G Leaguers. NBA teams were in desperate need of reinforcements—rosters would be full one day, then down five players the next—and naturally turning to their minor league affiliates for relief. That was exciting for G Leaguers, of course, but also tremendously nerve-racking. Clearly, no one—not even a group of healthy, vaccinated, and boosted professional athletes in their midtwenties—was safe from catching Omicron. Forward Stanley Johnson had been called up from the South Bay Lakers to the Chicago Bulls, only to test positive and be placed in the health and safety protocols immediately.

Around the Squadron was a noticeable shift in tone: less jovial, more intense; less distracted, more focused; less jokey, more apprehensive. COVID precautions previously unenforced were now being taken seriously. Players were hanging out less, wearing masks more. Johnson, a former lottery pick, had spent significant time in the NBA already, but for those who hadn't, the idea of what happened to him *happening to them* was unthinkable.

At one point, Harper let out a soft sneeze during practice, and Cheatham instinctively leapt in the opposite direction. "Oh, hell nah!" he exclaimed. "Where my mask at?" He was half kidding, but the other half reflected a real concern growing among members of the team, particularly Cheatham and Young. They would not—could not—screw up a chance at the NBA because they caught Omicron.

According to the NBA's COVID protocols, players had to be sidelined at least ten days or record two negative tests in a twenty-four-hour window before returning. Decimated organizations—such as the Bulls, who, with ten players and several staff members infected, saw two of their games postponed—had begun handing out ten-day contracts. Capitanes forward Alfonzo McKinnie was another to receive a deal from Chicago, shortly after his back-to-back dominant performances against the Squadron at Legacy Arena.

During a typical NBA season, teams aren't permitted to issue ten-day contracts until January 5. The deals that players like McKinnie were signing required a "hardship exception," granted to teams that had a player in the health and safety protocols or at least four players out with long-term injuries.

Though ten-day contracts generated little media buzz—especially in years unaffected by COVID—and didn't guarantee even a second of playing time, G Leaguers cherished them. Signing one was a realization of *the NBA dream*. "To spend any time in the NBA is a blessing," Cheatham had once said—even just ten days.

The compensation made those ten days even sweeter. The value of a ten-day contract varied based on previous NBA experience, but most players were paid more than double what they received for an entire G League season, sometimes triple or quadruple. Stanley Johnson, for example, was guaranteed over $120,000 when he signed his ten-day deal with the Bulls.

Suffice it to say, the stakes at the annual Showcase were always exceptionally high. About a dozen representatives from every NBA team would be in attendance, and production on the court wasn't the only factor they took into consideration. Somebody was always watching, lurking around the slot machines and roulette tables, taking mental notes.

"NBA teams are not looking for a reason to sign you. They're looking for a reason *to not sign you*," Pannone told the Squadron. "There's a plethora of players." More than three hundred were playing in the G League alone. It was difficult for NBA scouts to narrow down their lists, so they were constantly searching for an excuse to cross a name off, like college admissions officers combing through an endless stack of near-identical applications.

Instead of extracurricular activities, scouts nitpicked at factors like nutrition. At Showcase, it was unwise to be seen eating or carrying anything unhealthy. No Twix bars, which Harper liked to eat before games (a curious superstition since his college days at Auburn). No Monster energy drinks, which Young liked to use for a boost before practices. No Subway, Nathan's Famous, Pan Asian Express, Bonanno's New York Pizzeria, or Johnny Rockets, all of which were right outside the convention center where the games would be played.

"Somebody tell me what Travis Stockbridge looks like," Pannone said.

Crickets.

"Somebody tell me who Travis Stockbridge *is.*"

"I assume he's affiliated with the league?" Cheatham mumbled.

Stockbridge was the general manager of the Rio Grande Valley Vipers and a basketball operations coordinator for the Houston Rockets.

"It's the perfect example of 'You don't know who the fuck these guys are,'" Pannone said. "You don't know what they look like. You would have no idea he's out there. You don't know who the fuck he is. And you don't know who any of these guys are from the NBA. Every time you think you're not being watched, you're being watched. Somebody is there. Somebody is going to see and watch everything you do. They are going to *judge* everything you do."

"These are little things, but we talked at the beginning of the year about million-dollar decisions," Campbell added. "At Showcase, all of those things are heightened. Every decision you've made from training camp until now has been a million-dollar decision. At Showcase, everything is magnified. Every single thing you do is magnified. They may be like, 'Oh man, I remember Joe Young from the Pacers. Why does he have a Chick-fil-A bag?' All those little things that you don't think matter, they matter to someone else."

And because of Omicron, there were far more "little things" to consider. Forgetting to wear your mask could cost you millions. Inviting someone to your hotel room could cost you millions. Playing a hand of blackjack could cost you millions. Having dinner with a large group of friends could cost you millions. Wandering aimlessly on the Strip could cost you millions.

"Any kind of infraction that they see is not going to be a slap on the wrist," Campbell continued. He hated lecturing the team but knew, in this case, it was necessary. He desperately wanted to see Squadron players get called up in the ensuing weeks. To give them a chance, however, they had to hear this message. And they had to hear it *clearly*. "It's literally going to be, you are out of the bubble. Period. There will be no, 'Can you call Marc? Can you call the league?' If they see you doing this stuff, there is no *may* about it, they will absolutely kick you out."

The locker room was silent as players digested this new information. Showcase was going to look and feel a lot different than what they had anticipated at the beginning of the season. Some had questions. The protocols were vague, and guys were nervous about mistakenly breaking a rule.

"What about Uber Eats?" Cheatham wondered.

"They do not specify, but that should be no problem," Campbell replied.

Harper wanted to know if he could go to a private gym—alone—to get shots up. His request was reasonable, especially considering that after practice in Birmingham today—a Thursday—guys wouldn't have official court time until 5:00 p.m. PT on Saturday, when they would have merely an hour to go over their game plan for Sunday.

"We have asked about having a site for y'all to shoot," Campbell said. "This morning—like, literally ten minutes ago—they said that they would strongly, strongly, strongly recommend that you do not have a team practice off-site."

"If you go individually to shoot . . ." Pannone shrugged, implying that it shouldn't be an issue. "I know some of you guys have got connections to get into a gym. It's like going out to eat. From my understanding, as long as you're not at a bar or a nightclub, going out gambling, going to a concert where there are a bunch of people, that's on you guys. But from today at 2:00 until 5:00 on Saturday, that's a lot of time without getting in the gym and shooting—just so you guys know that."

It was a big adjustment. Given the significance of Showcase, it was a frustrating one too. All the players liked to get up extra shots outside of practice. In Vegas that wouldn't really be possible. For stars like Harper, who was already on the radar of multiple NBA teams, having to change routines now seemed unfair.

Everyone was having to adjust, though. By the morning of December 16, the whole world was adjusting to Omicron, and the G League was no exception. Showcase would create an environment about as anxiety-inducing as imaginable, but if players adhered to the rules, stayed out of trouble, and took care of business on the court, it also presented the best chance they would *ever have* to reach the NBA.

"You gotta know what's at stake," Cheatham said after practice. "My mindset going into Showcase is just consistency. I want to stay with all the things that I've been doing. As a team, stay with all the things that we've been doing. Don't get out of character. Don't try to do too much. Just play the game I've been working hard at damn near my whole life."

Such was the cruel irony of the G League. A damn near lifetime's worth of work could come down to three days—three *very unusual* days—at the Mandalay Bay Resort and Casino in Las Vegas.

13. SHOWCASE

Like most Las Vegas hotels, the lobby of the Mandalay Bay is never-ending. It bleeds right into the casino, where one can easily get lost in the overwhelming sensations: flashing lights and bright signs, the smell of spilled beer and powerful cologne, the sound of slots being pulled and chips being collected.

Upon arriving at the hotel, every member of the Squadron had to undergo a polymerase chain reaction (PCR) test. No one was experiencing symptoms, but given the rate of new cases, there was tremendous fear that somebody, or multiple people, would test positive. Fear quickly turned to relief; the results were immediate and the Squadron was COVID-free. The first of many hurdles had been cleared, which could not be said for every G League team. Toronto's affiliate, the Raptors 905, was dealing with an outbreak and would not be allowed to participate in Showcase.

At this stage of the season, the number of call-ups tended to increase. The fact that Omicron was decimating the NBA *just as* the Showcase was being held created a perfect storm for G Leaguers. Some were checking into the Mandalay Bay only to head right back to the airport. Others would have an opportunity to prove themselves as more NBA roster spots were becoming available. Of course, players never wished injury—or, in this case, illness— upon each other, but the reality of life in the minors was that one man's bad break was another's big break. One player entering quarantine meant that another got to realize his NBA dream. It was reassuring, too, that Omicron was proving far less harmful than previous variants, particularly to young and healthy individuals.

On December 17, the day the Squadron traveled to Vegas, the Orlando Magic called up *four* players from its affiliate in Lakeland—the same number of players the organization had called up over the previous two seasons combined. Nearly the entire starting lineup that had just faced the Squadron at Legacy Arena—that had just been *dominated* by the Squadron at Legacy Arena, no less—was now in the NBA.

A popular Vegas saying captured the sentiments of the basketball world at this time: "Goodbye reality, hello Vegas!" As everyone was flocking to the desert, the uptick of NBA signings from the G League felt like a departure from reality. It was all happening so fast. A player would be walking through the lobby of the Mandalay Bay, mentally preparing for the Showcase games ahead. Then the call would come from his agent: "You're not playing in the G League tomorrow. You're playing in the NBA. Hurry back to your room, repack your bags; you're on a flight in a few hours."

Goodbye Vegas, hello reality.

On the morning of December 18, Cheatham received a phone call from one of his closest friends, Westchester Knicks guard Myles Powell. Powell had just returned to the court after a ten-month absence due to knee surgery, playing his first game on the evening of December 17. The following day, the team was scheduled to travel to Vegas for the Showcase. While players were boarding a connecting flight in Dallas, Texas, Powell's agent called with unbelievable news: the Philadelphia 76ers were signing him to a two-way contract. Powell couldn't believe it. Finding his seat on the plane, surrounded by strangers, he started sobbing.

Cheatham was one of the first people he called, while the plane was still on the runway. "What happened? Bro, what happened?" Zylan kept asking. He could hear his friend weeping. It took a moment for Powell to collect himself. "Bro," he finally said. "I'm going to be a 76er."

The flight took off, and Powell switched his phone to airplane mode. For the next three hours, it was just him and his thoughts. He put his hood up to shield his face, rested his head against the window, and let the tears keep falling. "Damn near half the flight I was crying," recalled Powell. When the Knicks landed in Vegas, Powell left his teammates to join the Delaware Blue Coats, the affiliate of the 76ers. He would play one game at Showcase before going up to the NBA for a game against the Boston Celtics—his first taste of NBA action, just seventy-two hours after returning from nearly a year away from basketball.

$$\bullet \bullet \bullet$$

"It's going to create a lot of opportunities for people," Jose Alvarado said about the recent COVID outbreaks in the NBA. Alvarado had rejoined the Squadron for the Showcase. It was 9:15 a.m. on Sunday, December 19, and the team had convened in the Tradewinds A Conference Room at the Mandalay Bay for film. "I just hope they don't cancel the season."

Pannone assured Alvarado that such a drastic measure was unlikely. A pause in the season wouldn't make COVID disappear, so the league had to figure out how to endure as the virus raged on. Stricter policies were already being implemented—NBA players were now required to wear masks at team facilities and on the bench during games, and testing would be done more frequently.

The Showcase was held in a large convention center attached to the Mandalay Bay via a maze of hallways and escalators. It was the polar opposite of what one imagines when thinking of Las Vegas: a vacant, drab, colorless space. Entering through a set of inconspicuous doors from a wing of the hotel, the temperature seemed to plummet ten degrees. Thin black curtains surrounded each makeshift court. Most of the facility was empty, devoid of any purpose. It looked more like an abandoned warehouse than the site of a high-profile NBA event to be televised on ESPN.

Reserved tables—one for each NBA organization—were stationed around the two main courts, where team representatives huddled together. The set-up was rather formal, made even more daunting by the absence of fans and ambient noise. You could hear every whistle, every grunt, every squeak, every clank, every expletive.

NBA bigwigs—executives in attendance such as Masai Ujiri, Mitch Kupchak, Sam Presti, and Tim Connelly—typically used the Showcase as an opportunity to discuss potential deals ahead of the February trade deadline.

Those conversations were still happening, though they took a back seat to the more pressing issue at hand: the Omicron crisis. NBA rosters were depleted and moves had to be made *now*—not in February.

Birmingham wasn't competing for the Showcase Cup and the $100,000 cash prize that came with it. Despite a five-game winning streak, the team did not finish atop its regional pod—RGV led the group with a 9-3 record—or as one of the other top four teams across the G League. Nonetheless, the Squadron would still play two games in Vegas, and recent success warranted a closer look.

Birmingham's first matchup was against the Capital City Go-Go, the affiliate of the Washington Wizards. The Go-Go was 6-6 on the season, led by a balanced attack that included former Michigan State star Cassius Winston. The urgent need for G League players in the NBA only added more weight to the game. "It helps you get that little extra edge," said Cheatham. "I try to keep that consistent, but let's be honest, going into a game knowing that NBA teams are looking for guys to come in and play, obviously you gotta be a little bit more juiced about it."

"A little bit" might have been an understatement. Cheatham was clearly fired up; his deep voice rumbled through the convention center as he called out sets and communicated pick-and-roll coverages. On this afternoon, he checked all the boxes for a modern big man. He sprinted the floor, battled on the boards, set solid screens, moved the ball, buried open shots. His impressive stats (17 points, 10 rebounds, 7 assists) told only part of the story. Cheatham's energy seemed to inspire the rest of the team. Birmingham jumped out to a 14-point lead in the first quarter and never looked back, winning its sixth straight, 126–115, in front of countless scouts and executives.

Harper was engaged on both ends, finishing with 22 points, 9 assists, and 5 steals. The last time Young had participated in the Showcase—as a member of the Fort Wayne Mad Ants in 2017—he had forced the action and hijacked his team's offense. This time, he played unselfishly and with discipline, contributing 17 points on an efficient 8 of 15 shooting.

The biggest standout, however, was Hill. He loved playing in Vegas, which also hosted the NBA Summer League, because he knew that some of his opponents (less—if any—during the Omicron crisis) would indulge in the reckless nightlight scene, giving him an advantage on the court. While others nursed hangovers, Hill would be meditating and practicing yoga. All of his painstaking daily rituals contributed to what transpired against the Go-Go. Hill scored a game-high 25 points on 10 of 14 shooting from the field. He hit five three-pointers and had two dunks off timely cuts to the basket. On defense, he guarded multiple positions, even spending time on Capital City's six-foot-ten center Greg Monroe, who had over a decade of NBA experience.

Hill's was a quiet type of starring. His game lacked pizzazz—the type of flair that appealed to fans and landed one's name on the marquee. "He's just not super flashy," said Ray Hoffman, who coached Hill for three years at Belleville East High School. "Then you look up at the scoreboard, and he's made 12 free throws, and he has 30 points. He's just so steady. He doesn't really ooh and aah you. He's just a very good player."

In the absence of "oohs" and "aahs," Hill often wondered whether anyone was paying attention. His name was far less known than most of his peers. It was like every G Leaguer was running the same race, but Hill had started twenty yards behind. Over the past few weeks, he was doing a superb job of playing catch-up.

Several of the recent call-ups were former NBA players—recognizable names seen as reliable and trustworthy by NBA front offices. The situation was dire. Teams weren't looking for long-term projects; they needed guys who could come in and play meaningful minutes right away. Given those circumstances, when presented with a list of potential replacements, NBA coaches were more inclined to choose the players they already knew, not the Malcolm Hills. That was why numerous veterans with NBA experience had recently made a return to the big show: Alfonzo McKinnie, Isaiah Thomas, Langston Galloway, Justin Anderson, Justin Jackson, Luke Kornet.

Hill was used to being overlooked. Still, he could sense that things were maybe starting to turn, especially after such an eye-opening performance. The thought swirled in his head as he made the long walk back to his room from the convention center. Passing by one of the many food courts, a group of kids stopped him.

"Do you play basketball?" one of them asked, gazing up with astonished eyes. Hill nodded and politely introduced himself. Though the kids didn't *really* know him, their father insisted on taking a group photo.

"Can we have your shoes?" They gestured to the red and white Kyrie 7s in Hill's right hand—his "Jerusalems," as he called them, because it was the same pair he had worn while in Israel. Hill wanted to give them away; he just couldn't. He *needed* his shoes. Unlike players in the NBA, he didn't have a mountain of options to choose from. Hill also preferred to wear the same shoes for every game. The Jerusalems looked as though they had been run over by an eighteen-wheeler, but they were still intact and still serving Hill well. He viewed his basketball sneakers the same way baseball players viewed their gloves—the more broken in, the better.

"I'm so sorry," he responded, "I don't have it like that yet."

As Hill continued down the vast hallway, the father called out in his wake. "Remember us when you make it to the NBA!" he said.

Hill smiled.

• • •

A new NBA policy was introduced on the evening of December 19, paving the way for even more call-ups. Teams were now *required* to sign one replacement player when two members of their current roster had tested positive for COVID, two when three had tested positive, and three when four or more had tested positive. Joseph Hooven, head of PR for the Squadron, had advised the marketing staff to prepare a generic call-up graphic for social media.

Just in case.

Birmingham's second and final game was against the Grand Rapids Gold, coached by former NBA guard Jason Terry. Before the schedule was released, Squadron players were hoping for a matchup with the Gold, since Terry's roster was likely to attract curiosity. Grand Rapids had several basketball journeymen trying to get back to the NBA, including Mario Chalmers, Lance Stephenson, Shabazz Muhammad, and Nik Stauskas. As of a few hours before tip-off, the Gold apparently no longer had Stauskas. The former eighth overall pick in the 2014 NBA Draft was on his way to Toronto after being called up by the Raptors.

After six straight wins, confidence was soaring in the Squadron locker room.

It showed when players took the floor, despite facing a backcourt—Chalmers and Stephenson—with a combined twenty years of NBA experience. Alvarado buried a three-pointer to put Birmingham on the board. Then Young nailed a triple from the right wing. On the ensuing possession, Harper drew two defenders out of the pick-and-roll and fed Cheatham at the top of the key, who sunk yet another three.

All game long, Birmingham executed Pannone's offensive system perfectly: pushing the pace, spreading the floor, sharing the ball. The team finished with 28 total assists and a season-high 19 threes. On the defensive end, it held Grand Rapids to 20 percent shooting from behind the arc and forced 18 turnovers. Chalmers, a thirty-five-year-old guard and two-time NBA champion with the Miami Heat, was shut down by the Squadron, shooting 1 for 13 from the field. It all amounted to a 119–85 rout, the fourth largest margin of victory for any G League team to that point in the season.

Of all the supposedly over-the-hill veterans on the court, the twenty-nine-year-old Young made perhaps the strongest impression. Many scouts believed players were incapable of improving past their mid-to-late twenties. Young's performance against the Gold challenged that notion. Once ball dominant and disruptive on offense, he stayed within the flow of the game and still produced, notching 27 points on 10 of 16 shooting with 0 turnovers. Once disengaged on defense, he pressured his man, guarded with intensity, and recorded 3 steals.

Cheatham, who had 16 points and 9 rebounds, continued to catch the eye of noteworthy spectators. "Impressive outing from Zylan Cheatham at the G League Winter Showcase," ESPN draft expert Jonathan Givony tweeted. "Has really turned himself into a reliable shooter (42% 3P%), can really pass, versatile defender and plays extremely hard. Looks en route to a call-up based on what I've seen in Vegas."

It may have looked that way, but nothing was for certain. From conversations with his agent, Cheatham knew that NBA teams were at least paying attention. Hopefully, the past two days had stamped his ticket to the big leagues. He wasn't the only Squadron player who walked off the floor thinking his next game would be played in an NBA uniform.

"From a competitive standpoint, it's kind of hard not to look at some call-ups and guys you matched up with," Cheatham said. "But I think the good thing about me is, I've always mentally prepared myself for this type of stuff. I've always kept that mentality—no looking left or right, just focusing on my journey and being happy for the next person. Myles Powell is my brother; seeing him come back, play his one game, and get signed to a two-way, I felt like I got signed. I do everything with genuine love and genuine happiness, so shout out to everybody who's gotten called up. And I'm just going to keep working until I get my opportunity."

"Everybody's excited. It makes you think that you made the right decision— you came to the G League," added Young. "This is the first time the G League has ever done this, and they're calling people up that are high-level players. That's a free shot right there, and you're not going to see that anymore after this. For everybody in the G League, that's a great opportunity. We're lucky. So we just gotta stay ready."

14. GOING UP

Once the game against Grand Rapids was over, Squadron players were officially on break—well, most of them anyway.

Soon after the buzzer sounded, Chasanoff, Campbell, and Pannone pulled Harper aside for a private conversation. Birmingham's star point guard had struggled in the blowout victory, registering just 5 points and turning the ball over 4 times. It didn't matter. His fate was sealed regardless of what transpired that afternoon. Now Squadron brass was prepared to inform him of that fate.

Harper had been with Birmingham for nearly two months, averaging 21.2 points, 4.9 assists, and 1.9 steals, while shooting 41 percent from three and ranking second in the entire G League in total three-point field goals. He was one of the main reasons that the team had won seven straight, serving as a leader on and off the court. He deserved to be rewarded for his efforts. And so he was—the Pelicans were signing him to a two-way contract. Harper would be the first call-up in the history of the Birmingham Squadron.

His reaction to the news, which included a considerable salary bump, was not quite what one imagines in such a scenario. There were no tears shed, no screams in excitement, no dropping to his knees and triumphantly raising his arms to the heavens. That wasn't Harper. Besides, the news was, in his mind, *expected*. He was more concerned with next steps than reveling in the moment. *When would he fly out? Where would he meet the team? How would he get his car from Birmingham to New Orleans?* These were the thoughts that immediately rushed to his mind.

In a related move, the Pelicans waived forward Daulton Hommes, who had occupied Harper's two-way spot. Hommes, a six-foot-eight forward, was tremendously talented but had been dealing with nagging injuries that kept him sidelined. Both he and the Pelicans' other two-way player, Jose Alvarado, were excellent examples of what it takes to earn an NBA contract.

Hommes' story was an embodiment of the utmost perseverance. As a high schooler at Lynden Christian in Whatcom County, Washington, Hommes had torn the same ACL *twice*. He missed all of his junior and senior seasons, sitting out during the most pivotal time for his recruitment. The head coach at Western Washington University, a Division II school in Bellingham, had seen Hommes play when he was younger and was willing to give him a chance, especially since the kid had sprouted from six feet to six feet seven while injured.

"I was the eighteenth man on the roster, so he basically made an exception for me," Hommes explained. "Most teams carry fifteen, sixteen guys. We had eighteen. I really was just on the roster. I had no number—just basically a practice player."

After redshirting his freshman year to continue rehabbing, Hommes returned to the floor and worked his way to become the team's star, eventually transferring to Point Loma Nazarene University and winning Division II National Player of the Year in 2019. He spent the 2019–20 campaign with the Austin Spurs of the G League and then a season in Italy prior to getting the two-way deal from New Orleans.

Alvarado, a six-foot point guard originally from Brooklyn, New York, exemplifies the heart and passion that all NBA coaches seek from their players. His style is relentless. He defends the full length of the court, picking up his man as soon as the ball gets inbounded. He is aggressive, physical, intense, *annoying*—like a bug that never stops buzzing in your ear. He gladly does all the dirty work, whatever it takes to get a victory. As Jordan Usher, his teammate at Georgia Tech, once told the *Atlanta Journal-Constitution*, "Jose would cut off his fingers for us to win a game."[1]

One of Alvarado's signature moves—and a viral sensation on social media—is to hide in the corners of the court and then sneak up on whoever has the ball to get a steal. In a word, he is a *pest*. And every NBA team wants a pest. Squadron coaches would often encourage Harper to emulate Alvarado. In their view, fitting that archetype—the bug always buzzing in your ear—was the easiest way for an undersized guard to carve out a role in the NBA. Harper's game was different than Alvarado's; he had his own strengths that had carried him to this point, on the verge of signing with the Pelicans.

Now he and Alvarado held the organization's only available two-way roster spots. And they would be off to New Orleans—*to the NBA*—together.

• • •

Cheatham was content when he climbed into bed on the night of December 20. Birmingham had taken care of business at the Showcase, winning both of its games in emphatic fashion. Cheatham, himself, had excelled. Through the first stretch of the season, he was now averaging 14.2 points, 10.4 rebounds, and 1.2 steals and shooting 43 percent from behind the arc. He was the only player in the entire G League averaging more than 10 rebounds while hitting more than 40 percent of his threes. He had done everything within his power to put himself in a position for a call-up. Now he just had to wait and see what happened.

He was awakened early on December 21 by the sound of his phone buzzing. He let the call go to voicemail, still mustering the strength to get out of bed. When he finally dragged himself up, Cheatham saw that his agent, Drew Gross, had been trying to reach him. In a daze, he called back immediately.

"Have you left for the airport yet?" Gross asked.

"Nah, my flight is at 2:00. Why?"

"Because you gotta change your gate," Gross said. "You're not going to Phoenix. You're going to Miami. The Heat just signed you."

Cheatham's eyes widened.

I'm going to Miami? The Heat just signed me? The words replayed in his head, over and over. *I'm going to Miami? The Heat just signed me?*

It was one thing to get called up; it was another to get called up by the Miami Heat. Miami had a reputation for not just winning but also discovering talent in the G League. The team's current roster featured former G Leaguers Duncan Robinson, Gabe Vincent, Max Strus, Caleb Martin, Omer Yurtseven,

Dewayne Dedmon, and Chikezie "K. Z." Okpala. Call-ups from previous seasons included Kendrick Nunn, Derrick Jones Jr., Tyler Johnson, and Hassan Whiteside, all of whom had gone on to ink significant NBA contracts.

"Heat culture" is a well-known catchphrase used to describe Miami's unique approach to building championship-caliber teams. Not everyone is a good fit for Heat culture, capable of meeting the organization's strict demands. Players have to be mentally and physically strong, disciplined, committed, passionate. The fact that it was Miami who had pursued Cheatham was particularly encouraging. He wasn't just being summoned to the NBA; he was being summoned to one of the NBA's most respected franchises. He was being trusted to join Heat culture.

"I just felt an *overwhelming* excitement," Cheatham said. As soon as he got off the phone, he started running around his hotel room, jumping on the bed, yelling at the top of his lungs, dancing in front of the bathroom mirror in nothing but his boxers. Pannone came hustling down the hallway to join the celebration, emphatically knocking on Cheatham's door until it flung open. The two embraced, tears welling in their eyes.

When Cheatham told his mom, Carolyn, she reacted exactly as he did. She leapt up off her bed, screamed in jubilation, raced through their house in South Phoenix like a kid on Christmas morning. With all she was going through—Carolyn's battle with stage IV cancer had been intensifying—it was an indescribable moment for them both.

Cheatham's friend Darvis discovered the news shortly after, when it was first reported on Instagram. His initial thought was, *Miami is perfect for Zylan.* The organization fit his personality, his mindset, his approach to basketball dating all the way back to middle school. Darvis called him right away.

"Yo, Miami!" he said, his voice rising several octaves. "That's really where you're going?!"

Milestones like this always prompted Cheatham to reflect. Without the support of his mom and people like Darvis, he never would have pursued a career in basketball. He might never have left South Phoenix, let alone be bound for the clear skies and pristine beaches of South Beach.

In September 2018, as his final year at Arizona State dawned, Cheatham's mom texted him a photo of his "trophy wall" back home, where all his accomplishments were proudly on display. Her message along with the photo read, "Look how far we've come."[2]

Over three years had passed since then. There were more items to add to the wall, more accomplishments to be displayed. But with each step forward, Zylan tried to maintain the same perspective—a broader view of his life's journey. To not just look ahead but also remember the trophy wall and how far he had already come.

• • •

Like Cheatham, Malcolm Hill received a phone call early on the morning of December 21. He didn't answer.

The phone rang again—no answer.

Again—no answer.

It wasn't *that* early, especially by Hill's standards. He had made the rare decision that morning to sleep in—something about as rare as him eating doughnuts, which he had done the night prior.

Malcolm's mom, Machanda, had booked a trip to Las Vegas before the rules for the Showcase were abruptly changed due to Omicron. She wasn't permitted to attend the Squadron games and, to be extra cautious, had barely spent any time with her son while the event was ongoing.

By the evening of December 20, however, Birmingham was done. Malcolm was off until after Christmas. Though he had played another solid game against Grand Rapids, notching 12 points and 5 rebounds, he was more disappointed than satisfied with his performance. As usual, he was his own harshest critic.

If he zoomed out and considered the full season, there wasn't much to be critical of. Hill was averaging 16.9 points, 6.4 rebounds, and 1.6. steals per game. Since his player-development meeting in mid-November, he had upped his three-point efficiency and was now shooting 40 percent.

But zooming out was difficult for Hill, particularly at a time like this. Machanda sensed that her son would spend the night of the twentieth holding a magnifying glass to all his mistakes, wondering if each one might cost him a chance at the NBA. She proposed that they grab dinner at International Smoke, a restaurant colaunched by Ayesha Curry, wife of NBA superstar Stephen Curry, just to get Malcolm out of the hotel and, hopefully, out of his own head.

They didn't talk about the Showcase or the flurry of call-ups. Machanda tried to keep Malcolm's mind on other things. He was scheduled to fly back to Illinois on Wednesday and spend Christmas with the family, which would be a pleasant distraction. He needed a new iPhone, so Machanda offered to go with him to the Apple store the following afternoon. Then they could explore Vegas a bit, she suggested, seeing that they were both now on vacation.

There was a more urgent matter to address, however. Machanda craved dessert. More specifically, she craved doughnuts from Pinkbox, her favorite local spot. It was around 11:00 p.m., and Malcolm preferred to just go back to the hotel, but Machanda insisted. She punched the shop's address into the GPS and was surprised to see that it was twenty minutes away.

"You're not doing anything!" she teased Malcolm. "Come on, let's go!"

Machanda *did* want doughnuts, especially doughnuts from Pinkbox, a place with pastries so delicious they are "known to cause huge freaking smiles and excitement," according to the Pinkbox website. But Machanda's main goal was to keep Malcolm occupied, to do whatever she could to incite huge freaking smiles and excitement instead of huge freaking frowns and anxiety.

When they finally arrived at the shop, which actually resembles a pink box, Machanda realized that they had gone to the wrong location. The best Pinkbox—the one with the most variety—was by the Strip. Machanda certainly hadn't come this far to settle for less than the best. And Malcolm? Like it or not, he was along for the ride.

The entire escapade lasted over an hour, and it was well past midnight when Malcolm got back to the Mandalay Bay. Machanda's mission was a success: her son never had a moment to dwell on his mistakes or worry about the future. He expended all his energy pursuing and scarfing down doughnuts before collapsing onto his bed.

The next morning, after Cheatham had been called up to the Heat, Chasanoff was driving to the Mandalay Bay to pick up Pannone. The two had planned an epic outing to get pancakes. Not just any pancakes—*celebratory* pancakes from the renowned Mr. Mamas on South Jones Boulevard. Pannone, who considered himself a pancake connoisseur, maintained that Mr. Mamas made the best pancakes in the world. He usually laid off carbs, but after his team's success at Showcase, he had earned a generous stack of liberally buttered flapjacks drowning in maple syrup.

But the much-talked-about pancake plan had to be postponed. Chasanoff was en route to the hotel when he called Hill's agent, Adam Pensack, to inquire about a different player Pensack represented.

"Have you heard from Malcolm this morning?" Pensack asked, somewhat out of the blue. "Has he taken off yet?"

"No, I think his flight is later."

"He's getting a call-up," Pensack revealed. "Atlanta's going to call him up, but I can't get a hold of him."

Can't get a hold of him? That was surprising. It was late enough now that Hill was usually out and about. Chasanoff swung the car left and climbed a small ramp to the front entrance of the hotel, where an eager Pannone stood waiting, salivating, ready for pancakes.

"Ryan, you need to wait in the car," Chasanoff blurted out. "I need to go get Malcolm. The Hawks are calling him up."

He tossed Ryan the keys and called Dillon McGowan, the Squadron equipment manager and basketball operations associate, to get Hill's room number: 5-318. Chasanoff darted through the lobby, rode the elevator up to the fifth floor, and linked with Coach Huang in the hallway. Together they started banging on Hill's door.

"Malcolm!" Chasanoff hollered. "Malcolm, open up!"

After a brief pause, a voice from the other side mumbled, "I don't need housekeeping."

"Malcolm, it's Marc! Come get the door!"

"Oh, oh, I'm coming." There was movement—footsteps and shuffling. "Do I need to rush? I gotta put my shorts on."

"No, no, don't rush."

About a minute later, the door creaked open. Hill was shirtless, with deep bags under his eyes and a bewildered expression on his face. Chasanoff cut right to the point.

"While you were dead asleep, your agent's been calling you," he said.

"Oh, shit. What's going on?"

"I wanted to make sure you were awake so you can call Adam back. Atlanta is about to call you up."

"Oh, shit." Hill needed a second to process. He was still half asleep—still in a zombie-esque stupor—and the situation felt more like a pastry-induced dream than real life. Chasanoff and Huang watched as the truth slowly sunk in. Hill grinned wide. "Oh, *shit*," he repeated.

"Yeah, boy!" Huang shouted. "Yes, sir!"

With exactly ten days to go before the calendar flipped to 2022, Hill had achieved his improbable goal: *make the NBA by the end of 2021.*

"You couldn't think of anything to say besides 'Oh, shit'?" Machanda later cracked with a laugh, after watching a video captured by Huang. "That was the first thing that came to you?"

"Oh, shit" was the *only* thing that came to Malcolm in that moment. He was shocked. When he went to sleep the night before, he had zero suspicion that such news might be delivered to his door like room-service breakfast.

"He had no idea," Machanda confirmed. "I saw him the night before. It was two months into the season. You're playing well. You feel like you're doing well. It hasn't happened. [You're thinking], *When is it going to happen? Is it going to happen? What is it going to look like?* And then it happens, and you're just like . . . 'Huh?'"

• • •

Chasanoff, Pannone, and Campbell eventually made it to Mr. Mamas. The feeling they all shared that morning was hard to put into words. Chasanoff struggled to find the right adjective, describing it, simply, as "wow." Pannone called December 21 "one of the greatest days of my coaching career," even though he did no coaching. There was nothing bittersweet about losing Harper, Cheatham, and Hill to the NBA; it was *only* sweet. "This is what it's all about," Pannone said. During the course of a G League season, times like these were fleeting—moments when all stresses seemed to fade away, when the clock seemed to slow its ticking, when they could just sit in peace at a Las Vegas restaurant, munching on the best pancakes in the world.

15. CENTIMETER OF CHANCE

"This is the best time ever to be a G League guy," Boston Celtics head coach Ime Udoka told reporters on December 20, shortly after his team had called up Justin Jackson and C. J. Miles.

Udoka, a former G Leaguer himself, appeared in 136 games for the Charleston Lowgators and Fort Worth Flyers between 2002 and 2006. He was one of seventeen total call-ups to the NBA during the 2003–4 season—a mark that had already been surpassed in the 2021–22 campaign when Udoka uttered those words.

So, yes, Udoka was right. This was the best time ever to be a G League guy, no question about it. Since most teams were dealing with Omicron outbreaks, players were not only being called up at a never-before-seen pace but also being asked to play right away. Veteran guard Isaiah Thomas was called up to the Los Angeles Lakers from the Grand Rapids Gold on December 17. That night, he played twenty-two minutes and led the Lakers in scoring with 19 points. Two days later, he was in the team's starting lineup against Chicago—a game in which Alfonzo McKinnie, who was called up to the Bulls from the Capitanes, also logged seventeen minutes off the bench.

Harper would not join the Pelicans until their game on December 26. Because he had signed a two-way contract (as opposed to a ten-day contract) and New Orleans had enough healthy bodies at the moment, there was no need to rush him to Orlando for the team's next game. Harper was already familiar with the Pelicans' system, having been at their training camp in October. Birmingham also played a similar style to their parent club for this exact purpose—it made transfers up and down far more seamless.

Hill and Cheatham were off to join their new teams within hours. After a morning of celebrating, the message from Pannone was earnest: "Learn the playbook. Start watching film now. Be professional." Both players got their hands on the necessary material—film, sets, scouts, concepts, schemes—as soon as possible. The mindset had to shift from *I can't believe this is happening* to *I can't mess this up* over the course of a plane ride.

How to avoid messing up was straightforward, really: study. Or, in this case, cram. Hill and Cheatham had to treat the next ten days like a test. Pass that test decisively, and they could be in the NBA for good. Fail it miserably, and they could be out of the NBA for good. Those were the very real and very daunting stakes.

So they crammed.

Every waking second had to be spent preparing. Cheatham made flash cards in his room at the Gabriel Miami hotel on Biscayne Boulevard. Hill had to figure out how to maintain his daily routines, improvising as his schedule changed. Both pored through film and scouting reports.

Roughly twenty-four hours after arriving in Atlanta, Hill put on an NBA uniform for the first time. His jersey number was different. After rocking number 21 for over a decade—a tribute to his childhood friend who had passed away from cancer—Hill was in number 14. Hawks legend Dominique Wilkins had worn number 21, and his jersey now hung from the rafters, retired by the franchise in 2001. Hill was also sporting new shoes (courtesy of the team), swapping out the Jerusalems for a pair of black, red, and yellow Drew League PG 5s.

Having grown accustomed to much smaller, much emptier venues, Hill experienced State Farm Arena as the Eighth Wonder of the World. When the Squadron played the College Park Skyhawks—Atlanta's G League affiliate— during the preseason, he was in awe of their facility, of how legitimate the Gateway Center, with its capacity of thirty-five hundred people, felt.

The recently renovated State Farm Arena could hold five times that amount. On this night, it was packed with a little over fifteen thousand fans, many of whom were not wearing the protective masks that were now required on NBA benches. The lack of COVID restrictions in the building was strange, given how badly the virus was impacting the team itself. Five of Atlanta's players, including All-Star Trae Young, were currently out after testing positive for Omicron. Along with Hill, Lance Stephenson had been called up from the G League the morning prior. Two days after playing against each other at the Showcase, Hill and Stephenson were teammates in the NBA.

The Orlando Magic—Atlanta's opponent that evening—was even more undermanned. Six of the team's players were in the health and safety protocols, and another seven were sidelined due to injury. Freddie Gillespie, who was called up to Orlando from the Memphis Hustle, had joined the team so late that his name wasn't even listed on the roster sheets handed to the media.

Neither team was off to a great start on the season. Atlanta was underachieving at 14-15; Orlando had a dismal record of 6-25. Then again, neither team looked anything like it had a week prior, before Omicron struck. Several fans sitting courtside cheered as the newly added Stephenson, a popular player during his nine-year stint in the NBA from 2010 to 2019, went through warm-ups. None of those fans could tell Malcolm Hill from a random six-foot-six guy walking down Peachtree Street, however.

There were a lot more unfamiliar faces on the court than just Hill's. The game had the feel of pick-up at the YMCA, where teams are assembled arbitrarily. Guard Hassani Gravett, who played against Hill as a member of the Lakeland Magic in early December, started for Orlando. At one point in the first half, the Magic's entire lineup consisted of players on ten-day contracts. Five blank silhouettes—like created players in a video game—were displayed on a screen behind the basket in place of official NBA headshots. Because, well, none of them had official NBA headshots.

Hill went into that night unsure of what to expect. He didn't know whether head coach Nate McMillan—who, coincidentally enough, had coached Joe Young on the Pacers from 2015 to 2018—intended to play him. There was no hand-holding in the NBA. The constant refrain guys in Hill's position heard was "Be ready." It was equal parts encouraging and misleading—purposefully vague. *Be ready for what? For when?* On the other hand, disregard that advice and you could probably start packing your bags.

Hill was ready, but his name was never called. He was the only active player on the Hawks who did not check into the game. McMillan was familiar with Stephenson—he had coached the veteran guard for three years in Indiana—and clearly felt more comfortable throwing him out there. Stephenson received twenty-three minutes (tied for the fourth most on the team), shooting 0 for 4 from the field but adding 8 rebounds and 5 assists. Hill sat on the bench, perched at the edge of his chair, a heating pad draped over his knees. He looked antsy, prepared to spring to his feet the second he heard "Ma—" come out of McMillan's mouth.

During one huddle, McMillan criticized the team for not competing hard enough on defense. Hill bit his tongue. Perhaps his strongest asset was the energy he brought to that side of the floor. If *that* was the problem, how could McMillan not play him?

"When I look back at it, I'm a ten-day, fill-in guy. That's probably what they're thinking," Hill would later say. "I'm not coming from their organization. And I'm not, like, known in the basketball world like that."

Not like Stephenson.

Not like any of the players on Atlanta's roster.

In a "matchup of short-handed teams," as the Associated Press put it, the Magic prevailed, 104–98.[1] At the time, it was discouraging for Hill not to hear his name called—a flashback to the days when he was glued to the bench in Jerusalem. Still, it was reassuring to see guys that he had outplayed in the G League contribute on an NBA floor. He could make a difference if McMillan gave him a chance. He knew it.

"This isn't the end goal, obviously," he said after the game. "It's only the first step. And experiencing this—this only makes me want it even more. So I'm gonna go harder."

• • •

"Shit happens so fast. . . . This is crazy," Cheatham said, gazing in wonder at the twenty thousand red and orange seats around him. He had just finished an individual pregame workout at FTX Arena. Now he was enjoying a moment just to take in his surroundings. Three days earlier, he was playing in a drab convention center—on a different team, in a different league, at a different level.

"This is a championship organization," he added. Banners hanging from the ceiling—three of which celebrated titles claimed in the last twenty years—were proof of that. Cheatham had been at the practice facility for hours the day before, working out, watching film, listening to the rapper Future in the weight room with Jimmy Butler, trying to get up to speed. He went back to the hotel afterward to study his flash cards, all in preparation for this night—his first NBA game since the summer of 2020.

Cheatham had walked to the arena from the Gabriel, basking in the Miami sunshine. The five-minute route was sandwiched between the calm water of Biscayne Bay and the bustle of Biscayne Boulevard. Cheatham was in paradise. The city, the organization, the team—it all felt right. This was where he belonged.

Miami hadn't been impacted as severely by Omicron, though a number of key players were sidelined with injuries, including Butler, Bam Adebayo, P. J. Tucker, Victor Oladipo, and Markieff Morris. Cheatham was optimistic that head coach Erik Spoelstra would give him an opportunity, but he was also pragmatic. His expectations were tempered. He had just signed his contract on Wednesday morning, and to take the floor for a team with championship aspirations on Thursday night would be remarkable. Even Cheatham had to admit that.

He was determined, nonetheless, to soak up every bit of wisdom he possibly could. At the very least, he would have an inside look at how some of the best in the business operated. He would get to experience Heat culture, even if it might just be for ten days.

The transition to Miami—to the NBA—was jarring. Truth be told, it didn't make sense that the NBA was one step away from the G League. It felt as though Cheatham and Hill had leapfrogged *several* steps, like they had been upgraded to first class having been stuffed in an overhead compartment. The facilities and amenities were incomparable. Cheatham was no longer using the same bench press as a junior biology major at Birmingham-Southern.

Shit happens so fast. . . . This is crazy.

There was also a transition *down*, from the top of the totem pole to the very bottom. In Birmingham, Cheatham was at the center of everything. He was the team's leader, its star, its loudest personality. He was the one on the jumbotron, the one fans wanted to take pictures with after the game, the one who set the mood in the locker room.

With the Heat, though, Cheatham was a nobody. Fans would need to Google him. Teammates didn't look to him for mentorship—in fact, it was the other way around. Due to a lack of space, he was moved to the second row behind the bench, next to coaches, trainers, and security guards. Cheatham would eventually find his voice, figure out a role, ingratiate himself with Heat faithful. That is, if he stuck around long enough.

For now, he was ecstatic just to be there. It was a clear sixty-degree night in South Beach, the type of winter weather that makes one question living anywhere else. FTX Arena was at full capacity for Heat-Pistons. Cheatham was his usual animated self. He cheered for his new teammates like they were lifelong friends. During timeouts, he stood right next to Coach Spoelstra, leaning forward to catch every word. Cheatham remained on the bench—or just behind it—for the entire evening but smiled so much that his cheekbones might have required icing.

Miami went on to get the win that night, 115–112, thanks to a clutch performance from guard Tyler Herro. For Cheatham—and Cheatham only—that marked eight straight victories.

• • •

Hill would not get to spend Christmas with his family in Fairview Heights. Instead, he awoke on the morning of December 25 in a hotel room in New York City and would be working on the holiday. In a couple of hours, he would be off to Madison Square Garden (MSG) for a game against the New York Knicks.

Only a third of the NBA receives the honor of playing on Christmas each season. And it is just that: *an honor*. Players cherish the opportunity, perhaps more than any other afforded during the regular season. For basketball fans across the world, watching the NBA on Christmas has become a beloved tradition, as synonymous with the holiday as opening presents. Three days into his NBA career, Hill would be a part of that tradition.

Atlanta had faced Philadelphia two days earlier, eking out a 98–96 win on the road. Once again, Hill was the only available player on the team who did not receive any minutes. After a day off, the Hawks were scheduled for a 12:00 p.m. tip-off at MSG, the first of a five-game Christmas slate.

Hill had played at MSG before—as a member of the Fighting Illini—but quickly discovered that the environment was *a little* different for a Knicks game.

Okay, *a lot* different.

The fans were merciless. Atlanta had knocked New York out of the 2020–21 playoffs. Amid the five-game first-round series, Trae Young, who delivered a master class on how to dismantle a defense, became a Joker-level villain in the Big Apple. New Yorkers were still bitter, of course. And they didn't care that it was Christmas, nor that Young was still out with Omicron. Chants of "Fuck Trae Young! Fuck Trae Young! Fuck Trae Young!" broke out throughout the afternoon.

Hill tried to stay focused. It was easy to become distracted in such a raucous environment. The volume only grew when the Knicks jumped out to an early 19–3 lead: the deafening sound of long-awaited revenge. Atlanta would never recover from such a slow start. The game was decided by the ten-minute mark of the fourth quarter, after the Knicks buried back-to-back threes to take a 21-point lead.

With less than two minutes on the clock, and Atlanta trailing 99–80, McMillan called Hill's name. Almost three hours had passed since the game began; three hours that Hill had spent mostly sitting in a chair. The expectation remained the same: *Be ready.*

Most fans had cleared the building. Most television viewers had flipped the channel to *Home Alone.* To most of the world, those two minutes were completely meaningless. To Hill, they were a cubic centimeter of chance.

Watching from Fairview Heights, Hill's family displayed the body language usually reserved for car chases and horror films. In Miami, Cheatham was on the edge of his seat, yelling at the TV. "Skip it!" he hollered at one point, spotting Hill open on the weak-side. "Skip it to the corner!"

The ball was never skipped. In fact, it never found its way to Hill, which was just fine. His main focus was on contributing defensively, where Atlanta's struggles continued to drive the coaches mad. McMillan had been imploring his players to compete harder on defense, so Hill would compete like his life depended on it.

Centimeter of Chance

During one possession, he was matched up against the highly touted R. J. Barrett, the former third overall pick in the 2019 NBA Draft and an 18-point-per-game scorer. Barrett likely took one look at Hill and thought, *Mismatch! Give me the ball!* When teammate Obi Toppin threw it to him at the top of the key, Hill nearly deflected the pass, pushing Barrett further away from the basket. Now in control, Barrett drove hard to his left, but Hill cut him off. He spun, regrouped, and tried to attack the other way. Hill slid his feet and met him again. The two continued the dance for a few more seconds before Barrett admitted defeat, kicking the ball out.

McMillan stood on the sideline, arms folded, carefully observing. Atlanta won the final two minutes, 7–2, with Hill on the floor. There wasn't much of a difference between 99–80 and 101–87—except for Hill, there *was*.

"The biggest thing from that New York game was the fact that I had a plus-minus of 5," he later said. "I had no stats, but the plus-minus is huge for me because it can really show what type of impact you make on the game. Just looking back, do you know how hard it is to be ready for a game when you're coming in with two minutes left? I made sure I did *everything*."

● ● ●

Miami had another two games at home before embarking on the road. Cheatham would not receive playing time in either. The second game was against a decimated Washington Wizards squad that featured five players from the Capital City team that Birmingham had just faced—and destroyed—in Las Vegas. The title of the Associated Press's game recap that evening was "Depleted Heat Hold Off Depleted Wizards, 119–112." Emphasis on *depleted*.[2]

Although he wasn't playing, Cheatham's experience with the Heat was proving even more valuable than he expected. He was beginning to truly understand the level of focus and dedication needed to succeed in the NBA.

During his first shootaround, the team was running through various sets. The speed at which they operated blew Cheatham away. The motions had become second nature; players cut, screened, rolled, popped, relocated without a trace of hesitation. *No one* was making mistakes.

The vibe was different too. More serious—intense, even. For the first time in his life, Cheatham found himself genuinely nervous *at a shootaround*. The prospect of screwing up was terrifying. There was no "Oh, let's redo that" or "How do you do that again?" like in Birmingham. Either you knew the play, or you could get the hell off the court.

Of course, the sheer talent of Cheatham's new teammates was glaring as well. Shooters like Duncan Robinson and Gabe Vincent hardly missed. Playmakers like Herro and Butler (Kyle Lowry was out with COVID) made incredibly fast reads out of the pick-and-roll. Attacks were simple yet precise. Because players had memorized the scouting reports, they could easily antic-ipate what options would be open. The overall attention to detail, from the coaching staff down to the last guys on the bench, struck Cheatham the most. The preparation was so thorough that on game days, everyone seemed loose.

"I've always been a guy who works hard, does the little things, and plays hard," Cheatham reflected while he was with the Heat. "But I think there's another level that I can tap into as far as my approach, as far as my prepara-tion, as far as my seriousness for doing every little single thing there is on the floor to try to up my team's chances of winning. Seeing guys like Tyler Herro, Duncan Robinson, Gabe Vincent, Max Strus, Kyle Lowry, P. J. Tucker—to see these guys and the way they go about their preparation, getting ready for a game, was humbling to a certain extent."

• • •

The Bulls were walking all over the Hawks. It was December 27, two days after their embarrassing loss to the Knicks, and Atlanta's defense was still a wreck. Whatever the Bulls wanted, they were taking. Plain and simple.

Chicago's stellar forward DeMar DeRozan went into the half with 21 points. Zach LaVine, another All-Star, had poured on 23 of his own before the break. Atlanta was only down by six points (69–63), but it felt like far more.

Early in the third quarter, the Bulls expanded their lead to double digits. While Trae Young was back in the lineup, the Hawks had *eight* others in the health and safety protocols, including key pieces such as John Collins, Danilo Gallinari, and Kevin Huerter. McMillan was relying heavily on his starters, especially as Atlanta tried to claw its way back. As the third quarter was drawing to a close, however, he decided to give Hill a shot.

After not playing in the first half, Hill was surprised to be summoned so

Centimeter of Chance

late in the game. There was little communication outside of the proverbial "Be ready." Hill understood, nonetheless, what the coaches sought from him. His main task was to defend at a high level. Only one problem, a considerable one: Hill soon found himself matched up against DeRozan, who, at the time, was playing perhaps the best basketball of his accomplished career. In December, DeRozan was averaging 30.2 points on a staggering 53 percent shooting from the field. It was as cruel a "welcome to the NBA" moment as a player could possibly encounter. Hill's first meaningful minutes on an NBA court would be spent guarding one of the hottest superstars in the entire league, as some of Atlanta's biggest celebrity fans—Cardi B, Offset, Quavo, 2 Chainz—sat courtside.

Welp.

Hill wanted the challenge, though. "I was hoping to guard either him or LaVine," he later said. "I really wanted to because I knew off rip, especially coming into the game late, they're not looking for any offense from me." Hill's best chance to stand out was on defense. And if he could do a solid job against DeRozan, then he could probably do a solid job against pretty much anyone at his position.

Near the end of the third, DeRozan was isolated on the right wing and unleashed his go-to move: a nifty side-step into a midrange jumper. Hill played perfect defense—*textbook* defense. His contest of the shot was so close that DeRozan could have read his palm. And yet, it didn't matter. DeRozan still nailed the jumper. "There's nothing you can do about that," said Hawks color analyst Dominique Wilkins, "absolutely nothing."

In a group text, Hill would later joke with former Squadron teammates, including Cheatham, that some of the defensive techniques that worked so well in the G League didn't work in the NBA. Or, put more accurately, they didn't work against DeMar DeRozan. Few things did. No one was expected to shut down DeRozan completely—he would find ways to score even if the entire state of Georgia was guarding him. Hill spent much of the fourth quarter tasked with the impossible job and performed it well, as well as McMillan—or anyone, for that matter—could have possibly expected. Hill fought over screens, contested every shot, stayed mostly disciplined (DeRozan is known for his footwork and convincing pump fake). He was active and engaged, not backing down one bit from the Goliath opposite him.

With just under eight minutes left in the game and the Hawks on a small run, Hill picked up DeRozan full court. The four-time All-Star wasn't accustomed to dealing with pressure so far from the basket. He was gradually zigzagging his way up the floor when Hill poked the ball loose. As DeRozan scrambled to retrieve it, the referee blew his whistle. *Eight seconds.*

Eight seconds?

The fans erupted in approval. Eight-second violations—when a team fails to advance the ball past the midcourt line in less than eight seconds—are hardly ever called in the NBA. Why? Because players hardly ever try to force them. Doing so successfully was perhaps the best way for Hill to impress the Hawks coaching staff.

Atlanta cut Chicago's lead to four on the ensuing possession, but never got closer than that. Hill played the entire rest of the game—fifteen minutes altogether. He didn't attempt a single shot during those minutes. His role on offense was to stand in the corner, giving Atlanta's primary scoring options more space to operate, and cut when the lane opened up. So that's what Hill did. He managed to record his first NBA points at the free throw line, going 4 for 4 in the game. Overall, he finished with 4 points, 3 rebounds, 1 steal, and 0 turnovers. Nothing that would catch the eye of a fan perusing the box scores, but Hill had done his job.

As the dominoes were falling, time was also running out. Hill was already on day six of his ten-day contract. Soon he could be on his way back to Birmingham—back to the G League, where the chase would begin anew.

• • •

Atlanta's next game would be a homecoming of sorts for Hill. It was a rematch with the Bulls, this time in Chicago. Fairview Heights was just a four-hour drive away. Hill's mom, Machanda, and former AAU coach Patrick Smith made the trip down Interstate 55. It would be their first time getting to see Malcolm in the NBA.

When Trae Young arrived at shootaround that wintry morning, he looked around and wondered, *Huh? Who are all these people?* The Hawks were a *completely* different team. Down a whopping fifteen players due to a combination of Omicron and injuries, they had called up, in addition to Hill,

Chaundee Brown Jr., Cat Barber, Malik Ellison, Justin Tillman, Cameron Oliver, and Chris Clemons. Their active roster now consisted of more players on ten-days than standard contracts. And, given their opponent that evening, that did not bode well.

It did, however, mean that Hill was in position to receive significant playing time. Just past the midway point of the first quarter, McMillan called his name. Hill leapt up and bound to the scorer's table, adrenaline pumping. He was the first player off the Hawks bench.

Once again, Atlanta was struggling to check Chicago's high-powered offense, led by DeRozan and LaVine. Enter Hill for some assistance. Within seconds of checking in, he swiped the ball away from guard Coby White for a steal, resulting in a breakaway lay-up. He continued to bring the energy on defense—sometimes picking his man up full court—but as a team, the Hawks just couldn't slow the Bulls down.

On the other end, Chicago was determined to contain Young at all costs, packing the paint whenever the All-Star guard penetrated. It was the Bulls' way of saying, "We'll let the who's who of NBA fringe guys beat us tonight"—a sound strategy. Despite his unfamiliarity with many of them, Young was still willing to trust his teammates. With just over three minutes left in the opening frame, he attacked the basket, drew the defense in, and shoveled a pass to Hill in the corner. Hill caught it and fired a three-pointer in one smooth motion.

Good.

A couple of possessions later, Young maneuvered into the lane and rifled another pass out to Hill, who launched without hesitation.

Good again.

Machanda looked over at Patrick, her eyes wide, and asked, "Is this *really* happening?"

It *really* was.

Hill even buried a third three-pointer not long after, prompting Wilkins to say on the broadcast, "Hill is showing people, 'Hey, I got a wide range of things that I can do!'" Indeed, he did. By halftime, Hill already had 11 points and 3 steals.

"It was almost surreal," Machanda would later describe. "I've seen him work over the years and of course know what he's capable of, but to actually see it happen in front of you, not even on television, to actually be there and see it happen, it's incredible."

Such a decimated Hawks squad really stood no chance against the red-hot Bulls. They were blown out, 131–117, for a second straight game. Hill's performance was one of few silver linings. He defended exceptionally well (again facing DeRozan), limited his mistakes, and proved his shot-making ability. He looked like a prototypical 3-and-D guy, the most coveted type of player in the modern NBA. Of the Hawks who logged fifteen or more minutes that night, Hill had the best plus-minus.

There was one more game on the schedule before his ten-day deal was set to expire: a New Year's Eve clash with the Cleveland Cavaliers. It was a final opportunity for Hill to prove himself worthy of another NBA contract. Was there pressure? Sure. But Hill's confidence was also soaring. With momentum on his side, it felt like nothing could possibly go wrong.

16. CAN YOU PASS THIS TEST?

While Harper, Cheatham, and Hill made their transitions to the NBA, Joe Young traveled back to Houston. It wasn't what he expected, nor what he desired most, but there was a considerable bright side. Young would get to spend Christmas with his family for the first time in four years. Being closer to his pregnant wife—she was due in about a month—and two children was another reason he had chosen to sign in the G League.

As he was prone to do, Young went on an epic shopping spree ahead of the holiday. He bought a grand total of *162 presents* for his kids, a modest 81 for each.

Yes, that's right.

162 presents.

On Christmas morning, the family awoke at 6:00 a.m. and sat around their sparkling tree, its base enveloped by piles and piles and piles of gifts. Young was emotional, seeing the joy on his children's faces as they tore into wrapping paper. It was, truly, the perfect distraction.

• • •

Omicron continued to wreak havoc on the NBA, and the number of call-ups was climbing at an unbelievable rate. Between December 23 and 26, there were another twenty-eight call-ups, including Agua Caliente point guard Xavier Moon, who had participated in the Squadron's open tryout back in September.

Moon was at home in Alabama, having just left the Showcase, when he got the call that the Los Angeles Clippers were signing him to a ten-day contract. He was able to spend that night celebrating with his entire family. The next morning—Christmas morning—he was on a 7:00 a.m. flight to LA. Through the first chunk of the G League season, Moon had averaged 12.4 points, 7.2 assists, 4.4 rebounds, and 1.4 steals per game.

"There was never any doubt in my mind [that I would make it]," he said. "It was all about just getting that one opportunity. My opportunity happened to come when I started here [in the G League]. It happened faster than I expected it. If you would've told me last year that I was going to come to the G League, play as well as I'm playing, and get a call-up before Christmas, I would've been like, 'Man . . . stop!'"

Former NBA players such as Brandon Knight and Greg Monroe had recently earned call-ups from the G League as well. Anthony Tolliver, who had been working out on his own, was offered a ten-day contract by the Pelicans, which was later voided when Tolliver tested positive for COVID.

NBA front offices tended not to pursue journeymen like the thirty-seven-year-old Tolliver at this stage in the season. The more common approach—prioritizing youth over veterans—seemed to be on temporary hiatus during the Omicron crisis, which was a good thing for the twenty-nine-year-old Young. But if that were the case, why hadn't he been signed already? Far less talented players—many with no NBA experience—were getting called up every day. And then there was Young, a seasoned pro still in tip-top shape, just waiting by the phone.

In conversations at Showcase, Pannone had vouched hard for Young. Much of the feedback he received was the same: teams were hesitant to pursue Young because of his past mistakes, even as Pannone assured them that the former Pacer had changed. Regardless of what he and other Squadron personnel had to say, the hesitation remained.

With a surplus of capable players across the G League, NBA teams just figured, *why take any risk?* The difference between Young and the next guy was, in their minds, marginal. And how could they be positive that Young had changed? That would require a level of due diligence that teams were not prepared to do. In their view, it just wasn't worth it to dive that deep. They knew Joe Young from four years ago—and that was enough.

"Here's the thing that a lot of us hate, but we all know is true: it's always easy to destroy your reputation, and it's always twice as much work to build it," said Korey Harris, one of Young's assistant coaches in Beijing. Harris put the situation into context: "I know people who—I knew them years ago, and I knew them in a certain light. If I saw them today, I would still know them in that light. Just because they appear a little different for one day, or one week, or even one year, I don't even know if I would trust it. Depending on the situation, I would kind of move and tread softly. The NBA is big business. It's a lot of money. And there are a lot of people who are trying to take Joe's job."

It didn't help Young's cause that he had gone to the Chinese Basketball Association (CBA). Yes, Young had dominated the competition there, averaging 33 points, 5.9 assists, 4.9 rebounds, and 1.9 steals in 135 games. But in NBA circles, the CBA was viewed less favorably than other foreign leagues. The brand of basketball in China was more isolation-heavy, less team-oriented. It wasn't exactly fair for NBA teams to judge Americans for going to China, considering the CBA offered some of the most lucrative contracts. But that didn't stop them.

Young was already perceived as a somewhat selfish offensive player before he left the United States. While his rare scoring prowess was on full display in China, the many 50-plus-point games did little to quell concerns over whether he would buy in to an NBA system. Then again, those concerns had been addressed with the Squadron. Young had bought in and proven his ability to contribute to a winning team.

He wouldn't lose hope. There were aspects of his game that he knew could be improved for the second part of the G League season. Due to Omicron, the restart date had been pushed back from December 27 to January 5. G League rosters were suddenly depleted, and the postponement gave teams more time to fill gaps and safely return players.

The one thing Young and Squadron coaches couldn't fight NBA evaluators on was that Young hadn't shot the three-pointer well during the first stretch of the season. He went into the break shooting 31 percent from behind the arc on nearly six attempts per game—*not good*, but not a reflection of Young's capabilities. The three-point line in China, where Young connected on 36 percent of his attempts, was slightly closer. He was still getting reacclimated to the NBA distances.

When he was back in Houston for Christmas, Young went to a local high school gym with his dad, Michael, to work on his perimeter shooting. The challenge they set for Joe that day was to make three thousand threes—an absolutely ridiculous target, more appropriate for a week's worth of workouts than a single session.

Joe had multiple rebounders and multiple basketballs in rotation. "I was rebounding and passing to him, and I was tired," said Michael. "*Three thousand*—we've never shot that many at one time."

It took somewhere between three and four hours to reach the mark. By the time Young got there, his wrist was already starting to balloon. Gilchrist Schmidt, head athletic trainer for the Squadron, would later confirm that there was a fair amount of swelling in the area, just from pure overuse.

But the swelling didn't concern Young. He was confident now that his shot was fully readjusted, which was all that mattered. "That was the only thing that the scouts had to say—'We want to see him shoot a higher percentage on three-pointers,'" Young explained. "So, okay, I'm gonna go get it. I'm not gonna sit back and be like, 'Oh, man.' Nah. I'm gonna go make that percentage higher because talking about it is just talking about it. Actually going to do it is what makes success."

• • •

Young was feeling optimistic when he reported back to the Squadron on December 26—even more motivated than he was in October, when he first made the trip from Houston to Birmingham. "I'm not discouraged at all," he said. "I know I'm good enough to play in the NBA. I know I have the mindset for it. I know I can lead a team. It's all about, can you pass this test? Are you gonna fold when you don't get a call-up but your teammates did? No. Support your teammates, get better, go see your family. I'm back here now."

Young viewed much of the adversity he faced in this way—as a test of his willpower and commitment. "It's just a test," he repeated. "It's all about, can you respond? How are you going to respond when things get hard? I had to learn that when I was younger, but I didn't know how to respond. As I got older in this profession, I knew how to respond. When things don't go your way, you work harder, and you find a way. Anybody can get what they want; you just gotta go get it. I promise you. There's not one thing in this world that nobody can't go get. It's not going to be easy."

Coach Harris saw the adversity Young was battling as constructive. In the long run, he supposed, it would make Young stronger. If he were to be called up prematurely, before he learned the lessons that he needed to, it might not work out. But if Young endured through these tough times, he would become, as Harris said, "undeniable."

Of course, buried beneath Young's excitement and motivation was angst and frustration. How could anyone be immune to such emotions in his position? Every post on social media—reports of new ten-day deals, photos of former G Leaguers wearing NBA uniforms, stories covering the realization of, as Cheatham put it to the *New York Times*, "every hooper's dream"—was a painful reminder that Young wasn't where he wanted to be.[1]

By December 31, the previous record for G League call-ups in a season (sixty-three) had already been topped, as close to seventy players had made the jump from the minors to the NBA. For Young, some of those call-ups were harder to stomach than others. He was confused to see the thirty-five-year-old Mario Chalmers receive a ten-day contract from the Heat, given that Chalmers had shot 1 for 13 from the field and 0 for 8 from three in a loss to the Squadron at the Showcase.

As a father, Michael struggled with how to approach the situation. He was supposed to have answers for his son, but he, too, was puzzled. Surely Joe was worthy of an opportunity during this unprecedented time, when it seemed as though *everyone* was getting a call-up. Michael just encouraged Joe to keep working, to control what he could.

"I know he wants it bad, worse than when he got drafted," Michael said. "He wants his son to watch him play in the NBA. And he wants it *bad*. I don't know, man. Like I told him, 'I wish I could tell you why that opportunity hasn't come for you.' But he's not a quitter."

Joe took to social media to share some of his thoughts. On New Year's Eve, he tweeted, "Keep grinding they will call!! Believe and trust the process!! God don't make mistakes!!" Five minutes later, he added, "Basketball is life and I just wanna show my son when God gives you a gift you have to continue to praise him because he can take it at any second!!!"

The following morning, he posted, simply, "Psalms 27," a hymn that begins: "The Lord is my light and my salvation; whom shall I fear? The Lord is the strength of my life; of whom shall I be afraid?"

On January 2, he wrote, "I'm ready to pick up 94 feet and bring some energy!! Let's go." In a separate post, he wished his dad a happy birthday, referencing a phone call the two had shared recently.

Soon after Joe returned to Birmingham, Michael called to tell his son that he was proud of him. That he respected Joe's willingness to sacrifice. That he supported his decision to join the G League and chase the NBA again. During his own career, Michael had appeared in three NBA seasons before embarking overseas for good in 1990, never attempting to come back. "I didn't fight for it," he told Joe over the phone that day. "I know it's hard. I didn't want to fight for it—it was too much. You're actually taking the challenge."

Tears fell from Joe's eyes as he listened to his dad's words. "For my dad to call and tell me that, it was inspirational," Young later said. "It kind of touched me a little bit because it's not going unseen. Someone who is my number one supporter, he's going to tell me the truth."

Michael had one other message for Joe: "Don't quit. Keep going until the season ends."

"I was just telling him, I know his love for the game and what he's trying to accomplish," Michael said. "He had been there for half a season—finish it. And continue to play well and just remember to do what you have to do to provide for your family. He's going all the way through to the end—that's something that we talked about. I'm real big on finishing stuff. You don't start something and don't finish it. And he's always finished stuff."

Michael paused and took a deep breath before adding, "I'll tell you, I just don't understand it."

Can You Pass This Test?

17. A RUTHLESS BUSINESS

On the morning of December 29, after a whirlwind first week with the Heat, Cheatham tested positive for Omicron.

He was demoralized. It was the summer of 2021 all over again, when he caught the virus right before reporting to training camp with the Thunder. Except this time—at the height of Omicron—it seemed inevitable. Cheatham was arriving at the Heat practice facility every day to learn that someone else had been added to the health and safety protocols. Across the NBA, well over one hundred players were currently out with COVID.

Given the situation, Miami would not be re-signing Cheatham after his ten-day contract expired. Instead, since the team was in San Antonio to face the Spurs (a game that would have to be postponed because Miami did not have enough healthy bodies), he would be quarantining at a hotel for the foreseeable future. The Heat would leave for Houston soon after, but Cheatham would remain. He spent New Year's Day alone in a desolate room, feeling more frustrated than sick, wondering what the hell might happen next.

"That's honestly a great example of how ruthless the business can be," said Heat guard Duncan Robinson, a former G Leaguer himself. "Zylan did everything right. He really did. He showed up every day with great energy, played well in practice, did all the right things. The biggest thing that stuck out to me with him was just his attitude and his approach. Somebody that shows up and brings that type of spirit, I'll never count somebody like that out."

• • •

Before the Cavaliers traveled to Atlanta for a matchup against Malcolm Hill and the Hawks, they were in New Orleans to face Jared Harper and the Pelicans.

Nearly sixteen thousand people showed up at the Smoothie King Center that night—a fan base somewhat revitalized by the Pelicans' recent success. The team, which had struggled *mightily* through November (suffering a nine-game losing streak at one point), had won four of its last five and three straight at home. Against the Cavaliers, however, the Pelicans' woes seemed to have returned. New Orleans trailed by as many as 23 points in the first quarter and headed back to the locker room down 58–48 at halftime.

During the break, Harper, who had yet to play, was informed by coaches that he would be a part of the second half rotation. That he would get a shot—a *real shot*—to prove what he could do. It arrived at the 3:12 mark of the third quarter. Sauntering onto the court, Harper appeared . . . well, the same way Jared Harper *always* appears: cool, focused, emotionless, almost strangely calm. At times in Birmingham, while the team was getting fired up before a game, Harper would be standing there, hands in his pockets, blank expression on his face, like he was in line at a Starbucks. He *was* engaged and ready to go; his way of showing it was just different.

Make no mistake, despite the change in scenery, this was the same Harper entering the game for the Pelicans. The score was 78–65 in favor of Cleveland. These were pivotal minutes, as the game still hung in the balance. One bad stretch and New Orleans would be buried. One good stretch and the gap could be erased. First, the momentum had to be seized away from the Cavaliers. Life needed to be breathed back into the Smoothie King Center.

Harper picked up the tempo. He pushed the pace on offense, attacking the paint and kicking it out to open shooters. He hounded Cavaliers point guard Ricky Rubio—a former teammate of his with the Phoenix Suns, who is at least four inches taller—on defense. His assertiveness made an immediate impression on Jen Hale, Antonio Daniels, and David Wesley, the broadcasting crew for the Pelicans that evening.

A Ruthless Business

"This young man has a lot of confidence," Hale remarked. Seconds later, Harper caught a pass on the right wing, set his feet, and fired a three-pointer that sailed through the net. The crowd roared.

"You spoke it into existence!" exclaimed Daniels.

Harper kept rolling. On the next possession, he found Gary Clark in transition for another three-pointer. The crowd roared louder. As time ticked down in the quarter, Harper got into the lane and floated up a shot that softly bounced in. The deficit was down to seven, a very manageable number heading into the final period. "Jared Harper is very at ease," Hale said. "He does not look rattled by this moment one bit."

That was Harper—*forever* at ease. "Putting him in tough, adverse, challenging situations really helped with him being calm," explained Patrick Harper, Jared's father. "That also comes with your training. And he's confident. If he misses three in a row, the game is on the line, he's going to take the next shot."

The stage was never too big. In the 2019 NCAA Tournament, with a Final Four spot on the line, Harper scored 12 points in overtime to lift his Auburn Tigers over the Kentucky Wildcats. The game was so anxiety-inducing that somewhere in the crowd of more than seventeen thousand, Erica Harper, Jared's mom, couldn't bring herself to watch. But Auburn's "little maestro," as head coach Bruce Pearl called him, delivered again.

Jared would never even admit to *feeling* rattled. "He *could* be nervous, and I'll never know," said Jalen Harper, Jared's brother. "He would never tell me."

Jalen, who is three years Jared's junior, followed his brother's footsteps to Auburn. A six-foot-one guard, he strives to emulate Jared's composed demeanor on the floor. The two talk every day, though their discussions rarely center on the exciting goings-on of Jared's basketball career. That applies to game days too. They might discuss music and TV shows or send each other funny posts from Instagram but not a word about basketball. That part, according to Jalen, has always been understood.

And so it was understood, at least among the Harper family, that Jared would display this sort of aggressiveness on an NBA court. It was the style he had played since his first organized game in a Mableton youth league at the age of five, when parents had to introduce a made-up rule just to slow him down.

He kept the same mindset into the fourth quarter against Cleveland, connecting on a difficult runner over the outstretched arm of a much-taller defender. When he was guarding Rubio, he pressured the ball not unlike how Alvarado—presently out with COVID—would. "Ricky Rubio is *hating* Jared Harper," said Daniels, which was perhaps the nicest compliment he could pay.

When Harper checked out with 7:26 left in the game, the Pelicans were still in a hole, down 95–83. Without him, though, the hole surely would have been deeper. In just eight minutes, Harper had registered 7 points, 3 assists, and a block. His performance was, by no means, flawless. He launched one erratic midrange jumper, the kind of shot that would give Pannone nightmares. Just before being subbed out, he also turned the ball over, losing it out of bounds as he tried to corral a pass.

But overall, Harper was impressive—*very* impressive. He didn't just look like an NBA player; he looked like a good NBA player.

New Orleans went on to storm back, closing the game on a 25–9 run to grab the improbable 108–104 victory. It was the second biggest comeback in franchise history—an inspiring effort that required contributions from many, including Harper. This was the first time his fingerprints had been on an NBA win. "So what if it was seven points? That was a big seven points that was needed," Jalen said. "If he didn't do that, then they would've lost. It was his moment."

Jared, of course, would not be so gung-ho about it. Conversations with Jalen would swiftly return to music and TV shows, like this was any other game. Like Jared being in the NBA—and having an impact in the NBA—was run-of-the-mill. *Understood.*

"He gets his personality from me," Patrick said. "That's what he's gonna do [on the court]. He's doing what he's supposed to do. I think it's just that—a couple of years that you've kind of waited and *boom*. He was happy. We were all happy. His personality is very laid-back, but I know that inside, he was feeling real, real good about it."

Above all else, what Jared was feeling that night was a sense of validation. He always knew that he *could* do it. Now he had actually done it.

• • •

At precisely 10:41 a.m. on December 31, less than nine hours before Hawks-Cavaliers was scheduled to tip off, ESPN senior NBA insider Adrian Wojnarowski hit send on a tweet: "Atlanta Hawks guard Malcolm Hill—who had 13 points and 3 steals vs. Chicago on Wednesday—has entered COVID protocols, sources tell ESPN."

Damn.

Hill wasn't feeling sick that morning; on the contrary, he was peppy and eager to take the floor. His initial COVID test had come back inconclusive. Team personnel tested him again right after, and this time, the result was negative. *Phew*, Hill thought. *Close call*. But he wasn't out of the woods yet. A third test was conducted just to confirm that the negative result was accurate, and this one was . . . positive? Huh? How was that possible? Hill took three straight tests and received three different results.

He was stunned. This was more than just baffling; it was *inexplicable*. In the end, the strange sequence of events didn't matter. A positive was a positive. Hill would enter the NBA's health and safety protocols and begin quarantining immediately. Even worse, his ten-day contract would expire, and the Hawks would not re-sign him. His time in the NBA had come to a crushing end.

• • •

Upon returning to Birmingham, all members of the Squadron—players, coaches, executives, managers, trainers—underwent COVID testing. They would continue to be tested every day ahead of the team's regular season opener on January 5, an away game against the Stockton Kings. Records would be reset, and the top six teams from each conference—Birmingham was in the West—would earn a spot in the playoffs.

It seemed like a safe bet to assume that the full Squadron team would not be making the trip to Stockton. And sure enough, following two days of player-development workouts in Birmingham, John Petty Jr. tested positive for Omicron. With Harper, Cheatham, and Hill still gone, Petty projected to step into a much larger role. That would have to wait, however, and in the meantime, the Squadron acquired guard Marlon Stewart from the available player pool. Stewart arrived in town and was tested by Gilchrist Schmidt, head athletic trainer, right away. Schmidt couldn't believe the Squadron's luck: the COVID replacement for Petty . . . had COVID.

The back-up to the back-up was guard Nate Bradley, who spent training camp with the Squadron. Bradley, thankfully, was COVID-free. That left Birmingham with seven healthy bodies, which, while far from ideal, was enough to play. Two other key pieces would be missing when the Squadron flew to Stockton—both Pannone and PD coach Andrew Warren had also entered protocols.

So, on the team's first road trip of the regular season, it would be without four of its top players—Harper, Cheatham, Hill, Petty—and its head coach. "I think we knew it would look a little different," said guard Riley LaChance. "We didn't really know it would be that extreme."

Associate head coach T. J. Saint would take over for Pannone. Saint was more than qualified, having worked as a video coordinator for the Detroit Pistons and on the coaching staffs at Belmont University, Butler University, and the University of Georgia. It wasn't exactly the fairest position to be thrown into, but Saint welcomed the challenge. He was as dedicated a leader as Pannone, a relentless worker who lived and breathed basketball. His goal was to get back to the NBA, and the experience as head coach would be an invaluable step in that direction regardless of the circumstances.

While Saint was busy game-planning, Schmidt was scrambling to try to get Stewart and Petty cleared in time to play. He was working around-the-clock, exchanging texts with Squadron reps as early as 4:00 a.m. on the West Coast. Since both players were five days removed from testing positive, they *could* be let out of protocols early if their CT (cycle threshold) values—an indicator of the amount of viral material present in one's system—were above 30. Stewart was the first to get the go-ahead, joining the Squadron a day after the team had arrived in Stockton. Petty's CT value was soon adequate as well, but there was a holdup. Suddenly, the league office wanted him to ship a test to a specific lab, instead of accepting the results obtained from a location closer to Birmingham. That course of action would take far too long for him to be cleared for January 5. After *many* conversations, Schmidt managed to get the necessary approval from the league, and Petty hopped on the next available flight.

A Ruthless Business

Saint was going to get his pregame coffee when Petty arrived at the hotel, less than three hours before tip-off. To make matters worse, the six-foot-five guard, fresh out of quarantine and fresh off a commercial flight, hadn't been able to work out in over a week.

• • •

Nothing about the game that night felt customary.

Not the setting—Stockton Arena, which can seat a maximum of twelve thousand people, had a recorded turnout of 440. It was a generous count. The venue, which also hosts hockey games, was stuck at a goosebumps-inducing temperature.

Not the staff—while Saint manned the sideline, Pannone was hosting a virtual watch party on Zoom, another effort to engage with the fans in Birmingham.

Not the roster—Joe Young was the only familiar face in the starting lineup, joined by Tra Holder, Ra'Shad James, Riley LaChance, and James Banks III, all of whom came off the bench during the Showcase.

And not the outcome—after seven straight wins, Birmingham came crashing back down to earth, losing 103–80. Young could get nothing going, shooting 1 of 9 from behind the arc. Petty was able to contribute twenty-three minutes off the bench but looked, understandably, rusty. Holder, who had averaged just thirteen minutes per game through the Showcase, was the team's best player, recording 15 points and 7 rebounds.

The good news was that Birmingham would get a shot at revenge the following evening. The bad news was that the team would face all the same obstacles. It would take a true heroic effort from someone to give Birmingham a chance, and Young was the closest thing to Superman the Squadron had.

After the team put up a paltry 80 points in its opener, Birmingham needed "Joey Buckets," the unstoppable scoring alter ego of Young, especially since the Sacramento Kings had assigned guard Jahmi'us Ramsey and transferred two-way forward Louis King to Stockton before the game.

Less than four minutes in, Young sunk his first shot attempt, an off-balanced three-pointer from the corner. "That's a good sign there," said Squadron play-by-play announcer Eli Gold.

"You're not kidding," replied his partner, Rick Moody.

Young went on to nail *six* more three-pointers. He would flash every bit of his offensive repertoire: the deep range, the midrange pull-ups, the tough floaters in the lane. This was, in a way, payback—Stockton could have selected Young in the G League Draft, instead opting to trade the number twenty-one pick to the Squadron.

He finished the game with a sensational 40 points on 13 of 23 shooting, to go along with 8 assists and only 1 turnover. The performance earned him immediate praise on social media.

"Joey Buckets I see ya lil bro. Been a killer!" wrote Jonathon Simmons, who went from G League tryout player to $15 million man in the NBA, on Instagram.

"Certified Bucket Getter. Ain't no way a team can't use him rn [right now]!" tweeted Indiana Pacers center Myles Turner, Young's former teammate.

The official G League account posted a video of Young's highlights with the caption, "58 seconds of pure scoring."

And yet, it made no difference. Birmingham got demolished, 137–119, anyway. Stockton shot a ridiculous 58 percent from the field and an even more ridiculous 64 percent from behind the arc. The loss guaranteed that Young's masterful outing would garner far less attention from the people who mattered most: NBA scouts. On a night where he flat out dominated, the Squadron were still outscored by 30 points when he was on the floor.

• • •

Help soon arrived. When the Squadron returned to Birmingham for a home game against the Iowa Wolves, an old friend was there to meet them: Jared Harper.

Harper had been transferred down by the Pelicans. Since his breakout game against the Cavaliers, he had yet to receive another second of playing time, which was, for Harper, as puzzling as it was disheartening. "Of course, with me playing well, I thought that after I would get more of an opportunity to play," he admitted. "But at the end of the day, everything is going to work out for itself."

His presence may not have been essential in New Orleans, but it *was* in

A Ruthless Business

Birmingham. With Harper back, the 3,375 fans who dedicated their Saturday night to Squadron-Wolves could feel a whole lot better about that decision. Legacy Arena was regularly drawing solid crowds, at least by minor league standards. The experiment in Birmingham was so far proving successful, and the organization hadn't even come close to tapping into the full market. Locals still saw ads for the team and wondered, *Who the hell are the Squadron?* Or saw ticket prices and thought, *What am I paying that much for?*—despite seats being available for less than $20.

Harper, though, was worth the price of admission. He single-handedly seemed to tilt the odds in Birmingham's favor. As a backcourt, he and Young formed as dangerous a one-two punch as there was in the G League. Iowa had no answers for either of them. Harper would lead Birmingham in nearly every statistical category, registering 28 points, 8 rebounds, and 7 assists. He was matched up with Wolves two-way guard McKinley Wright IV, another under-sized guard (five feet eleven) who was known more for his pesky defense than his scoring. Squadron coaches constantly reiterated to Harper the importance of focusing on defense, as Wright did. For both of them, coaches reasoned, that was the ticket to a solidified spot in the NBA. *Be like Jose Alvarado.*

Coming off his 40-point outburst, Young would tally 27 points (on an efficient 10 of 15 shooting), 3 steals, and a few stitches versus Iowa. During the third quarter, he knocked the ball away from Wright and dove to the floor to retrieve it. The effort was inspiring; the consequences dire. Young's face collided with the hardwood, leaving a gash on his chin and a cut over his left eye that required stitches. He was forced out with 5:46 left in the third quarter and Birmingham up 75–65. He returned at the start of the fourth, when Birmingham's lead had been trimmed to 87–82.

The game came down to the final possession. Birmingham secured a defensive rebound with just under seven seconds remaining, down 115–113. Coach Saint, who was still filling in for Pannone, elected not to call timeout. The ball found Harper. He raced to the front court. Fans at Legacy rose to their feet. *Five seconds, four, three.* With little space to maneuver, Harper tried to cross over and . . . was stripped by Wright. *Ball game.*

"What a difficult, difficult loss for the Birmingham Squadron," Moody said. Indeed, it was.

● ● ●

"Iowa Wolves mount second-half comeback to defeat Birmingham Squadron," read the team's press release that evening. Less than twenty-four hours later, Joseph Hooven, head of PR, sent out another release: "Pelicans sign Gary Clark to two-way contract." Which also meant "Pelicans waive Jared Harper off two-way contract."

That was, unbeknownst to Harper, the organization's expectation from the beginning. New Orleans wanted another guard in the mix for the end of December, especially as Nickeil Alexander-Walker and Alvarado entered COVID protocols. It was also a well-earned financial reward for Harper, given his stellar play with the Squadron.

Once forward Didi Louzada, who was serving a twenty-five-game suspension for taking a banned substance, returned in mid-January, he would take Clark's standard roster spot and Clark would take Harper's two-way spot. That was the plan, and while it was not set in stone, the team ultimately stuck to it. Harper was reacquired by the Squadron and back on a G League contract.

"I think Jared handled it as professionally and as well as anybody could have handled it," said Squadron general manager Marc Chasanoff. "Right now, it wasn't the right opportunity. But it doesn't change the fact that you're good enough. It doesn't change the fact that you need to keep going. You can go back through the G League—I'm sure there are people that have come back [from the NBA] and you can let it define you, or you can use it as your motivatian to push through."

Harper's motivation never diminished. Every day that he was in the G League, he told himself the same thing: *I'm another day closer.*

● ● ●

While they were stuck in quarantine, both Cheatham and Hill were receiving interest from other NBA teams. It was a positive sign, sure, but it also made their situations that much more infuriating. After years of grinding for opportunities in the NBA, there were finally organizations prepared to sign them—and they could do nothing about it.

Cheatham was the first to get out of isolation. He immediately flew from

A Ruthless Business

San Antonio back home to Phoenix for a few days. Having missed Christmas break, Cheatham wanted to spend some time with his family, especially since his mom was in the throes of a battle with stage IV cancer. His plan was to return to Birmingham soon—the Squadron organization supported his decision to take time away—unless one of those interested NBA clubs pulled the trigger on a ten-day offer.

Hill was able to travel from Atlanta to Birmingham and settle into his apartment at Lumen. Still, even though he was freed from quarantine by the CDC's guidelines (five days of being asymptomatic), he remained ineligible to play. The G League was now exclusively using a company called BioReference Laboratories (BRL) to analyze and report CT values. Unfortunately for the Squadron, BRL headquarters was in New Jersey. Schmidt tested Hill right away and shipped the contents out through FedEx. The chances of it arriving at the lab in time to be examined the next day were slim. In Hill's case, the procedure was further delayed and complicated because of a winter storm that swept the Northeast. Schmidt continued to conduct tests and send them out, worrying that the others were not being delivered or dealt with.

Days went by. Hill's patience was dwindling. He wanted answers. He *needed* answers. His agent kept contacting Chasanoff, wondering when this would all be sorted out. Chasanoff had the clever idea to ask the Atlanta Hawks if they would test Hill, seeing that NBA teams were getting results much quicker. The Hawks agreed, so Hill woke up at 4:30 a.m. to make the drive from Birmingham to Atlanta. (The earlier he was tested, the earlier he would have answers.) It was a five-hour round-trip journey, and Hill never even got out of his car. He pulled up to the Hawks facility, got swabbed, turned around, and drove right back to Birmingham. He did that *twice*, in consecutive days, to confirm what he already knew: his CT level was above 30. Hill was finally cleared.

18. KEEP GOING

The Squadron looked a lot different when Hill returned to practice on the evening of January 12. Marlon Stewart and Nate Bradley—the two replacement players added before the restart—remained on the roster. Birmingham had also acquired thirty-two-year-old guard Darius Adams, who, like Young, was a former star in the Chinese Basketball Association. Adams was the CBA Finals MVP in 2017, the scoring champion in 2018, and the league MVP in 2019, but had never played in the NBA. He was staying in shape at home in Indianapolis when NBA teams started handing out ten-day contracts like business cards and thought, *How do I get one of those?* The answer, he realized, was to go through the G League, so Adams entered the player pool and was scooped up by the Squadron.

Seven-footer Zach Hankins, who had missed the first few months of the season recovering from two knee surgeries, was back on the floor. After his initial knee injury (a torn ACL), he had contemplated retiring from basketball forever. Financially, it seemed the practical move; he had played just one season overseas and recently gotten married. As soon as he could walk again, Hankins was delivering packages around Oklahoma City—where he lived with his wife—and using much of his earnings to pay for rehab. He was invited to join the Phoenix Suns for the 2021 NBA Summer League but, as the tournament got underway, still felt significant pain in his knee. Further examinations would reveal torn cartilage, meaning Hankins would require a second procedure.

I don't know if I can do this anymore, he told himself. Again, he pondered quitting. But the Squadron staff was willing to bring him in and exercise patience with his recovery. Now healthy and moving well, Hankins credited the organization—and its team of trainers and coaches—with saving his career.

Hill wouldn't be in Birmingham long enough to build chemistry with Hankins or get acquainted with Adams. In fact, January 12 would be his only practice in the G League before the Chicago Bulls called.

During his stint with Atlanta, Hill had played against the Bulls twice, thriving in both games. Chicago's front office was impressed by his defense, particularly on DeMar DeRozan, who continued to play at an MVP-caliber level. At the turn of the New Year, DeRozan even hit back-to-back game-winning shots on consecutive nights, something never before done in the NBA. Hill was watching it unfold while in quarantine. "I ain't gonna lie; that made me feel good a little bit," he said with a smile. "I was like, *Okay, I was playing solid against him.*"

Solid undersold it, and the proof was now in ink. On January 14, Hill signed a ten-day contract with the Bulls. Two weeks after guarding DeRozan, he was DeRozan's teammate.

• • •

Cheatham was all set to report back to Birmingham from Phoenix when he received the news that the Utah Jazz was calling him up on a ten-day contract. So, he would fly north, not east, and dress for a game against the Cavaliers right away.

Utah was coached by the highly regarded Quin Snyder, a former D-League Coach of the Year in 2009. The team had championship ambitions, sitting at fourth in the Western Conference with a 28-14 record. At present, they were in desperate need of big men, with centers Rudy Gobert, Hassan Whiteside, and Udoka Azubuike, as well as forward Rudy Gay, all in the health and safety protocols. Facing a Cleveland frontcourt that consisted of two seven-footers (Lauri Markkanen and Evan Mobley) and the six-foot-eleven Jarrett Allen (who towers over seven feet if counting his afro), the Jazz started Royce O'Neale at center.

Royce O'Neale is six feet six.

Adding a big through the hardship exception was the team's priority, and Cheatham appealed to Utah for many reasons: his athleticism, improved shooting ability, and, above all else, defensive versatility. The deal was made official in the early hours of January 12. After meeting the team at shootaround in the morning, Cheatham was active for the game that night. The turnaround was unimaginably fast. Cheatham thought he was going to Birmingham, blinked, and then he was at Vivint Arena, wearing a Utah Jazz uniform, peering out at 18,306 fans.

Midway through the third quarter, with Utah behind 71–58, Cheatham checked in. It was his first time appearing in an NBA game since August 13, 2020. Over an eighteen-monthlong journey, Cheatham had been traded, waived, injured, sidelined by COVID *twice*, and impacted by personal issues away from basketball. But he had persevered through it all to get back.

While the journey was remarkable, the culmination would be anything but. Cheatham's three-minute stretch in the third quarter went about as poorly as it could have. He missed his only two shot attempts, one of which touched nothing but air. His team was outscored 12–0, turning a manageable deficit into an insurmountable one. To top it all off, Jarrett Allen caught an alley-oop dunk that wasn't exactly *over* Cheatham, but he was definitely in the poster-worthy frame.

Cheatham reentered with 2:02 left in the contest and the outcome long decided. On one possession, he darted to the rim and threw up an errant floater that, again, failed to hit anything. When the buzzer sounded on his much-anticipated return to an NBA floor, Cheatham had recorded 0 points, 0 rebounds, 0 assists, 0 blocks, and 0 steals and shot 0 for 3 from the field. He was also a -13 in five total minutes of action.

Was it disappointing? Of course. Irritating? For sure. Worrying? Absolutely. But Cheatham couldn't afford to let any of those emotions affect him. Not now. This was day one of ten. "It's easy to believe when everything's going right," he posted on Instagram after the game, over an image of his number 6 Jazz jersey. "I see beauty and progression in every struggle . . . Bounce back Z."

• • •

Would others call this a miracle? Hill would later ponder the question, hunched over a computer, working on a blog post about his debut for the Bulls. He eventually typed, "For me, it's still an adjustment, but I believe miracles can be just a normal occurrence if you believe and allow the universe to work in your favor."

With all that led up to that mid-January night in downtown Boston, the word *miracle* felt appropriate. Almost a year prior to the day, Hill had written down his goal to make it to the NBA. Now he was playing for the NBA team from his home state, about to take the floor at the historic TD Garden. On the opposing side was superstar forward Jayson Tatum, a player that Hill had known since they were both coming up in the Metro East area. Hill's father had even worked at the same high school in St. Louis as Tatum's mother.

For Malcolm and Jayson to be meeting again—here—was incredible. A miracle, some might say. "Man, I'm telling you, I'm, like, *living it*," Hill stressed. "I used to think this stuff was *talk*, you know what I mean? But the more I'm experiencing this, the less I believe in things being chance or lucky; it's just things that people *think* and how they go about their routines in their day that allows them to have the opportunity."

Chicago was coming off a humiliating 42-point loss at the hands of the Warriors. This was a chance to bounce back against a loaded Celtics team, led by Tatum and fellow All-Star Jaylen Brown. Still hampered by COVID and injuries, the Bulls would need minutes from Hill, despite his recent—like *twenty-four hours ago* recent—arrival.

He played sparingly through the first three quarters, going 1 for 3 from the field and defending well. Bulls head coach Billy Donovan liked his competitiveness. Though Hill was still shaky on the team's system, Donovan decided to employ him down the stretch. Chicago held a 106–100 advantage with 4:25 on the clock when Hill jogged to the scorer's table.

"So Billy Donovan, with 4:25 left, brings in Malcolm Hill, in his Bulls debut, in just his fourth NBA game, to try to play some very key minutes down the stretch," said Bulls play-by-play announcer Adam Amin.

Watching on television, fans back in Chicago were likely thinking, *Why are we putting in Malcolm Hill?* and then, *Wait a second . . . who the hell is Malcolm Hill?* It wasn't as if Donovan was out of options. Alfonzo McKinnie,

Troy Brown Jr., and Matt Thomas were all available and all more experienced. Putting in Hill meant trusting a near stranger.

For what it's worth, Amin and color analyst Stacey King were not so skeptical of the decision. Clinging to a slight lead, the Bulls needed defenders, and Hill had already proven to be one of those.

With just under three minutes left and Chicago up 110–104, Tatum attacked an open lane to the basket. His eyes widened as he got closer, timing his steps to elevate for a dunk. Then, suddenly, his path was impeded. Hill had slid over from the weak side, squared his body, and braced for impact. Tatum barreled right into him, throwing up a wild shot in the process. The call was easy: charging violation—Celtics turnover.

"These are the kinds of things that keep you in the league right here," said King, a former NBA player and D-League head coach himself, "doing the little things."

A minute later, Hill was matched up against Brown, an athletic wing averaging 28 points per game in January. Brown controlled the ball up top, licked his chops, and tried to go one-on-one. He drove hard to his left, but Hill stuck with him the entire way. As King described, "Malcolm Hill's on him like a cheap suit . . . too tight!"

Brown spun and spun again, attempting—and failing—to create separation. He rose for a jumper but couldn't get the shot off with Hill's outstretched arms in his face. It was too late to change plans. Brown's feet landed back on the ground. The ref blew his whistle: traveling violation—*another* Celtics turnover.

Hill pumped his fist and flexed his muscles, more emotion than he was prone to exhibiting. The game was far from over, however. Spurred on by the Garden crowd, Boston strung together an impressive run in the final minute. Hill missed a short jumper that could have put Chicago up four with 45 seconds remaining. Instead, the Celtics would get several clutch free throws from center Robert Williams and steal a 114–112 victory.

Afterward, Hill and Tatum found each other on the court. Cameras captured the moment as they embraced. Tatum shared a simple, yet powerful message: "Keep going."

• • •

The Bulls were sold. One game, albeit a loss, was all they needed to see. On January 17, the front office offered Hill a two-way contract, which would be guaranteed for the rest of the season. He wasn't just a ten-day replacement player anymore. Hill was in the NBA to stay.

Receiving that offer was vindication, proof for Hill that his obsessive approach was working. That miracles could be normal occurrences.

"I knew he was NBA ready," said Clayton Hughes, Hill's stepbrother. "But I didn't expect him to get a two-way contract in the NBA *that* fast. Here's the thing about Malcolm, and I reiterate it all the time. He never gets satisfied. I used to hoop, so I've worked out with this man my whole life. People really do not understand how hard he works. There's no doubt that's why it's working out."

The deal was also vindication for Malcolm Sr., Hill's father, who had previously made himself two promises. One, he was never going to attend another NBA game *unless* his son was playing in it. And two, the next time that he watched his son play in person would be in the NBA. "It was just kind of my silent protest," he explained, "because Malcolm was an NBA player to me all along, even coming out of college. I don't think he was ever really given the respect he should have been given."

The respect would come sooner or later, Malcolm Sr. figured. Until then, he would carry out his protest. His vision all along was that Malcolm would go overseas, make good money, come back to the G League, and then jump to the NBA. It happened that way *exactly*.

Malcolm Sr. made the drive down to Memphis, Tennessee, for Chicago's next game against the Grizzlies. Tickets were waiting for him at the box office. This would be the first time he would see his son play live since the 2017–18 season, when Malcolm was suiting up for Telekom Baskets Bonn in Germany. Dad had followed every step of the journey on the internet, tuning in to crappy streams at odd hours of the day, always pushing his son to *keep going*—from the Philippines to Germany to Kazakhstan to Israel to the G League and, finally, to the NBA.

Standing in a jam-packed FedExForum as his son came sprinting out of the tunnel was one of the proudest and happiest moments of Malcolm Sr.'s life. "Outside of the birth of my kids and weddings and things like that . . . it was, like, pure joy," he explained. It was even more surreal because Malcolm Sr. had already been a Bulls fan. "To see him run out on that court with the Chicago Bulls just brought me pure happiness," he continued. "And to hear the Memphis Grizzlies fans boo him, it was like music to my ears. I was, like, man, wow. He has made it. It was an unbelievable experience for me."

With his roster spot secure, Hill seemed determined to justify the organization's decision. He logged thirty minutes off the bench, recording 12 points (on an efficient 4 of 6 shooting) and 8 rebounds. Chicago lost the game, 119–106, but for Malcolm Sr., the night was unforgettable. He was overwhelmed with emotion before the clock even started running. "And then for him to play the way that he did," Hill's father said, "I just felt like God was treating me that day."

1. Harper pleads his case to a referee during Birmingham's sole preseason game against the College Park Skyhawks on October 30, 2021. Photo by Rod Abernathy, Rodtee Media.

2. Young launches a shot during a game against the Texas Legends on November 13, 2021. Photo by Cooper Neill, NBAE via Getty Images.

3. *From left to right*: Head athletic trainer Gilchrist Schmidt, Coach T. J. Saint, Coach Perry Huang, and Coach Ryan Pannone watch from the sidelines. Photo by Rod Abernathy, Rodtee Media.

4. Coach Pannone (*left*) and Hill (*right*) during a practice at Birmingham-Southern College. Photo by Rod Abernathy, Rodtee Media.

5. The team celebrates Petty's (*middle*, holding the cake) birthday on December 2, 2021. Photo by Rod Abernathy, Rodtee Media.

6. *From left to right*: LaChance, Schmidt, Cheatham, and Young chat during practice. Photo by Rod Abernathy, Rodtee Media.

7. Legacy Arena, home of the Birmingham Squadron. Photo by Rod Abernathy, Rodtee Media.

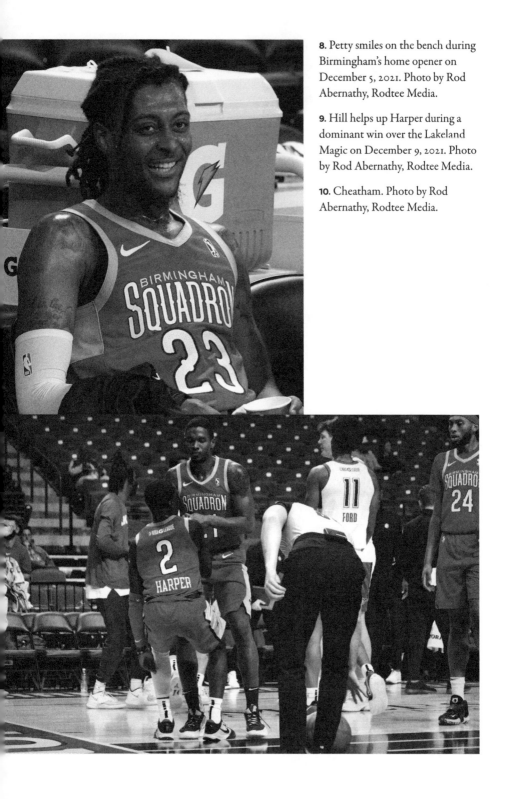

8. Petty smiles on the bench during Birmingham's home opener on December 5, 2021. Photo by Rod Abernathy, Rodtee Media.

9. Hill helps up Harper during a dominant win over the Lakeland Magic on December 9, 2021. Photo by Rod Abernathy, Rodtee Media.

10. Cheatham. Photo by Rod Abernathy, Rodtee Media.

11. Young. Photo by Rod Abernathy, Rodtee Media.

12. Coach Mery Andrade (*left*) talks with Daulton Hommes (*middle*) and Jose Alvarado (*right*) on the Squadron bench. Photo by Rod Abernathy, Rodtee Media.

13. The team huddles together after practice at Birmingham-Southern College. Photo by Rod Abernathy, Rodtee Media.

14. Cheatham elevates for a floater during a game against the Grand Rapids Gold at the G League Winter Showcase in Las Vegas. Photo by David Becker, NBAE via Getty Images.

15. Harper gets his chance to play for the New Orleans Pelicans in a game against the Cleveland Cavaliers on December 28, 2021. Photo by Sean Gardner, Getty Images.

16. After signing a ten-day contract with the Miami Heat, Cheatham celebrates on the bench during a game against the Washington Wizards on December 28, 2021. Photo by Issac Baldizon, NBAE via Getty Images.

17. After signing a two-way contract with the Chicago Bulls, Hill rises for a three-pointer during a game against the Oklahoma City Thunder on February 12, 2022. Photo by Jeff Haynes, NBAE via Getty Images.

18. *From left to right*: Hankins, LaChance, Adams, and Young on the floor against the Santa Cruz Warriors on February 24, 2022. Photo by Jack Arent, NBAE via Getty Images.

19. Xavier Moon (*middle*) is defended by Trey Murphy III (*left*) and Ra'Shad James (*right*) during the Squadron-Clippers game on March 1, 2022. Photo by Juan Ocampo, NBAE via Getty Images.

19. MALCOLM HILL'S HERE

Malcolm Hill would not be returning to Birmingham. His apartment at Lumen would be cleared out soon, making room for newly acquired big man Ike Anigbogu to move in. Hill's remaining belongings would be shipped to Chicago—his new home—right away.

Coach Pannone was ecstatic for Hill but also troubled by something— not many people knew the details of Hill's journey. Not even his former Squadron teammates did. *How could one truly understand the weight of Hill's accomplishment without knowing those details?* Pannone pondered. If the Squadron players were searching for inspiration, here it was. The dream had been lived out right in front of them.

Pannone voiced his concerns during the coaches' meeting on January 17. The staff came up with a plan to address the matter. In film the next day, they would tell the story of Malcolm Hill. The *complete* story, no details spared.

The gym was empty on that frigid morning, which was rare. Players typically shot around for thirty-or-so minutes before film started at 10:30 a.m. The coaches took their absence as a sign that practice would lack the necessary focus and energy. With a tough matchup against the South Bay Lakers, one of the best teams in the G League, approaching on Friday, they really couldn't afford any lazy practices.

Film began as it always did following a game. Saint broke down their impressive 123–110 win over the Salt Lake City Stars—their first victory of the regular season. Young shined in the contest, leading the team with 32 points on 11 of 19 shooting, to go along with 7 assists. His confidence was clearly rising; at the end of the third quarter, he fired a three-pointer from the left corner and knew it was good the second it left his fingertips, twirling to face the crowd. His back was fully turned to the basket when the ball dropped through the net. The 4,143 fans in attendance erupted, perhaps the loudest ovation at Legacy Arena yet.

Young hit four of the Squadron's twenty-two total threes, which tied for the most in a game by any G League team so far in the season. Saint, who was still at the helm (Pannone served as an assistant, after missing the lead-up to the game due to COVID), secured his first win as a head coach.

After fifteen minutes of recapping the game, Saint passed it to Pannone, who sat in the middle of the locker room. On the screen to his left was a chart with Hill's recent numbers—from the Champions League, the Israeli Basketball Premier League, the Las Vegas Summer League, and preseason with the Pelicans.

"I want you guys to describe Malcolm Hill to me as a person," he began. "How would you describe him?"

The players looked around, wondering who might venture an answer first. A few words were thrown out: "consistent," "disciplined," "a good guy." Pannone offered some himself: "trustworthy" and "humble," to which everyone nodded in agreement. Next, he asked the guys to describe Hill as a player. A lot of the same adjectives were suggested: "disciplined," "trustworthy," "you can count on him."

That Malcolm Hill, however, wasn't the same Malcolm Hill from overseas. During his five seasons in Europe and Asia, he had sometimes been detached, sleepwalking through the motions instead of attacking each day. "There were times when I was just going with the flow of things," he would later admit, "and being *whatever* about things—if it happens, it happens."

Now his mindset was the complete opposite. He vowed to do everything with purpose, to *always* be present. He wouldn't allow himself to be distracted or disengaged. Earlier that season, Pannone had caught a glimpse of Malcolm's iPhone—the same one he was once glued to overseas—while

Malcolm Hill's Here

they were on the team bus. The screen was so severely cracked that it looked dangerous to touch.

"Why don't you just get a new screen?" Pannone asked.

"Oh . . . I don't really use my phone," Hill responded.

As a player, Hill had also transformed. He was known as a pure scorer for most of his career, graduating from Illinois with the third-most points in school history. As a member of the Philippine Basketball Association's Magnolia Hotshots in 2017, he averaged 26 points per game. In Kazakhstan shortly thereafter, he was the second-leading scorer in the entire VTB United League.

One of his primary weapons was the midrange shot, which, of course, was rapidly vanishing from the NBA in the era of pace and space. So he concentrated on expanding his range to the three-point line. "The focus of his training was the corner three," his father, Malcolm Sr., said. "That's where most of our work was done in the gym—shooting from both corners of the court, from the NBA three-point line. He shot thousands and thousands of shots from the NBA three."

Most notably, though, Hill was never regarded as a defender. Previous coaches did not see him as a consistently reliable option on that end. He had flipped that script entirely in his pursuit of the NBA, shedding significant weight and evolving into an elite and versatile defensive player. It was his defense that had grabbed the attention of NBA front offices, eventually leading to his two-way contract.

"We always thought of him as like a slow-mo wing—smart with the ball, good with the ball, but a little bit playing his own game or whatnot," explained basketball scout Sam Meyerkopf, who concentrates on the NCAA, G League, and EuroLeague. "Old school, midrange, pretty physical, pretty strong, could even play some small-ball four. Didn't necessarily have the speed or even the three-point shooting of a typical wing. He's always been smart, high IQ, understands the game, point-forward-y kind of player, but to evolve from that to being able to just shoot threes at a more consistent percentage and shoot more of them is huge—and having the flexibility and athleticism to guard all different types of players and be there defensively."

In other words, Hill had streamlined his game to fit the modern NBA—something that sounds a lot easier than it is, especially when you've learned and mastered the sport in a completely different way. His development was also temporarily put on hold when he suffered a torn ACL while playing in Germany in 2018.

"Malcolm Hill has accomplished something that I've seen very, very, very few players do," Pannone told the Squadron. "This is year eighteen for me. You guys don't really know, but a big part of my career is working with NBA players individually—sixty different guys. I've been around some guys who have figured it out, some guys who didn't. I've been around very few players that can change as a person and as a player. What he's done is extremely difficult. He's not tall. He's not athletic. He wasn't known as a defender a year ago. What he's been able to do is un-fucking-believable."

Pannone gestured to the television, where, in a neat table, was all the evidence he needed. "I put these stats up there because I want you guys to see it," he said. "In the Champions League, he averaged 6 points a game, shot 15 percent from three. In the Israeli League, he averaged 9 points per game. He only played twenty minutes. In Summer League, they didn't play him. Jared, how many minutes did he get in preseason for the New Orleans Pelicans?"

"Zero," Harper mumbled.

"And how often did he check in in practice?"

"He didn't."

Prior to the season, when discussing his roster with other coaches in the basketball world, Pannone often heard a comment along the lines of "Malcolm Hill's starting for you guys? You must not be any good." To most people, Hill was an obscure prospect; to others, he was a bad prospect; and to very few, he was a prospect with actual NBA potential.

Pannone went on:

> There are some really good lessons in here for all of us. . . . Malcolm Hill is a player who has torn his ACL, has basically been cut and told he wasn't good enough—wasn't good enough to check in during Summer League; wasn't good enough to check in during practice. For all of you guys, there are a few things. One—don't let anyone ever crush your dreams. A lot of people told Malcolm Hill he ain't good enough—people who I know.

Don't let anyone fucking tell you guys that you're not good enough to achieve your dream—never. Doesn't mean you're arrogant. Would anyone describe Malcolm Hill as arrogant? He's not arrogant. He's very humble. Don't let anyone tell you guys you're not good enough. Don't let any scout or GM tell you that you can't make it. You can list the reasons—Malcolm Hill's not athletic enough, he's not this, he's not smart enough, he doesn't guard. Don't let anyone fucking tell you guys that you can't achieve your dream. Don't let any coach, including me, take away your confidence—ever, ever, ever, ever. *But* your fucking work ethic better match that shit, because I can tell you right now, Malcolm Hill works his ass off.

No one in the locker room would dispute that. In Birmingham, Hill took the court almost every day before film to work on his ball handling. After practice, he always stayed behind with Coach Huang to shoot more threes. His off-court routines might have seemed odd to some, but his dedication was impossible to deny.

Pannone loved to recount one specific story about Hill—a story that he thought perfectly summed up what it takes to reach the NBA level. He repeated it again now, even though many of his players had already heard it. During Pelicans training camp in New Orleans, there was an 8:00 a.m. staff meeting inside head coach Willie Green's office. Just as it was getting underway, someone entered the adjacent gym and began shooting around. Without swiveling in his chair, Green said to the rest of the coaches, "Malcolm Hill's here."

"He did something that is so hard," Pannone continued. "He simplified his game. All of the little shit that he was asked to do, he did it. A lot of guys can't do something in practice, take it to a game, implement it, and then take it to an NBA game and implement it there. It's just very difficult. I would say his ability to—and this is a skill—see something, practice something, focus on something, and implement it into a game consistently is extremely difficult. It's fucking hard to be the low man all the time. It just is. And that guy has done it."

Everything the coaches had asked for during his player-development meeting back in November, Hill had applied to his game. He wasn't the primary option on the Squadron as he had been on teams in the past, but he had followed the blueprint exactly, committed to the details, and taken no shortcuts.

"Does anyone know where Malcolm Hill ranked as a scoring leader on this team?" Pannone asked.

Crickets.

"Fourth. Throw in Jaxson and Trey—he was sixth."

The slide changed and a montage began to play on the screen. Coach Huang had assembled the best clips of Hill's defense in the NBA. Pannone talked through all the action.

"Look at that ball pressure, cancel the pick-and-roll, get into the ball, get under, beat him to the spot, chest him up, effort to get out, high hand."

"And do you guys notice what part of the game he was in?" assistant coach Mery Andrade chimed in. Several of the clips were from the fourth quarter. "We talk about trust. I will tell you, as a former player, you might not start a game, but if you finish a game and it's a close game, that says a lot about your character and what kind of player you are. And why are you on the floor at that time? Most likely, it's not going to be for offense."

The film continued to roll.

"Pretty good ball pressure, slowing them down. In the gap, early gap, high hand," Pannone narrated. "Good physicality. He's aware where Tatum is. He's in help. He sees Tatum. He's in help. Close out, high hand."

After three minutes of footage—three whole minutes of Hill going toe-to-toe with some of the best players in the NBA—the screen went black. Pannone took a deep breath and wrapped the film session with this:

> Now, everyone in here can do the same shit that he just did. I'll never lie to you guys. . . . I'm telling you guys right now, if you embrace all of the little shit defensively and you just are consistent and you go hard and you're smart and you can be trusted, you are going to have a far more successful career. There has never been a coach that you guys have played for that has been like, "Hmm, he's too good defensively, I don't want to play him." Never. It's not for everywhere in the world, but for the NBA, if you guys are going to get signed, it's because of your defense.

Malcolm Hill's Here

No one needed Malcolm Hill at the end of the game to go in and score. They got DeRozan and Vucevic—they don't need that. But they did need someone to guard Jayson Tatum and Jaylen Brown at the end of the game. And what Malcolm Hill does defensively, everyone in here can do, because he's not super athletic, he's not really tall, he's not super long. And that is what it's got to look like in everything that we do.

You guys know that Malcolm didn't bullshit drills. He didn't bullshit practice. He didn't bullshit anything. That's what we gotta see today in practice, every fucking possession, every shell, for where we want to go, for where you want to go. Upstairs, what was told to me about how practice is going to be today? What was being said? "Oh, it's not going to be a good practice. See—no one is up here shooting. Guys aren't going to have the energy. We had a practice like that last week, and they came out sluggish." That better not fucking happen for where you all want to go. We kickstart this—every fucking day, all the little details, all the little shit. We've got to dominate the simple, with great effort. You got it?

There was no response, but the silence spoke volumes. They got it.

● ● ●

Four days after losing to the Squadron at Legacy Arena, the Salt Lake City Stars were delighted to welcome a new player: Zylan Cheatham.

Cheatham wasn't getting an opportunity to play for the Jazz, so he was sent down to the organization's G League affiliate. Coaches and executives wanted a better look at him before his ten-day contract expired. Over the ensuing seventy-two hours, Cheatham would bounce back and forth between the NBA and the G League. He first arrived in Salt Lake City for a shootaround on the morning of January 19, ahead of a 7:00 p.m. game against the Memphis Hustle. The situation was, essentially, the following:

Stars head coach Nathan Peavy: Hey, Zylan. Welcome.

Cheatham: Hey, Coach. Thanks. Great to be here.

Peavy: So, the locker room is here. This is our team. These are our coaches. Here's our playbook. And oh, you're starting tonight.

Cheatham spent the afternoon studying the plays and excelled as the team's starting power forward that evening, notching 14 points, 17 rebounds, 3 assists, 2 steals, and a block in thirty minutes. With him in the mix, the Stars rolled to an easy 120–98 victory.

Coach Peavy was struck not just by Cheatham's impact on the floor but also his ability to mesh with the team in such a short span. "He made a big impact on us winning that game," Peavy said. "Even when he was on the bench, he was yelling at his teammates. It felt like he had been with the team the whole time. As a coach, you can very much appreciate that. That shows how great of a person, great of a teammate he is. I believe stuff like that is what's going to get him far—just being positive all the time, and no matter where he's at, he integrates himself with the team."

The next day, Cheatham rejoined the Jazz for practice. Then he went right back down to the Stars, who were about to embark on the road. The team would be going straight from its facility to the airport for a flight to McAllen, Texas, home of the Rio Grande Valley Vipers. As guys were running through plays, Cheatham remembered that he still had to go back to the hotel. Since his ten-day contract would be expiring while the Stars were in Texas, he needed to bring *all* of his belongings on the trip. He still wasn't sure whether the Jazz intended to keep him or let him walk. Neither was Coach Peavy, who checked his watch and implored Cheatham to hurry.

Hurry? That wouldn't be a problem. Cheatham was accustomed to hurrying. Hurrying to catch flights, to join teams, to learn playbooks. NBA fringe guys, especially at this time, were like contestants on *The Amazing Race*. When it came to packing in a rush and going with the flow of things, Cheatham was a seasoned veteran.

That wasn't by choice, of course. What he wouldn't give to stay in Utah, to truly settle into one place for once, to have the same home for longer than a basketball season. Even as a kid, Cheatham was constantly on the move, bouncing from one side of Phoenix to the other, attending three different high schools.

His life on the go would continue. Following the game against RGV, the Jazz decided not to re-sign him. Cheatham's contract was up, and he was a nomad once again.

Malcolm Hill's Here

Later, he would describe his ten days with Utah as "the experience of a lifetime." He got to learn from Coach Snyder and All-Stars Donovan Mitchell and Rudy Gobert. He saw LeBron James play live when the Jazz visited the Lakers on January 17. He emerged with three keys for himself going forward: adjust quickly to whatever opportunities arise, be consistent with his daily routines, and stay confident when his chances come.

Signing deals with two of the top teams in the NBA had proven to be, in Cheatham's words, "a blessing and a curse." "Going to those types of organizations, you can't expect to play," he said. "Everything is earned, not given. With a ten-day contract, obviously you want to try to get as much opportunity as possible, but when you go to a championship contender, or at least a Western Conference Finals contender, then the odds of you really coming in and getting minutes are pretty slim. I think it was a learning experience to say the least."

For Coach Peavy, it was tough to see Cheatham go. Their time together, though brief, left Peavy a huge fan. "I wish we would've kept him longer or signed him, but obviously the NBA is a business, and there are a lot of factors that go into making decisions like that," he said. "But as a coach, especially in the G League, you feel for these guys, and you root for them to really, really succeed, even when they're not with you."

So began the all-too-familiar routine. Cheatham bid Peavy and the Stars goodbye. He figured out his next move. He repacked his bags, checked out of the hotel, and left for the airport. After more than a month away, he was finally returning to Birmingham.

20. AT PEACE

Another practice at Birmingham-Southern had just wrapped up, this one more crowded than usual. The Pelicans had assigned forward Naji Marshall and rookie Trey Murphy III for the Squadron's next game against the Austin Spurs, sending down Brandon Demas, a player-development coach, along with them.

Pannone, content with the day's work, settled into a chair and rested his head softly against the wall. There were still more than two months left before the G League playoffs, and yet, it wasn't too early to deem the season a success. Pannone's primary goal was to help players reach the NBA—three of his guys had been called up, and one of them was never coming back.

It was easy to forget that Pannone, too, was chasing the NBA dream. In fact, he had been chasing it for far longer than any of his players. His coaching career had already spanned nearly two decades, beginning right after he graduated high school. The pursuit of the NBA was no less arduous for a coach; in a lot of ways, it was *more* demanding and required *more* sacrifices.

Pannone had traveled the world in search of the best opportunities, accepting meager salaries—$700 or $800 a month—to build his résumé. Along the way, he had picked up many side hustles (working camps, training players independently, running a website) and sold many of his belongings to make ends meet.

When he was an assistant coach for the D-League's Erie BayHawks in 2014–15, he found himself handling duties such as doing laundry, cleaning the locker room, and—literally—scrubbing toilets. "It didn't necessarily go the exact way that I was told it was going to go," Pannone said. "It was a very frustrating season professionally, probably the hardest season of my life." He earned just $1,000 a month, and the team did not provide housing or insurance. The only building where Pannone could afford to live would later be condemned. He couldn't cover the cost of heat, so he slept in multiple sweatshirts every night. For dinner, he often ate peanut butter banana sandwiches.

Pannone remained alert for any opportunities to advance his career. He paid for his own plane ticket and hotel to attend the D-League Showcase—held in Santa Cruz that year—so that he could be with his team and establish more connections.

In 2016 Hapoel Jerusalem wanted to add Pannone to its staff but didn't have an open position. Pannone desperately wanted to make it work. He knew the experience with Hapoel Jerusalem would be invaluable, for both his growth as a coach and his quest to reach the NBA. "Whatever it costs to live in Jerusalem, that's all I need," Pannone told the team. "As long as I'm not accruing debt, I'll figure it out." The club eventually hired him as an assistant, and Pannone was able to parlay that opportunity into a head coaching job for BC Prievidza in Slovakia the following season.

The situation in Slovakia was ideal (great team, supportive fans, amazing city), except for one problem: the organization wasn't paying Pannone on time. Whenever it had the money to pay *either* him or his players, he deferred to his players. It was frustrating, no question, but Pannone stayed anyway. His club was winning, and his résumé was becoming all the more impressive. When the season ended, BC Prievidza had gone 25-11, and Pannone was still owed five months' salary.

Pannone built many of his relationships abroad but did what he could to expand his contacts in the United States, showing up to every important networking event that fit his schedule. For the annual NBA Summer League in Las Vegas—an affair that has the feel of a New York City happy hour—Pannone always rented a car just to drive people around. It afforded him quality face time to make an impression. "People always need rides, and they want to save money," he explained. "Then you get like ten minutes alone with them, and they also feel like you did them a favor, so from a psychological standpoint, they are now indebted to you."

Connections are *everything* in the coaching world. It is often about who you know or what circle you're in or how wide a net you've cast. Pannone conducted his own extensive study to find the easiest path to the NBA, beyond just having a first-rate LinkedIn profile. After poring through the backgrounds of every head coach, assistant coach, and PD coach in the NBA, he discovered that the best way to land one of those positions—for anyone not a former player—is to be an intern with an organization and work one's way up.

"When I started coaching, I didn't even know that was an option," Pannone admitted. The year before he became a head coach in the G League, at age thirty-two, he was seeking an intern job with an NBA team. And only one coach—Fred Hoiberg with the Bulls—even considered hiring him but ultimately could not get it approved.

The next best route, as Pannone's research indicated, was to go through the G League. Well over one hundred coaches have made the jump from the minors to the NBA, including prominent names such as Quin Snyder, Nick Nurse, Taylor Jenkins, Dave Joerger, Luke Walton, and Darvin Ham.

Still, it was hard for Pannone to determine why exactly certain coaches got an opportunity over others. The consistencies were lacking, so trying to make sense of it was futile. Pannone could figure out the blueprint for each of his players, but not for himself. He could tell Malcolm Hill how to get to the NBA, but he wasn't entirely sure of his own formula.

"Being a G League head coach is a phenomenal way to break in, but there is no guarantee—there is no pathway," Pannone said. "And if you're a G League head coach and you don't have a lot of relationships at the NBA level, because my career has been different and unique, it's like, what are you being evaluated on and how do you break in? There is no magic formula. Win games? Done that. Be the top offensive team in the league? Done that. Develop players into multiyear deals, two-way deals, call-ups? Done that. The reality is, for almost all of us, you have to get lucky, and someone has to take a chance on you."

• • •

The Bill Burch Gymnasium had gradually emptied out. Pannone remained, still sitting on the sideline, reflecting on his journey. He was thirty-seven years old, married with three children. He didn't need much more than that to be happy.

Pannone is a simple man. He doesn't desire fancy things; he prefers "Versace" robes designed by his kids and wears baggy sweatpants with a baggy T-shirt on most days. He once teased Joe Young about his designer Balenciaga shoes, comparing them to a pair of socks. His favorite restaurant is Olive Garden; he swears its Alfredo sauce is among the best in the world. During one road trip, Squadron staff members posed the following question to him: "Would you rather add $15,000 to your salary every year but never be able to go to Chipotle or Olive Garden ever again or keep the same salary but you can go to those places whenever you want?" Pannone, somewhat surprisingly, chose the $15,000.

As much as he loves basketball—and he *loves* basketball—Pannone's perspective has evolved through the years. It is more mature now, more pragmatic. He doesn't take the game *too* seriously. Even when the Squadron lost, he graciously thanked the fans as he walked back to the locker room and always brought out waters to the families who stuck around afterward. "There's never a wrong time to do the right thing," he would say. Perhaps his most popular saying during the season was "Character is who you are, every day, all the time, even when no one's watching."

"He's a player's coach," described Young. "He's more focused on how we're doing in the morning. That's his first question before we come in the locker room. 'How are y'all doing? Can I help you?' That's any player's dream to have a coach that really cares about him and wants his players to be great."

"Ryan is a once-in-a-lifetime coach," Cheatham added. "You just don't really meet coaches who actually give a fuck about you, whether the ball is bouncing or not, like actually still genuinely care for you. Ryan is a person who even when I wasn't on his team was still checking on my mom, still sending me clips or advice. He's just a good person. You'll see him helping with bags and shit as a head coach. In my opinion, you don't see that very often. You don't meet guys like him. He's shown me that there are genuine people in business sometimes."

In team meetings, Pannone often invited his players to consider the bigger picture, to keep in mind the things that *truly* mattered. As he told reporters on media day right before the season started, "It's basketball; it's exciting. In reality, especially in the current shape of the world, we're super fortunate. I get to coach a game for a living."

Whether he ever made the NBA or not, Pannone counted himself lucky. The game had brought him to some extraordinary places. The Pelicans front office had trusted him with an incredible opportunity to lead its G League program. It was a joy to come to work every day, to be around this Squadron team. He had other more pressing goals at the top of his mind—making the playoffs, winning the championship, developing his players—and Pannone wouldn't measure success based solely on whether he one day reached the highest level.

"If you can finish your career and look back believing that you did everything that you could, you just didn't get the break—I can live with that," he said, staring out at the Bill Burch court. Without the clamor of balls bouncing and sneakers squeaking, his voice seemed to carry throughout the gym. He continued:

> I can live with never receiving the break to be able to coach in the NBA if I can look back and say I worked extremely hard, I was extremely prepared, I did the right things, I treated people right, I treated the players right, I stuck to my beliefs, I had a core philosophy, and I just didn't make it. Hey, there are a lot of great coaches that are better than me that never made it. They just didn't get the break.
>
> But if I look back on my career and say I didn't work hard enough, I wasn't prepared enough, I wasn't a good person, I was an asshole, I was selfish, I was about myself, then that's on me. It's the same thing you tell the players. Making the NBA or not making the NBA doesn't determine the success of your career. If Joe Young signs another NBA contract tomorrow, he's not a better player than he was today. You can't evaluate the success of your career based on the opportunities that someone else has to give you. I can't sign myself to a contract. If I get an opportunity to coach in the NBA tomorrow, I'm not a better

At Peace

coach than I am today. And the reality is, there are coaches at the high school level, Division III, Division II, NAIA, junior college, second division in Germany, third division in Serbia that are better coaches than me. There are truly great coaches everywhere, all over the world, right? And when you realize that and you can accept that, then you can be at peace. To be an NBA assistant coach is my dream—it is my goal. But whether I achieve that or not won't determine the success that I had in my coaching career. It won't define my career at all. And it won't define my happiness.

Of course, being at peace did not mean the chase was over. Pannone would continue to do everything within his power to get to the NBA—to ensure, no matter what, that he would never look back at his career with any regrets. And hopefully, the break would come.

21. THINKING ABOUT LIFE

Roughly twenty minutes after the final buzzer sounded, Young reemerged from the locker room, still wearing his sweat-soaked black undershirt, uniform shorts, two arm sleeves, two leg sleeves, two pairs of Nike socks, and brown Jordan sneakers. Birmingham had just notched one of its most impressive wins of the season—107–102 over the Agua Caliente Clippers, the top team in the Western Conference—to improve to 5-5. After losing to the South Bay Lakers, the Squadron had won four of five and three straight with Cheatham back in the lineup.

It wasn't unusual for players to retake the Legacy Arena court after a game. Most of the time, guys who saw limited or no action wanted to get some shots up before going home. It was extremely unusual, however, for a player who logged thirty-eight minutes to come back out for extra work, especially when that player had been nursing a knee injury and the team was scheduled to play again the following evening.

Young hadn't shot well in the win—finishing 5 of 19 from the field and 1 of 8 from three—though he did contribute in other ways. His presence always made a difference on offense because he commanded so much attention. He actually had the best plus-minus (+11) on the team that night and turned it over just once against Agua Caliente's stout defense. Still, he was frustrated. After starting the regular season on fire, Young had cooled off. He had hit just four of his last twenty attempts from behind the arc and knew how important his three-point percentage was to scouts.

So, it didn't matter that the Squadron would be taking on the Santa Cruz Warriors in less than twenty-four hours—Young felt compelled to shoot his way out of his slump. The alternative, he knew from experience, was to go home and toss and turn in bed, thinking about his struggles. At around 9:30 p.m., he started a postgame workout with the help of two rebounders. On the opposite basket, Riley LaChance had begun a workout of his own.

Young led with midrange jumpers. He gradually worked his way out to the three-point line, hitting every spot on the floor. He shot in silence, eyes locked on the rim. Fans cleared the seats. Employees quietly went about sweeping the arena. Drowsy security guards lingered by the exits. John Petty Jr. caught up with some friends who had come to watch the game. Joseph Hooven, head of PR, sat at the scorer's table, punching keys on his laptop. LaChance wrapped up his workout and returned to the locker room. Young kept shooting.

And shooting.

And shooting.

He hardly missed.

He continued for forty-five minutes—far longer than the typical postgame workout. He made a total of 450 shots and wrapped up by going 50 for 50 from the free-throw line. After thanking and dismissing his rebounders, he parked himself on the sideline opposite the Squadron bench. He just wanted to sit for a moment and think. Breathe. Reflect.

There were over seventeen thousand seats in Legacy Arena, and only a few were presently occupied. Slouching in his, Young scanned the vacant building. Massive bags had formed under his eyes. He was clearly exhausted. How could he not be? The Squadron had played five games in the last eight days, and Young had played significant minutes in all of them. With defenses keying in on him and refs not blowing many whistles, he had also taken a beating. His right knee, which he massaged softly, had been hurt for a while, but missing games wasn't an option right now, nor was making it public that he was currently dealing with a nagging knee injury. It was better for NBA teams not to know about it than to know that he was fighting through it.

It was more than all that, though. Young wasn't just physically drained—he was mentally drained, psychologically drained, emotionally drained. He wasn't all the way there yet, but for the first time all season, he sounded defeated. He just couldn't understand why his phone wasn't ringing. He had done *everything* the coaches had asked of him, everything the scouts were supposedly looking for—more, even. He had embraced a leadership role and been the ultimate professional on and off the court. He wasn't playing selfishly. He wasn't forcing anything. He wasn't being sloppy or careless with the ball. He was competing on defense, averaging 1.6 steals and sometimes picking up ninety-four feet from the basket. Sure, his shot had been up and down, but he had shown his versatility and broader skill set: 40 points against Stockton, 32 points and 7 assists against Salt Lake City, 16 points and 3 steals against Oklahoma City, 14 points, 11 assists, and 7 rebounds against Rio Grande Valley. And now, with Cheatham back, Birmingham was winning games against good teams.

So why, then, was his phone not ringing? Well, at the moment, it was because his phone was dead. Young seemed content to go off the grid, briefly blocking out the noise. He had been hearing the same message from his agent recently: "You're close!" In some ways, it was encouraging. In others, it was gut-wrenching. He didn't care about being close. He was, just by being in the G League and not China, *close.*

"I've been hearing that this is the most talk there's been. But, you know." He shrugged. "I've done everything that you can do as an elite player that belongs in the NBA."

Yes, NBA teams had expressed interest. But the huge wave of call-ups was also beginning to ebb. High tide was turning to low tide. Young certainly could sense that.

Getting back to the NBA had proven far tougher than he thought it would be. He still couldn't fully wrap his head around the reasons *why.* "You feel like these people forget about you," he said. "You start to think, like, man, what else can you do as a player? What else do y'all want me to do as a player?"

He had understood, from the very beginning, that there were concerns about his past immaturity. But "it wasn't a *bad* immature," he explained. "It was just, like, I went shopping with Paul George, and I probably bought the same shit he bought. That's bad. He comes in with a Ferrari; I come in with a Lamborghini. They don't like me because of that.

"I'm just to the point where I feel like they're laughing at me," he continued. "But I don't know—who knows? People don't understand, I'm not going back overseas. If I don't get back, I'm just going—I'm just going to probably retire. I'm not going back out there. I already told [my agent], like, 'I'm done. Done over the water.' My fam is here. And then I can just put a story out, like, 'Shit, I tried everything I could do to get back.' I ain't a bad person—never been to jail, don't do drugs, I got a family, married. What else do you want out of a vet? Like, goddamn."

Young had mentioned the idea of retiring before in private workouts with strength and conditioning coach Jordan Kincaide (which had dropped off a bit as the season progressed), but jokingly. Here, he sounded more serious. If he wasn't getting a call-up this season—a season that *Sports Illustrated* had dubbed "the year of the replacement player"—then it was hard for him to imagine coming back to the G League.[1] For guys on the fringe, there would likely never be a better opportunity to reach the NBA than the few months when Omicron ran rampant. So if the door was closing on the NBA, and Young had no desire to return overseas, that left limited options. In this moment of distress, retirement seemed to be the most appealing. "It's not quitting," he added. "It's like . . . shit, it's enough when you've done everything. *Y'all want me to win a championship in the G League?*"

Schmidt, the Squadron's head athletic trainer, walked over to let Young know that an ice bath was waiting for him in the locker room. "I'm gonna ride back with you—I'm about to get in the cold tub," Young told him. "I'm just thinking about life right now, man."

He couldn't bring himself to leave the court—not yet. He spent some time studying the game's stat sheet. He pondered what scouts were *really* looking for, considering that he had shown an ability to do pretty much everything throughout the season.

Why hadn't it earned him a call-up? What were the real reasons he was still here? When Young thought *deeply* about it—taking into account his past and all the mistakes he had made—he still struggled to find an explanation.

"I think they just—I don't know," he said, his voice trembling. "I don't even know what to say." There was a long pause, a silence made even heavier by the sight of an empty arena, and the bright lights beaming down on him. "I'm going to take a little nap now and think about it," Young finally said, crawling down onto the court. It harkened back to his days with the Pacers, when he used to sleep at the team's practice facility, waking up throughout the night to get more shots up.

It was 10:30 p.m., quiet enough in the building now that falling asleep wouldn't be so difficult. Young requested that ten minutes be added to the arena's clock; the loud buzzer would wake him from his slumber. He sprawled out by the three-point line, cradling a basketball in his left arm.

"I'm trying to get back to my dreams," he said, "so I gotta sit here and dream real quick."

22. FOR THE LOVE

Billy Campbell was behind on *Billions*. As associate general manager, his free time was limited during the season. Tonight, though, he would catch up on one of his favorite TV shows. The team was at the Guest House at Graceland hotel in Memphis. Earlier that evening, it had won its fifth straight game—a 129–116 rout of the Memphis Hustle. Seven players scored in double figures, led by Harper's 23. Young pitched in 4 steals, Ra'Shad James buried 4 three-pointers, and recent addition Darius Adams contributed 21 points off the bench.

At the moment, all was well. Moods were lifted. Smiles were plentiful. Following their win over Agua Caliente a week prior, Birmingham had toppled Santa Cruz 122–110 on Classic Hip-Hop Night at Legacy Arena. Pannone coached part of the game in one of the free Squadron bucket hats distributed to fans. Cheatham, who posted 18 points and 10 rebounds, swaggered to the locker room afterward, screaming, "I love winning! Another one!" He blasted "Dreams and Nightmares" by Meek Mill while receiving postgame treatment, rapping along with Ra'Shad James and Zach Hankins.

So all was definitely well. Cheatham would even receive a ten-day contract from the Pelicans just before the Squadron went on the road. It was more of a nice gesture than anything else, as he would be staying with Birmingham ("on assignment") for the full ten days, but his pockets were suddenly much heavier. On the team's next flight to Memphis, he was sitting in first class.

Another decisive victory—this one against the Hustle—left Campbell overjoyed as he got back to Graceland. The team would travel to Sioux Falls via Dallas in the morning, leaving for the airport at 9:00 a.m. Campbell watched an episode of *Billions* and was about to go to sleep when his phone buzzed. It was a notification from American Airlines: the Squadron's flight from Memphis to Dallas had been canceled. Campbell looked at the clock: 12:44 a.m.

Ugh.

This needed to be handled. *Right away.* And it wasn't going to be an easy fix; icy conditions had been impacting travel in the area for a few days, so options were limited. Campbell called Chasanoff—asleep; he called Pannone—asleep as well. He texted the team chat and emailed the league office, just so everyone was aware of the situation, but Campbell was on his own.

Birmingham had one off day to reach Sioux Falls before a 3:00 p.m. game against the Skyforce the following afternoon. Campbell got on the phone with the travel agency's help desk. Making new arrangements would have been stressful enough if he was traveling alone—*this* was torture. Campbell had to figure out how to get twenty people to Sioux Falls as soon as possible. After roughly three hours of deliberation, he came to a less-than-ideal solution: divide the team into groups for several different itineraries.

Of course, those itineraries were not equal in convenience. Since arrival times to Sioux Falls varied, Campbell had to determine who should be on each flight. The starters should get there first, he reasoned, along with Pannone and Schmidt. Campbell plotted it all out in a spreadsheet, dropped the plan in the team chat, and finally climbed into bed at 3:30 a.m., setting an alarm for four hours later.

He awoke to more bad news: there were apparently fewer seats available than expected on the flights that Campbell had "booked." The painstaking process began again. A team meeting was called for 10:30 a.m. in the Blues Room at the Graceland. Everyone crammed in with their suitcases. Campbell wrote the options—now four of them, none of them particularly appealing—on a giant whiteboard. The room spiraled into chaos, with players voicing their preferences, Campbell fielding more phone calls, and changes being made in real time.

One way or another, everyone got to Sioux Falls. A few players flew from Memphis to Atlanta, from Atlanta to Minneapolis, and from Minneapolis to Sioux Falls. Pannone also *drove* a group from Minneapolis, pulling up to the hotel after 2:00 a.m. Saint and Huang did not arrive until closer to 11:00 a.m, right before the team gathered for a walk-through in the John Q. Hammons Room at the Sheraton (the same Sheraton where, almost fifteen years earlier, Renaldo Major had learned that he was going to the NBA). Coaches clutched extra-large coffees. Piled onto a luggage cart were bananas, protein bars, and waters. Now that everyone was here, it didn't matter how strenuous the journey. Two of the organization's standards—established during training camp—still applied:

It is a league full of excuses—don't have them.
Embrace the suckiness.

Birmingham (7-5) was expected to beat Sioux Falls (3-9). But while the Squadron experienced the travel day from hell, Skyforce players were at home, as comfortable as people can be in dreary 20-degree weather (according to locals, this was "T-shirt and shorts" weather for early February). The game would be a test of Birmingham's resiliency. Pannone would only play the guys willing to go "super fucking hard," even if that meant shifting his rotation. He did what he could to raise the team's energy, dancing into the locker room before his pregame speech.

Energy turned out not to be an issue, but when Harper tweaked his hip in the second quarter, it was hard to imagine that the demanding schedule and onerous travel experience had nothing to do with it. Up 62–51 at the break, Pannone received word from Schmidt that Harper would not be able to return, though the injury was thankfully not too severe.

"Who do you want to start for the second half?" Saint asked.

Pannone thought for a while, rubbing his chin. Harper, a player he once referred to as his "security blanket," was irreplaceable.

"Jared?" Pannone finally replied, smiling.

Petty, the rookie guard from Alabama, eventually got the nod. Squadron coaches were pleased with his development so far this season, and there was still so much more to unlock. The organization was hopeful that Petty—a six-foot-five sharpshooter—would become a significant contributor in the NBA one day. His growth was a credit to the staff and to veteran teammates like Young, whom Petty called his "big brother." Young offered him countless basketball tips—moves to try, workouts to do, pregame routines to follow—and shared details about his own past mistakes. He wanted to prepare Petty for *everything* a future in the NBA might present.

"He just told me about the league and how it is once you get there, once you start getting money and just how people treat you after that," Petty explained. "Like, everybody wants their handout. And he told me how people were always asking him for this, asking him for that. He said it got to a point where he was helping everybody so much, he forgot about himself. That's one thing he told me—make sure you take care of yourself."

Petty was glad to have Young around but, frankly, shocked that he still was. How had his "big brother" not been called up? He repeatedly told Young, "They can't keep overlooking what you're doing. They just can't." But, in all honesty, Petty didn't know if that was true. His understanding of the business side of basketball was still limited. What he did understand full well was that Young seemed to possess more talent than most of their peers—talent that Petty marveled at in every game.

Against the Skyforce, Young went for 28 points on 11 of 15 shooting. On one play, he picked up his man—the familiar Mario Chalmers, who was back in the G League after ten days with the Miami Heat—ninety-four feet from the basket, stole the ball, and lobbed it up to Cheatham for a slam.

Despite Young's performance, Birmingham saw its lead gradually diminish in the second half, eventually falling 111–104. With a normal day of travel and Harper in the mix—or even just one of those things—it might have been a different story. But a loss was a loss, and there were no excuses in a league full of them.

• • •

Hill didn't have to worry about last-minute cancellations anymore. He wasn't squeezing into middle seats on Southwest flights, either. Life was comfortable in the NBA. More than comfortable—it was *lavish*. He was flying private, staying in upscale hotels, getting generous per diems. Now that he was signed through the rest of the season, he had a nice apartment in downtown Chicago, close to the team's practice facility.

By mid-February, Hill was decidedly out of the Bulls' rotation. The worst of Omicron had passed, and previously injured players had returned to the lineup. Hill's situation made it easy to grow complacent. "You can just be like, 'F it. I'm in the league, this is good enough for me. Let me enjoy this,'" Hill said. "You just gotta keep going, man—every day, day by day."

Hill's grind was different now but just as demanding. His focus had shifted from "make it to the NBA" to "stick in the NBA." Accomplishing the former far from guaranteed the latter. Players in Hill's position often landed *right back* in the minors, enjoying merely a cup of tea in the NBA. Hill was signed through the rest of the season, but beyond that, it all hung in the balance.

G League call-ups couldn't afford to just fit in. NBA coaches did not assess Malcolm Hills like they assessed others on the roster. Hill needed to put in *more* work, to have no slip-ups. "You walk in there one day half-stepping, they got you," said Langston Galloway, a former D-Leaguer who turned a ten-day contract into seven seasons in the NBA. "They're going to be like, 'Look, we appreciate all you've done.' And you're out the door, just like that."

The definition of half-stepping is different for a fringe player. Half-stepping for Galloway and Hill might be full-stepping for a first-round draft pick. When Galloway was called up to the New York Knicks in 2015, he had this ominous sense that someone was always watching him. If he made a mistake, someone would catch it. If he slacked off, someone would notice it. In Galloway's mind, the solution was simple—well, not simple, but straightforward: *strive for perfection*.

That was Hill's mission now: be as close to perfect as humanly possible. He came in early to work out and stayed late to get up shots. He ate right and took care of his body. He studied scouting reports and analyzed film. He did whatever Coach Donovan requested of him.

These were things that Troy Daniels, a one-time D-Leaguer who played seven seasons in the NBA, called the "givens." Miami Heat guard Gabe Vincent, who appeared in 55 games in the G from 2018 to 2020, referred to them as "the baseline." Don't do those things, both Daniels and Vincent stressed, and you have no chance of sticking.

Fringe players have to be the teacher's pets, always willing to go the extra mile, catering to the team's every need. Want me to change positions? Done. Guard that superstar? I'm on it. Run sprints? No problem. Carry these bags? Easy. Sing a song? Let me just warm up my vocal cords.

"You can call it however you want to call it," said Daniels. "People might laugh at you or whatever, but you know, my career lasted a lot longer than those people that were laughing."

For Hill, the million-dollar question—literally, a question worth millions of dollars—was, how do I impact winning? Or, to be more specific, how do I impact winning when I'm not even playing?

Vincent explained, "I think that's something that people also struggle with in our position. Every night it's going to be something different. Your impact might look different, might be greater, might be smaller, it might be you clapping, it might be you keeping the star's head level or just being the ear for him to bitch to before he goes back out there and plays. It's just constantly evolving."

At the absolute least, Hill had to be a good teammate. A *phenomenal* teammate. That meant cheering like a Little League parent from the sideline and bringing nothing but positive energy to the locker room. Perhaps no one in the NBA performed this role better than Mavericks guard and former G Leaguer Theo Pinson.

Pinson, who mostly warmed the bench, was known as the NBA's premier hype man. Mavericks head coach Jason Kidd labeled him the MVP of the team. Every night, Pinson made the sideline his personal playground. He celebrated three-pointers like college acceptance letters and dunks like winning lottery tickets. He trash-talked opponents relentlessly. He barked out coverages and schemes.

"I think everybody looks at me like, 'Theo's just out there screaming and talking junk, blah, blah, blah,'" Pinson said. "I'm like, yeah, I talk a little junk, but most of it is helping my teammates and remembering the coverages. I say this all the time: it's easy when you're tired and you're getting a little fatigued to forget what the coverage is—you're just out there playing basketball. And if you got somebody helping you on the back end, talking, it helps out the whole team. It's something that I found value in and the team found value in, and I continue to do it."

Even the embellished celebrations—the synchronized dances and oh-my-God-what-the-hell-just-happened facial expressions—are valued by coaches. That stuff *matters*, so much so that during film sessions in Birmingham, Pannone would sometimes sprinkle in clips of the Squadron's best bench reactions. Not to get a laugh—he would encourage his players to do more. He once referred to guard Justin Wright-Foreman, who was acquired by Birmingham in February, as the team's "TikTok All-Star."

Not every call-up had to be like Theo Pinson; there wasn't enough coffee in the world for that. "I think it can look like a lot of different things," said Vincent. "I might not be as theatrical as Theo, but there is a way that I can impact my teammates and uplift them and move the needle even when I'm not in the game."

Hill recognized the importance of doing so. "You have to," he said. "That's the least I have to offer since I'm not playing. Being on a roster, it's more than just what you can do on the basketball court. What other things do you have to offer a team? Which I think allows guys to stick around—being vocal, encouraging, positive, good locker-room dude."

When opportunities to play did come, Hill needed to seize every one of them. It didn't matter how small or seemingly insignificant; every sliver counted.

"I think the *biggest* thing in my career was taking advantage of every opportunity," Daniels emphasized. The six-foot-four guard was called up to the Houston Rockets from the Rio Grande Valley Vipers in March 2014. For the next month, he barely saw the floor—a couple of garbage minutes here, a couple more there. But Daniels did not take a single second lightly.

On the final day of the regular season, the Rockets rested several of their key players, having secured the number four seed in the Western Conference. Daniels moved into the starting lineup and erupted for 22 points, shooting an efficient 6 of 11 from behind the arc. Houston lost the game, and maybe ten people in the world cared. Daniels was obviously one of them. Another was Rockets head coach Kevin McHale, whose trust in Daniels was mounting, despite the rookie logging just seventy-five total minutes throughout the season. *They were seventy-five* good *minutes*, McHale thought—good enough to give the D-Leaguer a chance in Houston's first-round playoff series against the Portland Trail Blazers.

During a thrilling Game Three, Daniels buried the biggest shot of the night. Tied at 116–116 with less than fifteen seconds remaining, he nailed a three-pointer to put Houston on top. Portland failed to answer, and the Rockets secured the 121–116 victory. Daniels was the hero. "Just a couple weeks ago, he was in the D-League," superstar James Harden said in his postgame press conference. "Now he saved our season."

Daniels would never return to the minors after that, appearing in seven straight NBA seasons and earning more than $14 million in contracts. "I'm pretty sure I was not going to play in the playoffs," he later reflected. "But when it came down to it, [McHale] looked down the bench and called my name, just because in those last eight games in the regular season, I took advantage of those opportunities. People probably had turned their TVs off at that time."

So every opportunity was crucial, even the ones that felt meaningless. Hill was mindful of that. On February 7, he checked into a game against the Phoenix Suns with 1:41 left on the clock and the Bulls trailing 127–112. As fans headed for the exits, Hill scored a quick 8 points, going 3 for 3 from the field. The performance garnered some attention on social media, since it turned a bunch of winning gamblers (who bet Phoenix on the spread) into shell-shocked losers.

Throughout February Hill's role fluctuated, then diminished, then disappeared. He grew discouraged at times, sharing those emotions with his father, Malcolm Sr.

"Don't be disappointed," he told Malcolm. "You're in the NBA! Look how hard it was and how long it took you to get there, and you did it. When you look back on this year, you're going to think, *Wow!*"

Dad was right. Hill would look back on this season one day with wonder. But right now, he was too caught up in the grind. He was fully committed to taking all the necessary steps to carve out a role. To *stick*.

Yes, that process was arduous. When Atlanta Hawks center Clint Capela, who played thirty-eight games with the Vipers in 2014–15, described it, he had to pause for several breaths: "Also show that you can defend, also show that you have energy, also show that you're a good teammate, also show that you can be on time, also show that you can cheer on the bench. There's other stuff too. It's a grind, man. It's hard."

At this point, nothing would deter Hill from that grind—not the private planes, not the upscale hotels, not the per diems. As he often said, "I do this for the love and not the benefit."

• • •

After a short break in mid-February for All-Star Weekend, the Squadron headed west. The team would play two games against the Santa Cruz Warriors, then fly to Ontario, California, for a back-to-back against the Agua Caliente Clippers. Both Harper and Cheatham would not make the trip.

Harper had been selected to join the USA World Cup Qualifying Team for two games in Washington DC. It was a nice addition to his résumé and gave him the chance to impress a new group of NBA-connected folks. The team was coached by Jim Boylen, the former head coach of the Chicago Bulls and a friend of Pannone's, and consisted of longtime NBA players such as Langston Galloway and Joe Johnson.

Harper shot poorly during the event, missing all seven of his attempts from behind the arc, yet his offensive skill set and athleticism still stuck out to teammates. Galloway was particularly awed by Harper's leaping ability. At five feet ten, the diminutive point guard could dunk the ball with ease. Harper's vertical jump was actually the fifth-highest recorded at the 2019 NBA Draft Combine and ranked first when Kincaide tested players on the Squadron. Galloway saw Harper as an "NBA talent"; he just needed the right opportunity.

"It's going to come," Galloway said. "He just has to continue chipping away and keep working, and I think it's going to open up, because he works hard, he wants to get better. And that's all you can ask for."

Cheatham was absent from the Squadron for a different reason: his mom's health was rapidly deteriorating. He had been quiet about her cancer battle throughout the season, always wearing a smile. Privately, though, he was hurting. Even amid her fight, Carolyn remained his biggest fan, messaging him after games to praise his performances.

Following an early-season loss to Texas, Cheatham was extremely hard on himself. He had been dominated inside by the seven-foot-two Moses Brown, one of the few times he looked completely overmatched. By the time he got on the bus, Cheatham had already received a text from his mom, saying that he played great. It made him chuckle. No matter what, she *always* said that he played great.

During the most important year of his professional career, Cheatham was carrying the heaviest weight imaginable. It grew heavier as the months passed. His season was becoming more hectic; her cancer was becoming more aggressive. Cheatham couldn't let it affect his game. He had to cope with the situation *and still* perform on the court.

"When you put on the jersey and you step on the court, unfortunately not everyone has all the context of everything," Squadron general manager Marc Chasanoff said. "You don't know who's watching you that game. Whether you play phenomenal or you play like shit, it could sway a decision one way or the other. You just don't know. Zylan's mentality, his perseverance—he wants it so bad."

Cheatham went back to South Phoenix for the All-Star break. He knew his mom was in bad shape, but it was heartbreaking to see her up close. She couldn't walk or talk; didn't have any energy. Cheatham vowed not to leave her side, not while she was suffering like this. He would put his career on hold, even if that meant sacrificing another shot at the NBA. He called Chasanoff and Pannone and told them that he needed to stay in Phoenix. They expressed their utmost support.

"As much as my career is important to me, my mom is the most important thing, so I felt like it was just a time where she really needed me," Cheatham said. "It was hard to not show up there for my guys, but I feel like anybody who has a mother would understand."

Cheatham developed a home routine—he would wake up early, eat a quick breakfast, work out, and then go to the hospital where his mom had been admitted. He would sit next to her for the rest of the day. Visiting hours went until 8:00 p.m., but Cheatham always begged the nurses to let him stay later. He could usually buy an extra thirty minutes, sometimes an hour. "I would just stay by her side until they kicked me out," he said.

"He loves that woman dearly," Darvis Fletcher, Cheatham's best friend, said. Fletcher was in Phoenix with Cheatham at that time. "He'll go above and beyond for her—anything necessary. He would go work out and go right back to where mom was at and sit with her all day. And he would repeat that literally every day. It was definitely a tough time. With Z, he won't really show you all the time, but I know because I've been around. He definitely wasn't himself. He was down."

Being home was always a reminder of how far Cheatham had come—*of who he was playing for.* He carried the city with him wherever he went. The Arizona Diamondbacks *A* logo is tattooed across his burly right bicep. Just below it is a rendering of the antennas that sit atop South Mountain, which overlooks downtown Phoenix. Part of Cheatham's motivation to reach the NBA was a desire to serve his community. When he signed a three-year NBA contract in 2020, he began exploring ways to give back, including through the establishment of a new foundation that would support the children of incarcerated parents. Only one year of his contract would be paid out, however, after Cheatham was waived by the Thunder. He could still help South Phoenix, and still did, but not to the extent he desired—not the way he felt the city deserved.

"I have mixed emotions about it because to a certain extent, I want to show them that before you get there, you can still show love and do shit for the hood, which I've done," he explained. "But at the same time, I want to get all the way there before I really come back and do it the right way, because I don't want to just do it one time. I want to be able to do it for a period of time and get some shit really started."

With Cheatham at home, his mom's condition gradually improved. Her energy increased. Her spirits rose. She was doing far better than when he first arrived. Cheatham reported back to Birmingham at the beginning of March. The team had just returned from its long West Coast trip, having lost three of four games without Cheatham and Harper.

Cheatham was excited to rejoin the group. The way that they embraced him as a leader, as a friend, meant a lot to him—more than they probably knew. And, of course, the court was his "happy place," his escape from reality. When he was playing, nothing else consumed him. He looked free, joyful, unburdened, like all that weight he was carrying was momentarily lifted. "That's why this team is just so important to me," he said, speaking after his first game back, a 123–109 victory over the Texas Legends.

"It's just great to be back, man," he added, grinning wide. "That's all I can say."

23. WE ALL WE GOT

There are fewer call-ups to the NBA come March, which means that the primary motivation for G League players is disappearing—*fast*. The carrot that's been dangled in front of their faces since training camp has been chewed down to its stem. For some teams, especially those out of playoff contention, this changes *everything*. The investment in winning plummets. Team basketball becomes hero basketball. Attitudes shift from *I'll follow the blueprint* to *Screw it, I'll make my own blueprint*. Of course, disjointed teams stand no chance of winning a G League championship. But also, disjointed teams *don't care* about winning a G League championship.

All of this was top of mind when the Squadron front office began assembling its team over the 2021 summer. Pannone and his staff had coached a group that was fragmented and at times apathetic during their first season together in Erie. It was a young squad, talented but not cohesive. Their unity crumbled when adversity hit.

This year's roster was constructed with more care, informed by those past mistakes. The move to Birmingham had provided a blank slate—an opportunity to establish a new culture.

"The culture that we're trying to build is based off of good people," Pannone said on the first day of training camp. "And anything that's built off of culture starts with the people in the organization, your coaching staff. That would be the foundation of your culture, and then the players are built on it. So if there's a crack within your foundation or within the building blocks of the house that you're making, your culture is going to break. And we had some experiences with that the first year, and that's why the point of emphasis, number one, is just get high character, good people that love the game. That's the very first thing we looked for."

That approach, however simple it sounds, was not ubiquitous in the league. For the Squadron, it had proven incredibly successful. The team was close-knit, unselfish, committed; it cared about the right things. Coaches were not the least bit worried about fracturing, even as the calendar flipped to March.

The house was very much intact.

• • •

There was another disease outbreak on the Squadron in mid-March. This time, it was the flu's turn to wreak havoc. Harper and Wright-Foreman tested positive first, leaving the team with just eight players as it traveled to Texas for a game against the Austin Spurs.

When Young awoke at the Hilton Garden Inn Cedar Park on game day, he, too, had flu-like symptoms. And center Zach Hankins had a concerning amount of swelling in his surgically repaired knee. So less than ten hours before tip-off, the Squadron were down to six players. Chasanoff called the league office right away, hoping to get the game canceled. Proceeding with six players was not just absurd; it was dangerous. This was Birmingham's fourth game in six days, and the threat of an injury was real.

Chasanoff and Campbell exchanged fifteen calls that afternoon, each with a different update on the process. It was dragging along, with no clarity from the league. Campbell knew, from his experience working as a basketball operations coordinator for the D-League, that officials were hesitant to cancel games unless the circumstances were extraordinary. And the definition of extraordinary was a bit different in the minors.

Everyone met in the lobby around 5:00 p.m., with the bus waiting outside to shuttle them to the arena. Chasanoff called again with a more definitive ruling: "We're not going to play," he told the team on speaker phone. "For your health and safety, we do not feel like it's appropriate. We don't want anyone to risk their career."

Players wanted to make doubly sure of the decision before switching gears mentally. "So . . . what's the percent chance that we're going to play?" they asked.

"We are 90 percent not going to play," Chasanoff replied.

Ninety percent? Okay, that was pretty conclusive. A few players returned to their rooms. Ra'Shad James and John Petty Jr. fired up *Call of Duty*. Others stayed in the lobby to watch the NCAA Tournament. Campbell was fidgety. The whole situation brought him anxiety. He didn't think guys should relax until it was *100 percent* certain that the game was off. He was concerned about the potential consequences of them not showing up without a formal cancellation. *What might the league do to discipline them?* he pondered.

Chasanoff called a last time, just an hour and a half before tip-off, with a new plan. "We're playing," he said. "We gotta get on the bus." The league had threatened the team with fines and other punishments. Rumors swirled that they could potentially be banned from the playoffs. A message was dropped in the team chat: "Game is on. Bus is leaving in five minutes."

What followed was something out of a sports movie. The Squadron pulled up in time for a very abbreviated warm-up. Birmingham had seven active players—six and a half, really, since Hankins was fighting through knee pain. One of those seven was Jordan Swing, a veteran forward acquired less than twenty hours earlier. Swing had been overseas playing for BC Kyiv in Ukraine but managed to escape just before the war with Russia began. Another was Daulton Hommes, who started the season on a two-way contract with the Pelicans, was waived in December, and rejoined the Squadron in late February.

Birmingham fell behind—*way* behind. Which, given its predicament, was to be expected. No Harper, no Young, basically no pregame. With a minute left in the third quarter, the Squadron trailed 91–69. Frankly, it made sense to just concede, to look ahead to the next game, to not risk any freak injuries. But the guys kept fighting. Riley LaChance and Ra'Shad James scored key buckets. The wounded Hankins hit a nice hook shot. Cheatham bounded all over the floor, swallowing every rebound and protecting the rim. Hommes couldn't miss from behind the arc, sinking seven total three-pointers in the game, including one that cut the deficit to 100–98 with thirty seconds left. Birmingham had a chance to tie or win it on the final possession. The ball was inbounded to Cheatham by the right corner, he took two dribbles to his left, elevated for a fourteen-foot jump shot and . . . *clank*. It hit the front rim.

Two-thousand fans breathed a sigh of relief. Cheatham fell to the ground, glaring up at the basket with an expression that said, *How did I miss that?*

The loss was heartbreaking, of course, but there was no reason for Cheatham—or any of his six teammates that evening—to hang his head. This was more than a moral victory; it was a confidence booster.

"That definitely gave us a mindset that we can kind of roll with the punches and deal with anything that's thrown at us," said LaChance. "I think that definitely gave us confidence going forward and put us in the mindset that we can rattle off a bunch in a row here and get ourselves in a good position for the playoffs."

• • •

Ra'Shad James was a star in the G League before it was even called the G League. He spent three seasons in the minors from 2013 to 2016—averaging 20.8 points in 2014–15—before embarking overseas, where he suited up for teams in eight different countries. This was year nine of his career, and although James was still hopeful for a call-up, he was very much at peace with his journey no matter what happened.

James was one of few players who had remained with the Squadron all season. Harper, Cheatham, and Hill were back and forth from the NBA; Holder and Adams had been waived; Banks had been traded to the Texas Legends. James was in Birmingham the entire time, with his role constantly shifting and his minutes constantly fluctuating. One night he would start; another he would play fifteen minutes off the bench. He was the ultimate professional regardless.

As Birmingham entered the final stretch of the season, James introduced a new team mantra: "We all we got." It was as fitting as it was catchy. The slogan reflected both the players' togetherness and their commitment to being present—to focusing on the opportunity right in front of them (a G League championship), as opposed to the one that might exist down the road (the NBA).

Given the condensed season, the playoff race was extremely tight. Only the top six seeds from each conference would make the tournament. Squadron coaches wrote the West standings on the whiteboard in the locker room at Birmingham-Southern, updating the order every morning. On March 20—two weeks before the playoffs were set to begin—it appeared as follows:

1. Rio Grande Valley (21-7)
2. South Bay (17-8)
3. Aqua Caliente (17-10)
4. Texas (14-14)
5. Stockton (13-13)
6. Austin (13-13)
7. Birmingham (13-13)
8. Oklahoma City (14-16)
9. Iowa (12-14)
10. Memphis (13-16)
11. Sioux Falls (12-16)

In the wake of a brutal home loss to Sioux Falls, which Pannone believed to be the team's worst of the season, Birmingham responded with two dominant victories. First, it got payback on Sioux Falls with a 136–95 drubbing; then it destroyed the Legends, 127–97, in front of a raucous Legacy Arena crowd of 3,233.

That resurgence put the Squadron in position to lock down a playoff spot with a win at Iowa. At 11:00 a.m. on the morning of the game, the New Orleans Pelicans announced that they were signing Harper to a two-way contract—*again*. The team had promoted Jose Alvarado to a standard contract so that the rookie guard—now a solidified part of their rotation—would be eligible for the NBA playoffs. That left a spot open, and New Orleans was quick to award it to Harper.

Harper wasn't going anywhere, though. New Orleans wanted him to stay in the G League and help the Squadron pursue a championship. Less than

We All We Got

twelve hours later, Birmingham got one step closer, defeating Iowa 114–106 to clinch its first-ever playoff berth. Harper put up 22 points and 5 assists, Young led the team with 24 points, and Hankins notched his fifth double-double of the season.

Back in the visiting locker room, the guys sprayed water like champagne. They mobbed Pannone, dumping what was left of the cooler on his shiny bald head. Music blasted from the speakers, including—*Wait . . . is that Zylan?* Cheatham rapped in his spare time and occasionally, when the vibe was right, played his music for the team.

Making the postseason was an achievement worth celebrating, but only for a couple of hours. The job was far from finished.

· · ·

The final game of the regular season was a matchup with the Hustle out in Memphis, a city the coaches loved to visit for one reason and one reason only: Gibson's Donuts.

The bus went straight to the little shop on Mount Moriah Road, with its beckoning neon sign. Pannone bought a dozen, and that was just to hold him over for the next twenty-four hours. He scarfed down five right away, bested only by player-development coach Andrew Warren, who devoured seven in record time. When LaChance and Hommes compared the shop's signature glazed doughnuts to that of Krispy Kreme, Pannone told them, with a straight face, "I feel bad for you that you think that." A Gibson's glazed, Pannone went on (of course, he would not let this go), was like a 40 percent three-point shooter. And a Krispy Kreme? That was like a 33 percent three-point shooter. One was great; one was *eh*.

There would be more trips to Gibson's, but there was other—more import-ant, even Pannone had to admit—business to attend to. Beating Memphis, which sat at 15-18, would secure the Squadron home-court advantage for the first round of the playoffs. That was no small thing, particularly for a new organization and even more so for a new organization *in Birmingham*. Locals appreciated winning. A playoff game—perhaps a playoff *win*—would help build significant fan support.

Not that support was lacking. It had grown steadily over the season, enough to give the staff tremendous hope for the future. Fans varied from business owners entertaining clients, to families enjoying an evening out, to UA and AU alumni who showed up with signs for Petty ("Petty's Platoon") and Harper ("Harper's Heroes"). Even a few superfans had emerged, including Kelvin Davis, the sixty-two-year-old man from open tryouts. Davis liked to stay close to the team in the rare event that it might need an extra player during a game. "I'm so optimistic; who knows what's going to happen during the year?" he said with a smile. "*I'm still here, guys!*"

By no means was Legacy Arena *rocking* for Squadron games. It was more like gently swaying. Part of the problem was the sheer size of the building. The average attendance for the season was 2,470, which ranked third in the entire G League (the average across the league was 1,598). But the atmosphere felt crazier at venues like Kaiser Permanente Arena, home of the Santa Cruz Warriors, because its full capacity was a mere 2,505.

The goal was "to throw twenty-four parties for twenty-four home games," said David Lane, the Squadron general manager of business operations, prior to the season. And the organization had succeeded at that goal. There was everything from HBCU (historically Black colleges and universities) Night, when the entire Miles College marching band occupied a section of the lower bowl; to Star Wars Night, when entry came with a free Squadron lightsaber; to Literacy Day, when the shrill screams of hundreds of kids left players plugging their ears. Halftime shows leaned more toward the absurd, with cookie eating contests and random three-on-three games between fans. A man named Andy, who worked at a popular local brewery, attended every game and led "Let's go, Squadron!" chants. These were parties, yes—just *minor league* parties.

A playoff game, though, would be the biggest party yet. Staff members had already begun preparing for the possibility, selling refundable tickets and organizing marketing efforts. It would all be for nothing if the team did not beat Memphis.

But the team beat Memphis.

Birmingham fell behind early, maintained composure, clawed its way back, and seized total control in the second half. Seven players scored in double figures. The ball zipped around the court, resulting in 35 assists and 18 three-pointers. It was a tutorial on how to run Coach Pannone's offense, and it

We All We Got

left the mastermind beaming on the sideline. The final score was 126–111, Birmingham's fifth straight victory. The team would return to Legacy Arena to host the Texas Legends in the playoffs.

Walking off the court, Pannone looked overwhelmed, as if a host of different emotions were hitting him at the same time. "Fuck," he mumbled quietly, smiling and shaking his head. He was otherwise rendered speechless. After pacing in the hallway for a minute, he took a deep breath and entered the locker room.

Most of his postgame speech focused on the Squadron's unsung heroes, players such as James and LaChance, who, over the past six months, had filled every conceivable role. It was an element unique to the G League, a product of the constant roster changes. Those who stayed put jumped from understudies to leads—from leads to understudies—as the season ran its course.

"I want to acknowledge something that is very important to me," Pannone said to the team, his voice quavering. "I know sometimes the rotations are frustrating, and I appreciate how well you guys handle it. Some games you might play twenty minutes, some games you might play two minutes. I understand it is very difficult. And the way that you guys have handled that is a big reason why we are here—a big, big, big fucking reason. It is not anything personal or intentional. I want to acknowledge that we would not be here in the position to host a playoff game without how professional you guys are and how well you've handled the role. So, I just want to say thank you."

"Appreciate that, Coach!" James hollered.

"Hell of a fucking job," Pannone continued. "Look at what we've done: five in a row. You guys have earned every bit of this. You've responded. You fought for this. Now we get home-court advantage in the playoffs. Tomorrow will be an off day. Recovery is mandatory. We have one day to prepare. On your off day, watch our last Texas game. Watch some of their recent games. How we approach this mentally is going to determine how we handle it. Also, Zylan asked to stop at the liquor store on the way home."

Players leaned forward in anticipation, like students waiting for the final bell to ring.

"You guys have earned it. . . . We will stop at the liquor store."

"HELL YEAH!" Cheatham screamed.

"I ask you to remain profess—"

Pannone's voice was drowned out by a rowdy ovation. *Professional*, he meant to say. But to hell with that.

The ride home felt like the perfect—almost storybook—ending to a surreal year. Bellies were full with Olive Garden, per Pannone's request. Leftover bread sticks made their way up and down the aisles. As the bus cruised on Interstate 22 through the pitch black, players sipped from beer cans and sang along to a playlist of throwback anthems. They took turns controlling the speaker, each player trying to top the last with his song choice, everything from "21 Questions" by 50 Cent to "Shawty Is Da Shit" by The-Dream to "Can You Stand the Rain" by New Edition:

Sunny days, everybody loves them
Tell me, baby, can you stand the rain?
Storms will come
This we know for sure (This we know for sure)
Can you stand the rain?

They snapped their fingers and danced in their seats. They talked about the upcoming playoff game, how electric Legacy Arena might be. They swapped stories and shared laughs. For four hours, no one even thought about the NBA.

For a fleeting moment, they were all exactly where they wanted to be.

24. WIN OR GO HOME

An empty gym is Joe Young's sanctuary.

The night before the Squadron's playoff game, Young met Coach Huang at Legacy Arena for a workout. Apart from them, the building was vacant. Peaceful.

Young had recently dreamed that he was called up to the NBA. His kids shook him awake, wondering why he was celebrating in his sleep. Even when he was conscious, he could still feel the energy of a rowdy Gainbridge Fieldhouse (home of the Pacers), still smell the buttered popcorn that used to waft out of the stands.

He missed it.

He longed to experience it again.

Albeit not the same, the looming playoff game against Texas still brought Young excitement. A smile never left his face as he went through his shooting routine. He worked on everything: floaters, bank shots, off-the-dribble pull-ups, three-pointers, free throws. By the time he slumped into a courtside seat, he was dripping sweat.

Four months earlier, the Squadron had held a players-only meeting on this floor. "We're here . . . might as well take full advantage," Cheatham told the team that day.

Those words resonated with Young, even more now than back then. *He was here . . . might as well take full advantage.* And maybe, just maybe, a championship would get him out of here.

• • •

It was win or go home. The first round of the G League playoffs is single elimination. Birmingham (the number four seed) would host a familiar opponent in the Texas Legends (the number five seed). The teams had met five times throughout the year, with Texas winning the overall series, 3-2. But in their most recent clash just ten days prior, the Squadron coasted to a 127–97 victory. Sure, the Legends might have been the better team earlier in the season. But now? No way. Birmingham felt untouchable.

If the team beat Texas—ahem, *when* the team beat Texas—the Squadron would face the one-seeded Rio Grande Valley Vipers two nights later. Vipers head coach Mahmoud Abdelfattah had privately admitted to Saint that Birmingham was the one team he did not want to meet in the playoffs. Flights to the Rio Grande Valley were already booked. A group would leave at 5:55 a.m. the morning after the Texas game; another contingent would be on a 7:30 a.m. flight; and the remaining would depart at 9:07 a.m. Players were advised to pack their suitcases *before* coming to Legacy. That way, *when* the Squadron won, they would already be prepared for the trip.

It stormed the day of the game. A combination of strong wind and torrential downpour made simple walks to the driveway daunting. Thick fog settled over Red Mountain, obscuring the statue of Vulcan. By evening, the skies were much calmer, and fans were willing to brave the elements. The first two thousand to arrive were rewarded for their loyalty with free Squadron playoff T-shirts. The shirts were red, as the event had been promoted as a "Red Out."

Just shy of four thousand people packed the arena that night. Among them were several representatives from the Pelicans (including David Griffin, the executive vice president of basketball operations), the Hueytown High School marching band, and Randall Woodfin, the mayor of Birmingham. Far more reporters and television crews were in attendance as well, enough that the media workroom—which served mostly as storage for equipment and Full Moon Bar-B-Que dinners during the regular season—would actually be used for press conferences.

The team's friends and family section, located right behind the bench, was nearly full. Harper's parents and younger brother Jalen had made the trip from Atlanta. Young's wife and kids had come all the way from Houston.

At exactly 6:21 p.m., the Squadron gathered in the locker room. Nipsey Hussle boomed through the speakers. Written on the whiteboard, in big upper-case letters, were four words: WE ALL WE GOT! The players wore custom warm-up shirts—designed by Dillon McGowan, the Squadron equipment manager and basketball operations associate—bearing the mantra as well.

Coaches went through the game plan and scouting report once more. Saint was the last to speak. "Six months ago, we met on the seventh floor of Lumen," he began. "We talked about building an identity, and we've done that. Back then, there were thirty teams left. Right now, there are twelve. At the end of tonight, there will be eight."

He pointed to the television, where a grainy clip recorded on an iPhone looped. It was from their first-ever practice. "This is where it started," Saint said. "The foundation of building a defense—a shell drill in Birmingham-Southern's auxiliary gym. And then it translates." Saint showed more film of the defense from throughout the season. The team had fully committed to the principles he had preached on day one: energy, effort, physicality, discipline.

"It starts again tonight in a new season," he went on, gesturing to the TV again. "That's character, that's identity, that's disposition—what you guys have all built for the last six months. It was a blank slate, first-year team, Birmingham, no identity. Keep writing the identity. The pen is not done. What are you gonna do about it? WHAT ARE YOU GUYS GONNA DO ABOUT IT?"

"Let's fucking go!" Cheatham said, and the locker room erupted.

• • •

A lineup of Harper, Young, Petty, Cheatham, and Hankins started for Birmingham. The opening tip was controlled by Texas. Chants of "defense!" instantly filled Legacy Arena. The Squadron responded, forcing a shot-clock violation.

On the other end, Young dished to Cheatham by the free-throw line. Cheatham surveyed the floor and rifled a pass to Harper on the left wing.

Harper hesitated for a moment, then darted to the paint and elevated for a six-foot floater. *Good*. Birmingham was on the board.

For the rest of the first half, though, the Squadron offense appeared shaky. There were far too many ugly turnovers and wild shots. Guys seemed tentative, out of rhythm. The floor wasn't spaced well enough to create good looks. Birmingham came in averaging 125 points in its last six games. But *this* wasn't the team that did *that*.

Still, despite their struggles, Birmingham held a 50–49 lead at the break, paced by Harper's 14 points. They were winning *and* they could play better. *Much better*. "Twenty-four minutes, let's do the same thing that we've done for the past few games where we take it to another level," Pannone told the team during halftime. "From the fucking jump! Play for each other, trust each other!"

The message was received, *loud and clear*. Birmingham came out of the half and started to seize momentum. Petty attacked the rim for a lay-up, then buried a three-pointer from the corner. Young navigated to the paint and tossed an alley-oop to Cheatham. A few minutes later, Cheatham had another dunk, this one over James Banks III, the former Squadron center who was traded to Texas in March. A free throw from Harper gave his team a 65–57 edge at the 5:28 mark.

But Texas kept fighting, quickly erasing the deficit. The score was 75–73 in favor of Birmingham as time ticked down in the third quarter. Legends guard Anthony Mathis launched a three-pointer that clanked off the back rim. Hankins secured the rebound with five seconds left. He tossed an outlet pass to Young, who raced to the frontcourt and heaved a prayer from thirty-five feet that was in the hoop—and popped out. *Ahhh*. Four thousand fans sighed together, collapsing back into their seats.

So the margin was just two heading into the final quarter when—who else but—Banks gave Texas a huge lift. The six-foot-ten big man spent the first five months of the season learning from the Squadron staff, particularly Coach Andrade, and then used what he learned *against* them. *Of course*, thought Andrade, *this was destined to happen*. Banks scored the Legend's first six points of the period. He was the spark that ignited an overwhelming fire.

Birmingham completely unraveled. Its defense, which was solid through three quarters, crumbled at the most crucial time. Texas got lay-ups, dunks, and wide open three-pointers. One of Birmingham's keys for the game was to limit the Legends to less than 25 points per quarter.

In the fourth, the Legends scored 42 points.

Feeling the game slipping away, Harper tried to save the Squadron. For a while he kept them in it, hitting several tough shots. But his jumper stopped falling, and the Squadron could not get a stop. When the buzzer sounded, the scoreboard read Texas 115, Birmingham 100. Harper had dropped a game-high 28 points but also turned the ball over an uncharacteristic five times, Young made just 6 of his 17 field goal attempts, and Cheatham was quiet for much of the evening.

Despite the outcome, fans at Legacy Arena rose to their feet. The conclusion was disappointing, yes, but it was a season—a team—still worthy of an ovation.

• • •

Back in the Squadron locker room, the silence was palpable. It was so silent, in fact, that the celebration happening in the visiting locker room—about a hundred feet down the hallway—could be heard clearly. Players slouched in their chairs, staring down with blank expressions. They hid their faces under towels and tried to stop their minds from racing. *This is it? Really? Six months of sacrificing amounted to this?*

The coaching staff allowed them a minute of quiet reflection, then filed in. Pannone rested against a table in the front of the room. All eyes gazed up.

"I love you," he said, holding back tears. "I love you when we win. I love you when we lose. I love you when we play great. I love you when we play bad."

He spoke softly, slowly, deliberately, pausing between sentences to collect himself. To see Pannone, normally such a facetious person, so overwhelmed was jarring. When he talked, players found themselves waiting for the witty remark—the corny one-liner that, despite their best efforts to resist, always forced out a smile.

"I'm sad—not because we don't advance in the playoffs but because I don't get to coach this group of *people* again," Pannone went on. "Eighteen years—that's how long I've been doing this. This is the most fun team I've ever coached. You guys have been amazing to work with. And I am sorry that

I did not prepare you enough to win. But I am so proud of you, because it took winning five games in a row to get here, and every person in this room, from the last two players that joined this team to the guys who were here from day one, sacrificed a lot to be here: family, money, other opportunities."

The thought of those sacrifices made the agony of defeat, the reality that this was over, even more difficult to swallow. *So, I spent all that time in the gym to be knocked out in the first round of the G League playoffs? I turned down millions of dollars to end up here?*

"I know it hurts," Pannone continued, taking a deep breath in. "But I'm telling you guys this—there is no team in this league that I would rather coach than you guys. Some of you are fathers, some of you will be. My son fell in love with basketball by watching you guys play. And it means something—because, of course, I don't care if my son loves basketball or if he grows up to be a basketball player, but it's still kind of special that he did because of you guys. He acts you guys out playing on a little hoop at home. Dunking, shooting threes, no middies—Joe, you know what I'm talking about."

Pannone pointed at Young and cracked a soft smile—*there* was the witty remark.

"But I am so proud of you guys, and I am so glad that I got to coach you," he added. "And I am so thankful that I got to spend every day with you guys. You guys have been amazing to coach because you are great people. Really good people. And I'm proud of you. Really proud of you."

A profound silence fell upon the room again, broken only by the occasional sniffle.

"Guys, we started this shit day one," Chasanoff said, stepping to the middle of the room. "No one here is a returning-rights guy. We had a blank slate this year. T.J. said it before the game, he said it day one of camp, we create the identity of Birmingham. What we did all year, it made the city proud, it sure as shit made the New Orleans Pelicans proud, and I couldn't be prouder of what we've accomplished. Ryan said it, everyone sacrificed for this team. And I couldn't be prouder of every single one of you. Thank you, guys, for all you put into this."

They huddled together one last time and that was it. *Really.* Lockers were cleared out. Plastic bags were filled with shoes and uniforms. The whiteboard was wiped clean. The court was broken down. Leftover merchandise was boxed up. Any traces of this year's Birmingham Squadron were erased.

One by one, the players exited. Only a few—if any—would be back next season. "Just that quick, it's over," Cheatham described. "It's very abrupt. There are guys you get close with, you connect with, you bond with. To know that—damn, you're about to go about your life, I'm about to go about mine, and we probably will never play on the same team again. It's just over that quickly."

They said their goodbyes, took one final glance at Legacy Arena, and walked out.

By the end of the week, they would all be gone from Birmingham.

25. NEVER ENDING

For Harper, the season was not yet over. The stars happened to align perfectly for him to get another opportunity in the NBA. On the same evening that Birmingham was eliminated from the G League playoffs, the Pelicans secured their spot in the play-in tournament for the NBA playoffs, beating the Kings in Sacramento. Harper reported to New Orleans the following day.

Only three games remained in the regular season. Since he was signed to a two-way contract (as opposed to a standard contract), Harper would not be eligible for the playoffs. On April 7 the Pelicans hosted the Portland Trail Blazers with a chance to clinch a home play-in game. Harper was able to check in with 5:02 left in the fourth quarter, as New Orleans held a comfortable 115–86 lead. By the 2:49 mark, he had already scored 8 points. Fans at the Smoothie King Center cheered wildly. Those watching at home voiced their support for Harper on Twitter:

> @FLURRAYTALKS: Add 4 inches to Jared Harper and we are un-ironically talking about a 20/7 guy.
>
> @COOLKANEMVP: If Jared Harper was 6′4″ he'd be a top 10 young guard in the league.
>
> @KINGCHRIS504: Jared Harper could've won us like 3 games this year, I'm not joking.

Two nights later, the Pelicans visited the Grizzlies in Memphis. The game was another blowout, this time not in New Orleans' favor. It was 131–90 with 7:03 on the clock when Harper replaced Alvarado. For those (often ugly) seven minutes, Harper was the best player on the floor. He scored on his first offensive possession, leading color commentator Antonio Daniels to remark, "He's not allowing the game to breathe. He's going to take his skill set *to the game*."

Harper finished with 12 points on an efficient 5 of 6 shooting from the field, also notching 3 steals and 2 assists. The performance earned him a spot at the podium for a postgame interview, during which Harper told reporters, "I know I deserve to be on the NBA level and play."

The final contest of the season was a nationally televised matchup against the Golden State Warriors. With the Pelicans locked in as the number nine seed in the West, head coach Willie Green opted to rest many of his key players. Harper received twenty minutes off the bench and, unsurprisingly, was productive again. A few times Golden State tried to capitalize on his size, taking him down to the post. But Harper hung tough. The end of the game marked the end of his season, at least on the court. During the playoffs, he could sit on the bench for the Pelicans but would not be active. He finished a stellar year on a stellar note, recording 10 points, 9 assists, 1 steal, and 0 turnovers in a 128–107 loss to the eventual NBA champions.

Watching at home, Patrick and Erica Harper were thrilled for their son. This game, they believed, would provide Jared with extra motivation going into the offseason. "Now you've got some fuel in your fire because there's a glimmer of hope," said Patrick. "You got a chance to play, and you did well."

A string of impressive games at the NBA level would add more fuel to his fire, sure. But it would also lead Jared to wrestle even further with the same exasperating question: *What more can I do?*

Harper had starred in the G for three consecutive seasons, made an All-NBA G League Team twice, contributed to a winning organization, shot a high percentage from three, gotten better each year. And now he had played significant NBA minutes—and thrived in them.

"I feel like that's always been my frustration," Jared said, "because it's difficult, especially when you're around people—NBA players or former NBA players or even front office [executives] or coaches, NBA circle people—and they're like, 'Oh, you're definitely an NBA player.' I don't think there's ever really been a question of, like, 'Am I?' It's just, I guess, when exactly it will happen or can happen."

"There aren't many things that I can say that bother him," Patrick added, "but I get the sense, like, 'Hey, I've done everything. I've gotten better. I've performed well. I've done this. I've worked on this.'"

What more can I do?

Of course, there was always more that he could do. For one, Harper's defense could improve. He occasionally took possessions off on that end. He wasn't quite the *pest* that Alvarado was—the type of undersized player that NBA scouts were drawn toward. Harper's scoring ability, while elite, wasn't going to be his ticket to the big leagues. Not by itself.

As a playmaker, Harper had also taken a major step forward, averaging 7.2 assists for Birmingham. But even he knew there was more room for growth. When the Pelicans faced the Phoenix Suns in the playoffs, Harper studied opposing point guard Chris Paul, a twelve-time All-Star regarded as one of the greatest ever at his position. *Paul makes the right play ten out of ten times*, Harper noted. With the Squadron, he reasoned that he had made the right play nine out of ten times. Coach Pannone agreed; he also believed that Harper, like Paul, could be a ten-out-of-ten player.

Still, even if he did develop further, Harper could very well find himself asking the same question next summer: *What more can I do?* Constantly hearing that he was an NBA player was reassuring but also frustrating. If he was an NBA player, then he should be in the NBA, right?

Not exactly.

The distinction between an NBA player and a player in the NBA exists for a reason. Only around five hundred spots are available in the NBA each year, and more than five hundred players are capable of filling those spots. And such a small number of those spots—just eleven in the 2021–22 season—go to players under six feet tall.

By the spring of 2022 Harper had already made up his mind about the ensuing year. If he was not offered an NBA contract after the annual Summer League, he would play overseas in Europe. He didn't care where or for what team; he just would not return to the G. He shared that decision with Squadron coaches during his exit interview in May. They understood. Pannone was a big fan of the EuroLeague and thought Harper would enjoy his experience there, should it come to that.

"You were really great to coach, really great to have," Pannone told Harper that day. "I'm sure fortunate that we were able to have you on our team and coach you. I was really excited to get you. We knew that we wanted you, and you were even better than what we thought. I fully believe—I'll say it and keep saying it until the day you retire—you are an NBA player."

"It was awesome to coach you and work with you," Saint added. "I learned a lot from you just in our little individual daily film sessions. You really are an NBA player."

That much—regardless of what the future held for Jared Harper—would always be true.

• • •

At the end of March, before the G League playoffs began, Cheatham flew to Milwaukee to work out for the Bucks, one of the best teams in the NBA. He was on a 7:00 a.m. flight out of Birmingham and went straight to their practice facility. That afternoon, he was put through a workout with three other G Leaguers: B. J. Johnson, Micah Potter, and Justin Tillman. They were all competing for one open spot on the Bucks roster.

Cheatham was pleased with his performance that day. Upon returning to Birmingham, he was hopeful that the Bucks would call with good news soon. For the time being, though, he had to focus on the Squadron. He proved crucial during the team's five-game winning streak to clinch a playoff berth, averaging 13.4 points (on 64 percent shooting) and 11.4 rebounds.

After Birmingham was eliminated by Texas, Cheatham remained optimistic that he, like Harper, might finish the year in the NBA. But the Bucks ultimately went in a different direction, calling up guard Rayjon Tucker from the Wisconsin Herd, their G League affiliate, on April 8.

Back to square one.

Once again, Cheatham had been so close to a big break, only to see it vanish. His professional career seemed cursed, beginning midway through his rookie season, when the COVID-19 pandemic shut down the NBA.

"I want you to keep your head up and keep going," Darvis Fletcher, Cheatham's best friend, repeatedly told him. "You're too far to give up now. You're right there. It's going to happen. It has to happen. You're doing everything right."

When he returned to South Phoenix, Cheatham reconnected with many of his childhood friends, including Fletcher. They sat around and reflected on his season together. There were a lot of highs to celebrate, but it was also one of the most grueling and emotional years of Cheatham's life—not just of his career. His message to his friends was encouraging, nonetheless.

"He was like, 'All of this is happening to me but I'm still here. I'm still standing,'" recalled Fletcher. "A lot of people can't make it through what he's been fighting through. He's just in a space where, 'I'm still here, so I have to keep pushing. There's no way I did all this and went through everything this year and I'm going to give up.' So he's still in it. He's still ready for whatever."

Cheatham continued to garner interest from foreign clubs, but he was not yet prepared to leave the United States, not while he was knocking on the door of the NBA. "I'm putting all my eggs in one basket this summer," he told Squadron coaches during his exit interview in May. "I'm going to give this NBA thing a real try. I'm going to put everything I got into my training, hit Summer League, and worst case, if I gotta spend some more time in the G, that's what it is. But I'm really taking it one step at a time, because I really feel like if I attack Summer League with the right team, doing everything that I'm supposed to do, I think I'll get where I want to be."

"Yeah, you're right there," Pannone replied. He, too, was constantly getting calls from international teams to inquire about Cheatham. "You're obviously right there. You got three call-ups this year, and if some bad luck didn't happen, who knows? Maybe you'd never have come back from Miami."

Cheatham nodded in agreement.

"I assumed that would be your path," Pannone continued, "that you'd try at least one more year and give everything that you have. I just wasn't sure."

"Yeah, so that's where I'm at with it," Cheatham said. "But obviously I'm not ignorant. I'm not oblivious to the reality of the situation. I am about to be twenty-seven. I don't have the cartilage I used to have in my knees. And at some point, I am a provider for my family. So I'm realistic with my approach.

But just being that I got those ten-days and those call-ups, I'm not really financially pressed at the moment."

With his sights still set on the NBA, Cheatham started training for the annual Summer League. At the same time, he was also caring for his mother, Carolyn, whose health was rapidly declining. Carolyn had always been there for him, working tirelessly to give him the future that he wanted. "It was just me and my mom through everything," Zylan said, reflecting on his childhood. "Us struggling, trying to figure it out, through everything, just me and her. There ain't really too much in the world I wouldn't do for her, because I watched her get up and bust her ass every day for me."

Sadly, Carolyn's condition grew worse as the days went by. Her long and courageous fight with cancer was nearing its end. Less than a week before Zylan was scheduled to leave for Summer League, she passed away.

Cheatham was heartbroken. He just didn't understand how something so cruel and unfair could happen. She was his best friend—his number one fan—and without her, he felt alone. Empty. Over the next several months, he would often find himself trying to text her, yearning to talk to her about whatever was on his mind.

Isolating was one of the ways that Cheatham coped. Another was playing basketball. With a heavy heart, he carried on with his career, joining the Bucks for Summer League. Of course, his presence there was about more than just chasing the NBA. For Cheatham, the court had always been a place of refuge; the game "an escape and emotional release."

When Cheatham first started to take basketball seriously in the eighth grade, there were no thoughts of making it to the NBA. It was just a way to keep him out of trouble. "I think basketball really saved my life," he said, "so I just try to give everything I got to the game every day."

From seven-hour gym sessions with Fletcher at the South Mountain Community Center, Cheatham's NBA dream was eventually born. As more time passed, he began to view that dream as much bigger than himself. He wanted to make it for Fletcher, who introduced him to the game at such a pivotal moment in his life; for his mom, who sacrificed *everything* to put him in this position; and for the entire city of South Phoenix, which raised him and supported him. He would keep going for all of them.

No matter the adversity, Cheatham's mindset would remain the same: *I'm still here. I'm still standing. And I'm not giving up.*

• • •

When Young would mention the idea of retiring during the season, strength and conditioning coach Jordan Kincaide would always reply with the same answer: "You wouldn't know what to do with yourself."

Kincaide was right. At this point, basketball was a part of who Joe Young was. He could not walk away from the game—or, ultimately, from his NBA dream.

Once the season ended, the twenty-nine-year-old Young returned home to Houston. He enjoyed some quality time with his family. It wasn't long, though, before he was back in the gym. He extended open invites to Petty and Cheatham to join him for workouts. His primary goals for the summer were to improve his three-point shooting and his finishing ability around the rim. The midrange shot, which had long been Young's greatest strength, was becoming a lost art in the NBA. So he wouldn't focus on it—or rely on it—any further. He would do whatever it took to grab the attention of scouts.

Young also began training with John Lucas II, a former NBA player (the number one pick in the 1976 NBA Draft) and current assistant coach for the Houston Rockets. Lucas put him through *extremely* rigorous conditioning drills that, while painful, left Young feeling eighteen again.

Young's overall outlook hadn't changed. He was still fixated on the NBA—still committed to chasing what he had lost—despite the arduous season he had just endured. He was still optimistic that his opportunity was coming. He would not participate in Summer League but worked out privately for eight different NBA teams.

"I'm ready to get back on an NBA floor!" he tweeted in July. And in August, "I be wondering why I'm not still in the NBA, but hey God knows and I will be back before it's said and done!!!"

There was no doubt that the past year had been difficult for him, that it had taken a significant toll on him emotionally. Young had left a $3 million contract on the table to sign in the G League, fully expecting to finish the season in the NBA. On the second day of training camp at Birmingham-Southern, he had sat on the sideline with a smile on his face and told a reporter, "We will get back. We're going to be back in the NBA."

He was so confident then, so full of hope. He spoke of new beginnings and opportunities and rechasing his dream. "If you know you belong somewhere and you know what it takes to get there, then you gotta do the things that you don't want to do," he said. "I knew that I would have to take a big pay cut. I felt like, no biggie. I can sacrifice that to get to where I want."

Of course, the longer Young spent in Birmingham, the more disheartened he grew. A record 117 players were called up to the NBA during the season, shattering the previous high of 50. And somehow, Young wasn't one of them.

The G League might have been a forgiving place, a place for second chances. But the NBA, ostensibly, was not—at least for guys on the fringe. Because the truth was, Young had done everything right. He had kept his word to Chasanoff and Pannone, fulfilling every promise he made back in October: to be a leader, play the right way, buy in to the team's system, work hard. He had persevered through a taxing six-month season, appearing in forty-four of forty-six games and logging the twelfth most minutes in the entire G League. He had never quit.

"It's something you should be proud about, because I'm proud of you," Pannone said to Young during his exit interview. "From day one, everything you said you were going to do, you did. A lot of people say a lot of shit, and they don't do it, especially when things don't go their way or when they hit adversity. You were amazing. And I loved coaching you. And I'm very, very, very grateful for what you sacrificed for our team and to be there every day."

The feelings of gratitude were mutual. "I really appreciate y'all for giving me an opportunity to show who I really am," Young told the staff. Call-up or no call-up, his season with the Squadron had allowed him to prove his reputation wrong. To demonstrate his maturity. *To change his narrative.*

"You were unbelievable," Saint said. "I've said this to other people: this whole year is an unbelievable real-life example of somebody who had to go through something mentally—a lot of stuff that was really tough—and you did that and you got better and you took people with you. That is really fucking rare. This world is a selfish world, con artists everywhere. I don't know what's going to happen with your career or my career or anybody's career, but you did an unbelievable job this year."

"I'm just going to build off of this," Young replied. "I just really appreciate y'all for giving me an opportunity to build off of something and change a red flag into something good, you know?"

"I'm truly honored," he added. "I'm telling you, I'm truly honored. Don't even think twice—*do y'all think Joe would come back?* Just know this—yes, Joe will come back."

• • •

Now that the season was over, Hill could take a moment to pause. He could finally look back and think, *Wow.*

A season that started with him in the G League, as a player—in his words— "not known in the basketball world," finished with him on the Chicago Bulls. He wore four different jerseys in a five-month span, appearing in eight games for the Windy City Bulls, Chicago's G League affiliate, in March. By the end of the year, not only were the Bulls still invested in him, but other teams around the NBA were expressing interest too. Chicago would soon extend a two-way qualifying offer, making him a restricted free agent. Hill was certain that he would either be back with the Bulls or on a different NBA roster when the 2022–23 season began.

After taking just a week off to reflect, Hill returned to the grind. "Why not enjoy myself a little more? The answer was simple for me," Hill wrote in one of his blog posts. "I am nowhere close to where I want to be, and I haven't accomplished the end goals. Not even close."

He could feel himself getting comfortable—*too comfortable*—with his daily routine, so he tweaked it. Or, to be more precise, he *added* to it. He incorporated more recovery techniques, including qigong, a form of traditional Chinese exercise similar to tai chi. He focused on new ways to stimulate his mind, picking up Sudoku and doing word searches and puzzles. "It feels like I'm unlocking more neurons," he explained. "I just feel at peace, at ease." He started listening to more podcasts and carving out more time to read, diving into Robert Greene's *Mastery* and David R. Hawkins's *The Map of Consciousness Explained.*

His two main goals for the offseason were to change his diet—eating more fruits and vegetables and less meat—and begin his days earlier. He got into a rhythm of waking up at 5:30 a.m., which allowed him to pack far more into his schedule. Before the sun rose each morning, Hill had already started his morning rituals: meditation, yoga, reading, journaling. It gave him time for two—often three—workouts throughout the day.

By now Hill fully trusted the power of his routine. He also knew that his trust was bound to be tested at some point. There were plenty of moments over the past year when he wondered, *How am I possibly going to make it to the NBA by the end of 2021?* After all, to most people, it was a laughable pursuit.

"I didn't know what it was going to look like or how I was going to get to the NBA," he admitted. "Good days, bad days. Good games, bad games. Good practices, bad practices. I dealt with all of the emotions that people deal with: happiness, sadness, anxiety."

During the bad days, Hill liked to perform self-checks. He challenged himself with questions like "Do you really believe?" and "Do you trust the work?" and "Do you want it *that badly*?" Of course, the answer—to all of the above—was always yes.

Even so, Hill needed a break to reach his goal. He couldn't sign himself to a contract, just like Pannone couldn't, and Harper couldn't, and Cheatham couldn't, and Young couldn't. What worked for Hill—what *pushed* him—on his improbable journey to the NBA was largely a feeling of being in full control. A sense that he could will his goal to fruition. That the onus rested squarely on his shoulders.

That he could *create* a break.

No, there were no guarantees that if he did everything right, then an opportunity would come. But for Hill, one thing was certain: if he didn't, then an opportunity would not.

"A lot of people think, with me especially, *Oh, he works hard. He's going to get it,*" Hill once said. "They don't know the fine details, because I used to think that stuff *just happens.*"

Stuff didn't *just happen* to Hill. In his mind, every decision he made, every action he took, every thought he had all factored into what transpired between

January 2021, when he was riding the bench for Hapoel Jerusalem, and January 2022, when he signed a two-way contract with the Bulls.

"As humans, we have this unique ability to go for something and to become something," Hill once wrote. "We have the ability to change our circumstances and our environment by the way we think. I'm not saying that this is easy. As a matter of fact, it's the opposite. It's probably one of the most difficult things you can do. It takes discipline and work to change your habits to *become*. Success does not far exceed personal development. We all have to do this type of self-examination. The ultimate question that you have to answer is: are you willing to become the person it takes to get what you want?"[1]

"Even if he wasn't my son, it's just an incredible story," Machanda Hill, Malcolm's mom, said. "To literally be on a roster on an NBA team—it's unbelievable. I watched the games and no matter if he played two seconds or twenty minutes, I'm like, 'He's literally on the bench for an NBA team.' But you can't just write something down and hope it happens. He worked incredibly hard. He believed. And it happened.

"I think Oprah said, 'Luck is preparation meeting opportunity,'" Machanda continued. "So you can get the opportunity, but if you're not prepared, it's not going to mean a whole lot. You can be prepared, but you need that opportunity. But when those things come together . . . *man*. They say, 'Oh, Malcolm's so lucky!' Not quite."

How can you be lucky when you don't believe in luck?

Acknowledgments

I should probably start by acknowledging Ben Osborne, who hired me as an intern at *SLAM* magazine in 2015 and has been an incredible mentor and friend ever since. When I had the idea to do this book, Ben was one of the first people I called. He encouraged me to pursue it, and here we are. Ben, I could never thank you enough.

To Adam Figman and the *SLAM* fam, I wouldn't be in this position without you. Thank you for your unwavering support and for making me a better writer and reporter.

Of course, I must thank the entire Birmingham Squadron and New Orleans Pelicans organizations for allowing me to be a fly on the wall for such an unforgettable season. Joseph Hooven, you're the best PR rep in the business. To the staff and players, words can't express how much I appreciate all of you. It was an honor to be a small part of such a special group. Malcolm Hill, Joe Young, Zylan Cheatham, and Jared Harper—you gave me your time, your trust, and your stories. For that, I am forever grateful.

I have to shout out a few more folks from Birmingham. Scotty Colson, Rick Moody, Eli Gold, Scott Adamson, Joseph Goodman, Kelvin Davis, and Griffin Levy, thank you all for being so welcoming and kind. Roderick Abernathy (check out Rod Tee Media!) and Mercedes Oliver, thank you for your friendship throughout the season and for contributing your work to this project.

Thank you so much to everyone who took the time to speak with me during my reporting: current and former players, coaches, executives, announcers, scouts, agents, family, friends, and so forth. I have to single out Andre Ingram, who wrote the outstanding foreword. No G League book would be complete without you! And thank you to Mike Bass, Joanna Shapiro, Philip Bausk, Shareef Abdur-Rahim, and all the wonderful people at the league offices for your assistance throughout the season and beyond.

A huge thank you to my agent, Joseph Perry. You made this process a million times easier, and I am so lucky to be able to work with you. Thank you to my fantastic editors Robert Taylor and Joseph Webb, and the entire staff at the University of Nebraska Press for believing in me and making my dream a reality.

Ben Simon, thank you for all your help editing and fact checking. Can't wait to read your book one day. Jeff Pearlman, Mirin Fader, Jake Fischer, and Paul Fichtenbaum—I look up to all of you, and your support for this project means the world to me. Thank you as well to Roger Hamilton, Ben Jadow, Jake Shapiro, Jake Rosen, and Gabe Davis for your feedback on the manuscript.

To all my friends, you picked me up when I was feeling down, discouraged, and stressed (which was often!). Without you, I wouldn't have made it to the finish line. And to Brodie, my best friend (also the greatest pug in the world), you were *literally* by my side from the first page to the very last. I couldn't have asked for a better writing buddy.

Most importantly, thank you to my family, the original Squadron. Jake and Sam, thank you for always being there when I need you. Dad, thank you for inspiring me and pushing me to pursue my dream. Mom, thank you for your endless encouragement and for being the best editor and my number one fan no matter what. I love you all, and I hope I made you proud.

Notes

Unless otherwise noted, all quotations are from interviews conducted by the author in person or on the phone between September 2021 and September 2022.

1. What's the G League?

1. Dwain Price, "Youth Not Served," *Fort Worth Star-Telegram*, June 25, 2000.
2. John Millea, "Running the Option," *Star Tribune*, June 28, 2000.
3. Carlos Castaneda, *Journey to Ixtlan: The Lessons of Don Juan* (1972; repr., New York: Washington Square Press, 1991), 234.
4. This American Basketball Association (ABA), a semipro minor league, bears no relation to the original ABA, which merged with the NBA in 1976.

2. Birmingham

1. "Legends Aren't Born, They're Forged," About, Vulcan Park & Museum, n.d., https://visitvulcan.com/about/.
2. New Orleans Pelicans, "New Orleans Pelicans Purchase NBA G League Team to Play in Renovated Legacy Arena in Birmingham, Alabama," news release, NBA.com, October 24, 2018, https://www.nba.com/pelicans/news/new-orleans-pelicans-purchase-nba-g-league-team-play-renovated-legacy-arena-birmingham-alabama.
3. Aubree Bailey, "Report: Alabama Is the State Most Obsessed with College Football," News 19, January 4, 2022, https://whnt.com/news/alabama-news/report-alabama-is-the-state-most-obsessed-with-college-football/.
4. Rick Bragg, "In the Nick of Time," *Sports Illustrated*, August 27, 2007, 54.

5. Harvey Updike, "**Original Audio** Al from Dadeville Admits to Poisoning Toomer's Corner," January 27, 2011, audio, 1:59, *The Paul Finebaum Show*, WJOX-FM, https://www.youtube.com/watch?v=Yyc7lcGCMI0.

6. Alan Solomon, "Jordan Already Bonanza for Barons," *Chicago Tribune*, April 1, 1994.

7. Paul Finebaum, "We Came, We Saw, We Saved Our Stubs," *Birmingham Post-Herald*, April 9, 1994.

8. Chet Fussman, "Panelists Pick Iron over Gold," *Birmingham Post-Herald*, July 15, 1996.

9. Exhibit-ten contracts are essentially training camp invites that allow players cut by the NBA team to earn a bonus of up to $50,000 if they sign with the team's G League affiliate.

10. Two-way contracts, introduced in 2017, allow an NBA team to have two more roster spots in addition to its normal allotment of fifteen. For the 2021–22 season, two-way players would receive a flat salary equal to 50 percent of the minimum player salary applicable to someone with zero years of NBA experience ($462,629). In most cases, two-way players are expected to split time between the NBA and the G League.

3. Tryouts

1. Lorne Chan, "Chasing the Jonathon Simmons Dream at Austin Spurs Tryouts," NBA.com, September 25, 2016, https://www.nba.com/spurs/chasing-jonathon -simmons-dream-austin-spurs-tryouts.

2. Kendra Andrews, "Why JTA Felt 'Destined' to Sign Standard Contract with Dubs," NBC Sports, May 13, 2021, https://www.nbcsports.com/bayarea/warriors /juan-toscano-anderson-felt-destined-sign-warriors-contract.

3. "Atlanta Vision Selects 47 Year Old for Vet Camp," Our Sports Central (website), August 2, 2006, https://www.oursportscentral.com/services/releases/atlanta -vision-selects-47-year-old-for-vet-camp/n-3355650.

4. Karen Rosen, "The Oldest Rookie," *Atlanta Journal-Constitution*, February 22, 2007.

5. Kelvin Davis, *The Oldest Rookie* (self-pub., April 24, 2021), 39.

4. Draft Day

1. Eric Koreen, "Q+A Pop Quiz with Raptors' Thaddeus Young: Torching Toronto, Pounded by Andre Miller Passes, and Forgetting Pop," *The Athletic*, March 16, 2022, https://theathletic.com/3187954/2022/03/16/qa-pop-quiz-with -raptors-thaddeus-young-torching-toronto-pounded-by-andre-miller-passes-and -forgetting-pop/.

2. *Returning rights* meant that if Devearl Ramsey was to sign a G League contract, he would automatically be acquired by the Stockton Kings.

5. Training Camp

1. Alex Caruso, "Episode 24: Alex Caruso," November 5, 2020, *The Old Man and the Three*, hosted by J. J. Redick and Tommy Alter, podcast, audio, 1:12:38, https://chartable.com/podcasts/the-old-man-and-the-three-with-jj-redick-and-tommy-alter/episodes/70155902-episode-24-alex-caruso.

6. Winning Matters

1. Josh Vitale, "Jared Harper Came to Auburn to Play on an NCAA Tournament Stage Like This," *Montgomery Advertiser*, March 29, 2019.
2. There are several small rule differences between the G League and the NBA. Overtime, for example, is two minutes in the G and five minutes in the NBA.

8. November 17, 2021

1. Michelle Gardner, "ASU's Zylan Cheatham Plays to Honor Late Brother, Who Was Shot and Killed Saturday," *The Republic*, January 3, 2019, https://www.azcentral.com/story/sports/2019/01/03/asu-basketball-zylan-cheatham-brother-shot-killed/2469407002/.

10. The Price of a Dream

1. Steve Irvine, "Former UAB PG Squeaky Johnson Is Finally Living His NBA Dream," *Birmingham News*, December 31, 2011.

14. Going Up

1. Ken Sugiura, "Jose Alvarado, Georgia Tech's Prince of Thieves, Shines as a Senior," *Atlanta Journal-Constitution*, February 15, 2021.
2. Jordan Kaye, "No 'Outside Noise': Zylan Cheatham Vows to Stay off Social Media," Rivals (website), October 1, 2018, https://arizonastate.rivals.com/news/no-outside-noise-zylan-cheatham-vows-to-stay-off-social-media.

15. Centimeter of Chance

1. Associated Press, "Magic Beat Hawks 104–98 in Matchup of Short-Handed Teams," ESPN.com, December 22, 2021, https://www.espn.com/nba/recap/_/gameId/401360294.
2. Associated Press, "Depleted Heat Hold Off Depleted Wizards, 119–112," ESPN.com, December 28, 2021, https://www.espn.com/nba/recap/_/gameId/401360328.

16. Can You Pass This Test?

1. Tania Ganguli, "'Every Hooper's Dream': NBA Hopefuls Get Their Chance during Crisis," *New York Times*, December 29, 2021.

21. Thinking about Life

1. Rohan Nadkarni and Michael Pina, "The NBA's Replacement Players Are Enjoying the Ride. They Don't Want It to End," *Sports Illustrated*, January 6, 2022, https://www.si.com/nba/2022/01/06/nba-replacement-players-daily-cover.

25. Never Ending

1. Malcolm Hill, "Success . . . Luck or Skill?," *In the Know w/ Finke & Hill* (blog), April 12, 2022, https://finkeandhill.com/2022/04/12/success-luck-or-skill/.